Samuel Beckett's Self-Referential Drama

THE SENSITIVE CHAOS

It's myself I hear, howling behind my dissertation . . .
Samuel Beckett, *The Unnamable*

Samuel Beckett's Self-Referential Drama

THE SENSITIVE CHAOS

Shimon Levy

sussex
ACADEMIC
PRESS
Brighton • Portland • Toronto

2 4 6 8 10 9 7 5 3

First published 2002, reprinted 2012, in Great Britain by
SUSSEX ACADEMIC PRESS
PO Box 139, Eastbourne BN24 9BP

Distributed in North America by
SUSSEX ACADEMIC PRESS
ISBS Publisher Services
920 NE 58th Ave #300, Portland, OR 97213, USA

British Library Cataloguing in Publication Data
A CIP catalogue record for this book is available from the British Library.

Library of Congress Cataloging-in-Publication Data
Levy, Shimon, 1943.
Samuel Beckett's self-referential drama : the sensitive chaos / Shimon Levy.
p. cm.
Partly based on the author's work of the same title, published in 1990, with new chapters and sections added.
Includes bibliographical references (p   ) and index.
ISBN 978-1-902210-54-4 (acid-free paper) —
ISBN 978-1-902210-46-9 (pbk. : acid-free paper)
1. Beckett, Samuel, 1906—Dramatic works. 2. Self in literature. I. Title.

PR6003.E282 Z77134 2002
842'.914—dc21
                2002018781

Typeset and designed by G&G Editorial, Brighton
Printed and bound in Great Britain by TJ International, Padstow, Cornwall
This book is printed on acid-free paper.

Contents

Preface

By the year 2000 Beckett criticism will equal that of Wagner and Napoleon, considered the most written about personae in history. In 1970 the Beckett scholar Melvin Friedman wrote that "Beckett criticism has reached such an enviable and almost unbelievable level of sophistication that any kind of overview of his life and works is at least ten years out of date".[1] Five years later Ruby Cohn, in her introduction titled "Inexhaustible Beckett", said that the "Beckett canon has elicited highly sensitive criticism".[2] The year 2000 is now behind us, and both scholars are proven right.

Given the social, artistic and literary context of scholars, translators, directors, actors, readers and audiences who have been involved in varying degrees of intensity, dedication and commitment to Beckett's works, it would certainly be impossible to gain agreement about *any* aspect of Beckett's craft that would satisfy all and sundry. Indeed, there are compelling reasons why such a task should not be attempted. Nevertheless, despite the wide and critical diversions there remain certain less disputed artistic notions that stand above and beyond the critical minutiae. An indispensable notion for coming to terms with Beckett's universe is that of self-reference.

Beckett, like "no other modern writer, has integrated the act of creation so consistently and ironically into his own creation".[3] Wolfgang Iser says that Beckett's "anatomy of fiction" (and, for that matter, of his drama as well) "is itself conducted through a fictional medium. The attempt to reveal the basis of fiction through fiction itself means that the process of revelation can never end".[4] Hanna Copeland rightly maintains that "Beckett's art culminates in rigorously self-conscious, and, hence, self-reflective works, works in which the creator and the act of creation are of ultimate importance in the thing created".[5]

There is, in fact, hardy a serious critic who has not observed the high degree of self-consciousness in Beckett's works, though some critics find this quality to be a flaw. Gadamer says that "if self-consciousness is to be true self-consciousness . . . it must find another self-consciousness that is willing to be for it".[6] This holds true, in a uniquely theatrical way, in Beckett's plays. Characteristically, in all his plays, the basic situation is that of appealing to another "self-consciousness" in order for the speaker, the dramatic character, to give "the impression he *exists*".[7] The attempt is made to "reach out" for the necessary self-consciousness of another so that the dialogue that takes place in the dramatic and theatrical "vehicle" reflects a desired dialogue between playwright and audience, and hence expresses a concern for humanity. Because the playwright has already done his share in the "dialogue" by the very act of writing and presenting the play, it is up to the audience and the individual people that constitute it to do their share. Thus the mode of existence of the playwright and his self-reflexiveness can only be detected through the self-reference of the medium and the audience. Self-reference is not only a literary or dramatic technique but, at the same time, the subject matter of the work. The chapters that follow detect and reapply a number of critical notions that ensue from the Beckettian dramatic texts themselves. Moreover, the very act of performance of a given play is an intrinsic part of whatever it means and communicates.

The **Introduction**, "Self-Organisation in the Middle of Chaos", presents the question whether Chaos Theory achieves the status of providing a solid interpretation for a Beckett play or even for theatre in general? Other than for its entertainment value of playing with analogy (and so-called "family resemblance"), Chaos Theory is considered to be non-reductionist and can be characterized as "organic" "holistic" and even "homeopathic". In this respect, at least, it is shown to provide a highly "theatrical" method in which the observer (or "audience") changes the observed.

Chapter 1, "Philosophical Notions," deals with the more traditional philosophical approaches to Beckett's work. It proposes a "performative" interpretation to the Cartesian *Cogito, ergo sum* and its relevance to Beckett's plays, and discusses philosophical notions of Logical Positivism and Existentialism.

By these means a hermeneutical approach is established, based on Beckett's own (self) critical works and his distinction between the medium-oriented expressive means, the artist and the audience.

Beckett's dramatic practices and theatrical techniques are discussed in **chapter 2** through a close reading of both text and stage instructions, along Beckett's dramatic volume.

Offstage, in the context of "The Poetic of Offstage", is presented in **chapter 3** as a unique theatrical device that Beckett employed with amazing ingenuity. He harnessed actual theatrical Void not merely as an aesthethic principle, but as an "active nothingness". Various offstage characteristics are discussed, such as "Selves", rituals and spaces.

Chapter 4, "The Radioplays", examines the specific modes in which self-reference is enhanced by the radiogenic nature of radioplays, in counterdistinction to the stage plays.

Chapter 5, "Spirit Made Light", focuses on the unique "spirituality" of Beckett's six film and TV scripts, as well as on their medium-oriented self-reference.

In **chapter 6**, "Godot – Resolution or Revolution?", Beckett's most famous play is discussed out of its traditional ambience. Godot is presented as an Israel Culture Hero, in fact, a daring socio-dramatic "Crritic", with whom Israeli theatre-makers have criticized Israeli society since 1955.

In closing a hermeneutical cycle, **chapter 7**, "I's and Eyes", concentrates on the foundations of the theatrical situation: Playwright, Actor, Role, Audience, Critic. Whereas the playwright can be described as extending an invitation, through the medium (stage, screen, radio) to the audience, Beckett hides implied audiences in his plays, and many critics too. Beckett's dramatic works are a true and courageous attempt at communication, achieved through the very act of performance. The intensely original and sophisticated modes of presentation bring with them an implied *moral* demand extended to the audience, for help.

"Six She's and other *Not I* Proxies" is a personal report on my work with six actors with whom I have been searching and researching Beckett's *Not I* over the last 25 years. As the predominantly theoretical parts of this book imply that theory alone does not suffice to "explain" Beckett's plays, because (theoretically!) the plays must be performed in order for their "meaning", "message" etc. to come across at all, I conclude with some of my – and others' – real "Not I" experience.

Acknowledgements

This book is partly based on my *Samuel Beckett's Self-referential Drama: The Three I's* (London: Macmillan, 1990), with the new chapters and sections added. The text has been substantially rewritten and revised througout.

The new and additional material has appeared in various forms over the last eleven years. "Self-Organization in the Middle of Chaos" was published as "Does Beckett Admit the Chaos?" in the *Journal of Beckett Studies*, vol. 6, no. 1 (Florida State University, 1997), 81–96. Sections of "Poetics of Offstage" were published as "On and Offstage: Spiritual Performatives in Beckett's Drama", in Mary Bryden and Lance St John Butler (guest editors), Beckett and Religion, *Beckett Today/Aujourdhui*, 9 (2000): 17–30; and in "I on the Threshold of Offstage", in A. Jenkins and J. Saxton (eds), *The Beckett Papers*, University of Victoria, Canada (1996): 268–75. "Spirit Made Light" appeared in Catharina Wulf (ed.), *The Savage Eye* (Amsterdam and Atlanta: Rodopi, 1996), 65–82. "Godot – Resolution or Revolution?" was published as "Godot, an Israeli Crrritic" in *Theater Three*, Final Issue Nos. 10–11 (1992): 78–89. "Six She's and other *Not I* Proxies" has been accepted by Angela Moorjani (editor) for *Beckett Today/Aujourdhui*.

My thanks to all the editors for the privilege of reproducing the above material in this volume.

Permission is gratefully acknowledged to Faber and Faber Ltd and The Grove Press Ltd, for permission to reproduce copyright material from Samuel Beckett, *The Complete Dramatic Works* (London and Boston, 1986).

The jacket picture is used with the kind permission of John Minihan.

Abbreviations

Waiting for Godot	WFG
Endgame	EG
Happy Days	HD
All That Fall	ATF
Act Without Words I	AWWI
Act Without Words II	AWWII
Krapp's Last Tape	KLT
Rough for Theatre I	TI
Rough for Theatre II	TII
Embers	EM
Rough for Radio I	RI
Rough for Radio II	RII
Words and Music	WM
Cascando	CAS
Play	PL
Come and Go	CG
Breath	BR
Not I	NI
That Time	TT
Footfalls	FF
A Piece of Monologue	POM
Rockaby	RB
Ohio Impromptu	OI
Quad	Quad
Catastrophe	CAT
What Where	WW

Quotations from the above plays are by permission of Faber & Faber, and Grove Press, from Samuel Beckett, *The Complete Dramatic Works* [CDW] (London and Boston, 1986). The paging follows this edition.

Special thanks go to

Naomi Paz

friend, colleague and wise editor.

Introduction: Self-Organization in the Middle of Chaos

Bearing in mind that "The danger is in the neatness of identifications" (Samuel Beckett, *Dante . . . Bruno. Vico . . Joyce*), theatre, as a chaos system, has yet to be sufficiently thoroughly explored. Like the waves of the sea, the accumulation of clouds, the behaviour of cars on a highway, human heartbeats or the flow of a river – theatre is equally a "chaotic" multi-system. Whereas contemporary theatre semiotics can be compared with particle research in physics, chaos theories applied to theatre research may show the way back to the phenomenon as a whole, using criteria that ensue from any theatrical event as a live and changing process.

Just as we may be familiar with the basic data relating to the weather yet are unable to make a precise forecast, so too are producers, actors and audiences alike unable to foretell whether tonight's show will be successful. As a system that includes dozens of individuals, as well as repertoire and financial considerations (and the weather conditions too, as they affect the state of mind of all those attending the theatre), even the tiniest detail may influence the modes of presentation and the receptiveness of the audience. The technical language of chaos theory speaks of "sensitive dependence on initial conditions".[1]

While the study of drama is primarily engaged with written plays as its given subject matter, in theatre performance analysis is obliged to treat an actual performance as a dynamic live and unique event. A performance is an immediate, irreversible, surprising encounter – a process rather than a final "result". In theatre, chaos is intrinsic to the nature of the medium: there are no two identical performances of the same production and it is difficult enough to step even once into the same theatrical river. Artistic, political, psychological and commercial reasons apart, one of the crucial components of chaos in theatre is the audience's live response, without which there would in any case be no theatre. The collective as well as individual audience reactions simultaneously condition and change the theatrical event.

Beckett's works are particularly suited to a study of Chaos Theory including the plays' theatrical context. Not unexpectedly, chaos theoreticians wish to broaden their horizons and apply their methods to anything that moves, and the visual arts are no exception (especially computer graphics). The question to be addressed is not whether chaos may benefit from Beckett but, rather, could a Beckett play benefit from chaos-related scientific observations? Is the methodic shift from science to art justifiable? Can chaos, other than for its entertainment value of playing with analogy (and so-called "family resemblance"), achieve the status of providing a solid interpretation for a Beckett play or even for theatre in general?

Chaos theory is considered to be non-reductionist and can be characterized as "organic", "holistic" and even "homeopathic" in its treatment of its subject matters: As Gleick notes: "They had a taste for randomness and complexity, for jagged edges and sudden leaps. Believers in chaos – and they sometimes call themselves believers or converts, or evangelists – speculate about determinism and free will, about evolution, about the nature of conscious intelligence. They feel they are turning back a trend in science toward reductionism (*the analysis of systems in terms of their constituent parts*). They believe that they are looking for the whole."[2] According to its scientists and a growing number of aficionados, chaos promises a high level of integration between related elements.

For Beckett students, this may ensure a lesser degree of separation between the writing of pure theory on the one hand and the teaching, translating, designing, directing, and acting of Beckett's plays on the other. Chaos promises to supply a more comprehensive approach and supports the casting of a closer look at processes and "flow". Gleick's introduction to his book is likely to find an attentive response in Beckett fans. Students of Beckett (like some learners of the chaos language) try, in their scholarly efforts, to give vent not only to pure thoughts but to feelings and beliefs too. "For what characterizes much of the most recent literary theory has been its willingness precisely to question the forms of authority and command invested in theory itself." Connor also quotes Foucault, who adds, perhaps inadvertently, an extra touch of chaos: "After all, what would be the value of passion for knowledge, if it resulted in a certain amount of knowledgeableness and not, in one way or another and to the extent possible, in the knower's straying afield of himself?"[3] Chaos is quite explicit about the need to learn from the subject matter itself – "how it is" and how to approach it.

In this context it is noteworthy that Beckett saw his dramatic texts as complete only after he had made the necessary line or stage instruction changes, when he himself was directing. He related, no doubt, to the particular chaotic circumstances of each production, inherent to each individual actor, whether he directed or supervised his plays in French, English, or German. It would appear that it was not in spite of but because of his profound understanding of the nature of the medium that he was so meticulous with the smallest detail, down to the minutest rhythm beats or precise movement he found necessary.[4] This fact may also serve as an answer to Beckett directors who deliberately ignore his remarkable exactitude of notes, and treat them freely in the name of artistic creativity: even an obsessively exact carrying out of Beckett's instructions leaves (as I can testify from experience) an enormous amount of artistic freedom to all involved. It is not only the technique that constitutes – self-referentially – a good portion of the "message", or that the technique "owes far more to suggestion and ambiguity than it does to reference".[5] Knowlson's view can be supported with an argument ad chaos: because of the intrinsically chaotic nature of theatre, Beckett was fighting for the minimal rather than the exclusive directorial rights of authorship. As we shall see, it is the central role of the observer of the examined Beckett stage that is more essential for the present discussion.

Not I, a "steady stream . . . [of] mad stuff . . . " – can be regarded as an apt representation of any chaos theory that tries to reconcile between order and disorder. The play is a unique synthesis between a series of conflicts, the most basic of which is that it actually expresses "that there is nothing to express, nothing with which to express, nothing from which to express, no power to express, no desire to express, together with the obligation to express".[6]

Having translated *Not I* and directed it, I submit that the play seems to respond well to chaos theory in more than just this basic paradoxic mode. (In the following discussion I relate to an "ideal" performance.) *Not I* excels in great simplicity, presenting a relatively simple motif of a woman who is being born, living and dying right in front of the audience, while trying to find some meaning in her unique existence as a mouth on stage. Against this simplicity, her life and its delivery on stage is portrayed as highly complex and sophisticated. As in chaos, here too complexity and simplicity are complementary.

Thematically, the play stretches beyond the life and death of the character since it begins with a kind of pre-performance "pregnancy" of barely audible words and continues after her (stage, at least) death. Structurally, *Not I* is a combination of a free, partly repetitive flow of the character's associations that are moulded nevertheless into a classical five-acter, in which the four movements of "Auditor" supply brief pauses. The play exposes an integration between Beckett's inclination towards entropy, and the "I" of Mouth, posited as the focus. Frail, split and tentative, it constantly and vehemently attempts to pull itself up by its own words, like Baron von Muenchhausen, stuck with his horse in the swamp. Physically this attempt is absurd, because one needs an external "lever".

Psychologically, the chance to receive an Archimedian lever in the form of compassion from the "other", the on-stage Auditor, is indeed attempted – but his hands are too short. Potential help from the actual audience in the auditorium goes against the convention of proper behaviour in the theatre. The audience is not supposed to rescue tortured characters but to watch and hear them out. Moreover, the act of "rescuing" is dependent on the audience's free will to "reach out". Such a willingness is implicitly invited but it cannot be guaranteed and it definitely cannot be imposed. Beckett may assume that in their inability to help, the audience's compassion will even be enhanced.

Spiritually, only if and when "I think" here and now, "am" I also here and now.[7] Rather than a syllogism, the Cartesian dictum is performance act.[8] From a spiritual point of view, the self indeed sustains itself in mid-air, like Alice in the rabbit-hole: falling, "but . . . so far . . . ha! . . . so far . . . " (NI, 378)[9] managing to transfer marmalade jars from one shelf of consciousness to another. As long as Mouth speaks, she is, since "the whole being . . . [is] hanging on its words" (379).

Not I is one of the most striking cases in theatre history to use speech about birth as the birth of speech – " . . . out . . . into this world . . . ". She describes what she does, does what she describes, at one and the same time. This performative "self birth" is performed on the verge of stage and offstage, here signifying both womb and tomb. Offstage delineates the threshold of the theatre as well as the limits of theatre and life "out there". It marks the borderline between (stage) Being and Nothingness and expresses them in theatrical terms. Not I is a creation from and out of chaos, highly sensitive to the initial conditions of Mouth's biography. In her maddened speech, as in her position in stage space, she expresses her whole life. Space and speech are the basic elements of theatrical presentation, which Beckett often made quite explicit in other plays: WI, for instance, says "Silence and darkness is all I craved" (PI, 316), and the lines "they give birth astride of a grave" and so on, are almost too often quoted. She in Not I is portrayed not as presenting her self, but rather representing her self, aided by the organic participation of a "ray or beam" of light – a theatre light? – and her posture ("standing", "sitting"). These are the very expressive means of the medium into which she, "tiny little thing", is thrown.

Gleick's description of the three-dimensional Lorenz-attractor – "like a pair of butterfly wings interwoven with infinite dexterity . . . when the rolling motion stopped and reversed itself, the trajectory would swing across to the other wing . . . ".[10] – is an apt description of Mouth's reaction, to herself and, implicitly, to the audience. To enhance this point with chaos theory, Peitgen and Richter explain: "there is no arbitrariness involved . . . the sequence is determined by its initial value – and yet, it cannot be predicted other than by letting it run."[11] Once her vagitus is heard, as the "initial condition" expressed in "out", Mouth's life runs its course. But can these two centres, the "butterfly wings" in Lorenz's experiment, serving here as mutual "attractors", be regarded as Mouth's attempts to reconcile her "conscience positionelle" with her "conscience réflechie" (Sartre) which only together constitute her "not I-ness"? The immense physicality of this emotionally highly-charged play gives the spectator the impression that it takes place on a strange threshold. Secluded in space, it "happens" along the borderlines: "The focus has shifted to the nature of *boundaries between* different regions. We can think of centres – attractors – which compete for influence on the plans . . . "[12] The mixture between linear and non-linear dramatic and theatrical processes in Beckett's plays often leads to branch points, certainly for the audience, and probably also for the playwright. The decision, according to Peitgen and Richter, of which way to follow has the character of amplification. Science, as chaos theory shows, turns from reductionism back to the phenomenon itself and cannot ignore the observer.

From the point of view of the actress, as director Xerxes Mehta describes, "Beckett finally arrives at works that successfully join the intense subjectivity of personal experience to shape that 'accomodates the mess'" and yet survives the demands of a "gross and public medium."[13] Even one step without the actress's total involvement in her real "Not I" will prevent the audience too from being able to posit their real selves in this theatrical gap. Lorenz's attractor can therefore be seen in its *Not I* context as a graphic design on three theatrical levels: Mouth's own double consciousness; the unbridged gap between her and "Auditor"; and, most importantly, the yearned for communication between "her self" (as both role and actress!) and the audience. This typical chaos pattern can be observed in many other Becket plays, where the fictitious on-stage relationships reflect with great precision the relationships between stage and audience.

"In a universe ruled by entropy, drawing inexorably toward greater and greater disorder, how does disorder arise?" The Beckettian solution to Gleick's somewhat rhetorical question is funny, courageous, and sophisticated, but quite tentative. It can be found in his dramatic structures ("find a form to accommodate the mess"), strongly enhanced by self-referential use of light, sets, movement, and so on, as well as using their absence, namely the "being" (of) offstage. Fractals in chaos are recurrent patterns, becoming smaller and smaller according to a constant ratio. Similarly, the device of flaunting the artifice through the play-within-a-play dramatic device presents this Russian-doll effect. It has been well used, abused, and misused in theatre history from Aristophanes through medieval mystery plays, and from Shakespeare through Molière to Goethe, Ibsen, and Chekhov. Beckett, however, harnesses his dramatic fractals, as we can call his play-within-a-play odds and ends, in a Mandelbrot-like design. In Mandelbrot's process the mathematical values and their spatial image become constantly smaller as their sequence approaches zero. The points in the module stretch between 1 to 0 (or vice versa) and "their sequence lies on the boundary between the two domains of attraction . . . ".[14] The asymptotic movement from being to non-being is certainly nothing new to Beckett's writing. Many of his protagonists are always on the way from 1 to 0, but as long as they are on stage, on film, on video or on sound-tape, they can never reach "there." They are rarely able to finish what they feel to be their one true story – "finish this one . . . then . . . rest" (*CAS*, 297).

Beckett's drama is an inevitable mode of self-organization in the midst of chaos.[15] Since there is no external "organizer" (God?) or any other absolute, objective system of values (to which and in which classical plays were performed), consciousness itself creates dramatically existential patterns that maintain and hold each other. The aesthetic result, at least, is a delicate balance between order and chaos: confronted with nothingness, a dramatic tentative order must sustain itself, as does the consciousness of Beckett's Muenchhausen-like characters. It is the principle of internalized infinity as an anthropocentic, human answer to the absence of an exterior (theocentric) power, or possibly its arbitrary irrelevance. Hence the playfulness of theatrical self-referentiality of play-within-a-play patterns is, in *Not I*, the chaos-like expression of an order seeking consciousness *vis-à-vis* the void.

In *Not I* we experience how Mouth plays her own consciousness to herself and plays it unknowingly also to Auditor who is allowed to react with only four brief movements (described in certain manuscripts as "compassionate helplessness"). As a kind of "mousetrap", the entire first part of the play up to movement (I) is a prologue; only later is it developed in details, a play-within-a-play within a play. Beckett does not need to specify all the members of an infinite series of fractals – the basic logics of the audience can well continue where he leaves off.

As in Chaos Theory, *Not I* too is composed of a "hierarchical organization of living systems". Being still alive, She shows a typical chaos-like "sensitive dependence on initial conditions" known as "The Butterfly Effect": Mouth presents her particular situation as ensuing, at least partly, from "no love such as normally vented on the . . . speechless infant . . . " (*NI*, 376). She is in fact an unmediated chaotic consciousness trying to make sense to "her" self, imagining how and whether things could have been different. The notion of punishment, for instance, does not make sense. Having nothing but her consciousness to explain herself to herself, any "butterfly wing effect" is considered, then rejected.

It is "The principle of *self*-similarity" (emphasis added) and Beckett's dramatic macro-structures (acts, bigger "scene" units) and micro motif-and-variation repetitions in *Not I*, that both create and fight the void. Looking at the many motiphemes ("beats") in *Not I*, a similar though not identical pattern can be detected as repeating in macro- and micro-structures. But whereas Peitgen and Richter describe Mandelbrot's process as "The aesthetic charm correlates with a fundamental meaning," the fractals in *Not I* are indicative of an aesthetics that bears extreme pain. The tortured consciousness of Mouth is depicted in the play, suggesting a chaos-like Mandelbrot coastline. Apparently the line becomes longer the finer the scale on which we measure it, provided we have enough time (unlike scientific chaos . . .) between life and death. For Beckett's characters the coastline becomes gradually more excruti-ating. As optimists, we may say that this coastline runs its curves between the material medium of theatre and a possible spiritual message. Both the amount and unique quality of Beckett's ghosts and spirits, Mouth perhaps included, provide a tentative support for a more spiritual approach. In any case, scientific chaos "coastlines" end when the show is over, while Beckett will go on searching in his next play.[16]

Fractals, designed graphically (by computer) and applied to theatre, draw further attention to Beckett's extraordinary use of Offstage, a uniquely theatrical mode he uses to "presentify" nothingness on stage. The way spaces are formed determines "unformed" spaces as well. On the *Not I* stage (gradually though not consistently shrunk from play to play, exposing more nothingness, more offstage than "stage") the black area or aura is vastly bigger than the lit area. Following Mandelbrot's visual image, we observe a minute magnification of a tiny particle, an "advanced" stage in Mouth's vortex, quite close to a state of being unable to differentiate anything anymore. The required speed of the delivery avoids instant recognition of the pattern though it may be perceived, retrospectively, as a whole. She is both metaphorically and literally on the verge of offstage in the end becoming smaller and smaller. The correspondence between a diminishing light and the fading voice takes "technical" care of this stunning effect, which virtu-ally sucks the audience into Mouth's offstage space rather than just letting her dwindle out there – a lingering vocal and visual dissolution.

In "Implications?" the last chapter of his *Shadows of the Mind*, Roger Penrose asks: "How is it that the mere counterfactual possibility of something happening – a thing which does not actually happen – can have a decisive influenc upon what actually does happen? There is something in the mystery of the way that quantum mechanics operates that at least seems much less closer than in classical physics, to the kind of mystery needed to accommodate mentally within the world of physical reality."[17] Albeit to judge the scientific implications, I can nonetheless transplant the above observation into the body of Beckett's theatre, provided we overcome the antibodies "quantum mechanics" and "classical physics" and replace them with "stage" and "offstage".

In examining elements of chaos in *Not I*, the audience observes the "result" only as a methodic starting point that the mind actually advances as a process, rather than as a process detained for the mind to regard as a result. The status of the observer is as essential in experiencing *Not I* as it is in chaos theory. In order to explain this point a brief survey concerning the observation of self will assist. Following the Copernican revolution (1543), human consciousness was endowed with a constitutive status, not just the "observing" ("conscience positionelle") position it had had before. As soon as the real cosmic relationships between the sun and the earth became clear, we lost our previously alleged centrality in the universe, but gained instead a new insight into our observing consciousness itself. Indeed we were cast into the offstage of the universe, but compensated with the centrality of the observing consciousness, now obliged to look at itself. From now on consciousness had to sustain itself without the security proven false of space around it. In Beckett's works this notion can be seen as (theatre) space first receding from consciousness, then replaced by it.

One of the first modern thinkers to deal with this interdisciplinary organic approach now called "chaos" was Goethe. He was particularly interested in the relationships between observer and observed phenomena and the interaction between theory and its subject matter. Goethe dedicated some of his studies to the *Urpflanze*, to the development of plants, and made fascinating observations on light and optics (as an ardent objector to Newton's theory!). Among Goethe's later followers were Rudolf Steiner and Theodor Schwenk. Steiner (*Philosophy of Freedom*, 1895) took to the spiritual explanations in his attempts to link science, religion, and art in as rational terms as possible, whereas Schwenk researched the formations and dynamics of water and how water forms its own course (like a river or the Gulf Stream creating its watery banks even in the ocean). Pioneers of Chaos Theory – Libchaber, D'Arcy Thompson, Feigenbaum, Peitgen and Richter – followed the Goethean rather than the Newtonian notions of flow as a dynamic combination between form and movement. In yet another insightful breakthrough, Arthur Zajonc explains why he prefers Goethe's understanding of light to Newton's. Beckett in his own way appears much more "organic" in his usage of theatre than meets the naive eye.

"Relativity eliminated the Newtonian illusion of absolute space and time; quantum theory eliminated the Newtonian dream of a controllable measurement process; and chaos eliminates the Laplacian fantasy of deterministic predictability."[18] Beckett's notions of time and space may be better understood in terms of an Einsteinian worldview. Beckett's attitude to matter (theatre sets, props, for example) is clearer when regarded through the principle of uncertainty. Following Heisenberg's principle, but probably inspired by a Goethean spirit, Nobel Prize laureate in physics John Archibald Wheeler showed how the existence of an observer is necessary for the creation of the world to the same extent that the existence of the world is necessary for the creation of an observer.[19] From a mystical, Jewish–Kabbalistic point of view this argument is quite old and well known,[20] but Wheeler's scientific approach enhances the argument about the status of the spectator in Beckett's plays.

The position of Beckett's audience is not only analogous to that of Wheeler's observer and maintainer of the universe, but a *sine qua non* for a fuller understanding of Beckett's entire theatre dynamics. A more complete "realization" of any given piece, as Iser has thoroughly shown, is conditioned upon the active participation of the spectator/listener qua receiver. Beckett gives ample examples of how he considers the audience in his plays, many of them ironic but nevertheless concrete and implicitly quite demanding: "morbidly sensitive to the opinions of others" may be taken seriously in this context of chaos and "if it's the connection, the least jog can do it" (*TII*, 243). These two examples, from a play that treats the "absence in presentia" of the author himself, indicate that Beckett does indeed "admit the chaos".

Beckett was well versed in Goethe's writing. "Wär' nicht das Auge sonnenhaft, Die Sonne könnt es nie erblicken" is a poetic, homeopathic formulation for a theatrical means Beckett uses not only in reference to physical light but to the light as a metaphor of understanding as well. If the self does not perceive something of the "other", he or she cannot identity it in him/herself either. As Hans-Georg Gadamer puts it: "If self consciousness is to become true self consciousness it must find another self consciousness that is willing to be for it."[21] In *Not I* the existence of "another self consciousness" is not only indispensable because of the medium as such. It ensues just as much from what the play (text and performance) implies. The self of the other is reflected in *Not I* in the double consciousness of the character, and is made clear through the one-way attitude of Auditor, who at the same time represents the audience on stage, thus "inviting" them to participate. Yet another "doubling of presence"[22] can be seen between the actress playing the role and the role itself.

In Beckett's plays characters are never "really" alone on stage. If they seem so to themselves or to their audience, they immediately split into two or more selves. In one of his reflective lines, Vladimir says: "Now

. . . (*joyous*). There you are again . . . (*indifferent*) There we are again . . . (*gloomy*) There I am again." These lines not only reflect his particular state of mind. Retrospectively they can be seen as guidelines for treating selves throughout Beckett's drama, all the way to his last play *What Where*. The author practiced what Vladimir preached: moving from "you" to "we" to "I"; then split the "I" so as not to leave it in solitude. In theatre at least, a witness is a precondition. The relation I–it, I–Thou or even I–I creates "The dialogue" as the dramatic answer to the question "What is there to keep me here?" (*EG*, 120). Without it no speech and no being in space on stage make any sense. A Jewish Hasidic saying may be relevant here: "If I am I *because* you are you, then I am not I and you are not you; but if I am I *and* you are you, then I am I and you are you."[23] Deviating from scientific into philosophical and even mystical notions of chaos (of which chaos scientists are well aware), we again witness how components of chaos in regard to the existence of an other are not just analogous to Beckett's *Not I*. Part of the order in disorder is that "Sensitive dependence on initial conditions serves not to destroy but to create" – a theatrical situation if nothing else.[24] While *inlusion*, defined as experiencing participation in a theatrical make-believe situation, is a typically theatrical phenomenom, Beckett makes it a condition for his audience.

In her *The Fire in the Equations*, Kitty Ferguson attempts to link chaos with God: "Those who believe in God welcome chaos and complexity for other reasons beyond the fact that these theories reveal gaps which human knowledge will never fill: (1) these theories can be seen to demolish the concept of a deterministic, mechanistic universe; (2) chaos theory appears to allow an omniscient being to determine events through infinitely minute changes in initial conditions."[25]

Treating notions of determinism and the related reversibility of time is beyond the proclaimed scope of this book and certainly not an exclusive matter of chaos theory alone. However, Beckett's universe, deterministic as it is often presented, still allows for a complete spiritual freedom of consciousness (albeit practically impotent) of the acting self of the role, the "other" and the audience. The other is not an omniscient being like God, but in Beckett's theatre its active mental "self" participation is a prerequisite. In *Not I* the members of the audience are invited to posit their selves instead of the absent I in *Not I*. "Our act of observation creates a real situation where otherwise there would be only ghostly uncertainty,"[26] says Wheeler, inadvertently touching upon a major Beckett issue: but in *Not I* we do indeed create a ghostly uncertainty *because* of our act of observation. Is it the anthropocentric principle that guides Beckett all along? For it is our point of view that dictates what we find in *Not I*. To the question why do we "observe" (the universe, *Not I*) at all, the answer is that if we didn't, we could not be around to ask the question in the first place. It (the universe, *Not I*) exists because we exist. Goethe wrote:

> Not Art and science serve alone;
> Patience must in the work be shown.
> A quiet spirit plods and plods at length;
> Nothing but time can give the brew its strength.
> And all, belonging thereunto,
> Is rare and strange, howe'er you take it.
> The Devil taught the thing, 'tis true,
> And yet the Devil cannot make it.
>   (Goethe, *Faust*, The Witches' Cave scene)

Unlike Goethe who was both religious and a scientist, Beckett, as neither a mystic nor a chaos scientist, delineates the boundaries of both in his art. Rather than indulging in a Faustian repartee, he lets M say: "How could you have responded if you were not there? (Pause.) How could you possibly have said Amen if, as you claim, you were not there?" (*FF*, 403). The audience may choose Clov's words as an answer:

> What (*Pause.*) Is it *me* you are referring to?
>   (*EG*, 130)

1 Philosophical Notions

"Among those we call great artists, I can think of none whose concern was not predominantly with his expressive possibilities, those of his vehicle, those of humanity."[1] Beckett's remark on the painter Bram Van Velde should be seen as an assertion of the way in which the self-consciousness of an artist's mind reveals itself in a work of art. When applied to Beckett himself rather than to Van Velde, these words reveal a concise theory of art and communication. The "expressive possibilities" are those of Beckett or any great artist as the initiator of a hermeneutical circle. In an article on James Joyce, Beckett says that "his writing is not about something; it is that something itself".[2] This statement, whereby works of art can be regarded in terms of self-referential elements, is even more closely focused by Beckett's quoting of Proust's confirmation of his own self-consciousness, which discovers the self-consciousness of others only through itself. "Man is the creature that cannot come forth from himself, who knows others only in himself, and who, if he asserts the contrary, lies."[3]

Beckett's remarks can be regarded as referring to himself and his works as much as they refer to Van Velde, Joyce or Proust. Indeed, a number of critics see an analogy between Beckett's critical essays on other artists and his own literary and dramatic practice.[4] The main common denominator of the analogy lies in the strong emphasis on various aspects of self-consciousness and, more specifically, on the self-consciousness of the expressive artist. Due to the high degree of self-consciousness and self-reference in Beckett's works, many allusions to philosophers, from Descartes to Berkeley and from Wittgenstein to Sartre, can be found in relation to the problem of the self and its linguistic, gesticular, auditive etc. manifestations in Beckett's prose, poetry and, especially, in his drama.

Self-reference as a dramatic device can be seen in Aristophanes' snide remarks on his own character, craftsmanship and medium-awareness in *Frogs, Birds*, and *Peace*; and as an amusing inside joke in Roman plays; and even in the medieval *Second Shepherd's Play*, where theatricality itself is exposed. When *As You Like It, Midsummer Night's Dream* or *Hamlet* are examined more closely they reveal that the self-referential elements in them move from a peripheral function to a dominant position and become a focus that carries a substantial part of the overall meaning. Self-reference keeps growing in explicitness and sophistication through Goethe's *Faust* and Ibsen's *Peer Gynt* until, with Pirandello, it is the main axis of his forty-six plays. In the works of Weiss, Ionesco, Genet, Stoppard, Tardieu and Handke, to name but a few, the centrality of self-referential elements in the plays is inescapable: meta-theatrality becomes the subject matter and the message of the plays.

Samuel Beckett's volume of works relies strongly on the primal act of expressing the inexpressible. While allowing for methodological modification pertaining to the particular character of the material dealt with, I suggest that self-reference, reflexivity, medium-awareness and notions of an implied author, as well as audience, are all manifestations of a unified artistic course – a course that ensues from Beckett's expressed artistic self-consciousness. Textual as well as non-textual manifestations of self-reference constitute a central phase in the following analysis of Beckett's plays and prove to be of major importance in understanding Beckett's entire work.

The approach adopted here follows a number of notions developed by Paul Ricoeur and Wolfgang Iser's critical hermeneutical methods and insights. However, modifications were made because the works in question belong to the performing arts, whereas the respective critics are concerned mostly with texts and readers. The reason for choosing this rather than any other critical approach is that an overall theory – such as psychoanalysis, Marxism, structuralism, etc., and many combinations thereof – presents the problem of the relation of the universal and the particular. A singular work of art, such as a Beckett play or radioplay, will hence be interpreted according to the abstract and extra-artistic assumptions of the theory. When dealing with artistic *self*-consciousness and reference, a close reading of the text and the attempt to interpret it with critical tools (generously supplied by the author himself in and through the work itself) is the only justified approach.

Still, there exists the evident question about the *difference* between the following version of the hermeneutic interpretation and that offered by other "overall" critical approached, since, by being an interpretation, any critical approach necessitates a certain distance from the work criticized. In a hermeneutic understanding the problem of the universal and the particular is reversed: "It grasps individual life experience on its entire breadth but has to adapt a set of intentions centred around an individual ego to the general categories . . . "[5] The inevitable circularity of the hermeneutic approach fits Beckett's own literary devices, often just as circular in structure and style. According to hermeneutic traditions, "interpretation has subjective implications such as the involvement of a reader in the process of understanding and the reciprocity between text-interpretation and self-interpretation".[6]

In Beckett's case the problem is not only the well-known hermeneutic circle presenting itself as an applicable method of criticism, but the subject matter too, which is highly self-reflective and often deals, *within* a given work, with various possible interpretations of a situation. Thus the evaluating criteria of a work correspond and in fact ensue from the self-referential work itself. The difference between the *implied* Beckettian artistic method and the *explicit* methodology used here lies primarily in the structure of the latter. Notions of the self (of author, work, audience) are presented in Beckett's works in a unified way. It is the all-important factor of the direct and immediate presence of the live, *performed* act of presenting self-consciousness on stage that is the central mode here.

Self-consciousness can be defined as "an awareness of oneself by oneself, and an awareness of oneself as an object of someone else's observation".[7] *Artistic self-consciousness* is the more specified self-consciousness that reveals itself in the style, content and various devices of a particular work. *Self-reference* is perceived as a quality of either an utterance (such as "this sentence has five words"), or, by extension, a theatrical means of expression (lights, sets, etc.) that draws attention to itself. *Self-reflectiveness* refers to a situation or a process of reflection of a *self*, be it the author's self, the character's, the actor's, or even the self of the spectator or listener. *Reflexivity* (or "reflexiveness", depending on the critic or philosopher who uses the term) refers to the mirror-like image that a feeling, though or pattern of behaviour may have. In some philosophical texts it is used for what here is called self-reference.

Many of Beckett's protagonists are physically reduced to agonizing existential variations of "I think, therefore I am". They may be paralyzed or blinded but their consciousness keeps flickering, and often quite energetically so. They may say "silence and darkness were all I craved" (*PL*, 316) but as long as they live they cannot avoid self-consciousness. The latter can be considered sheer self-deceit as in Sartre's "mauvaise foi", or as a goal to be attained only by hard work of the will and the mind or by a performative act as Hintikka implies. According to Steiner, it can also be regarded as an act of creative freedom and independent spirituality. An exclusively human phenomenon, self-consciousness also needs a body in which it can function.

The self-conscious elements in Beckett's plays can be divided, according to his own words on other artists, into three aspects of consciousness which, though closely woven together and practically overlapping, are nevertheless clearly distinguishable. Beckett's notion of "expressive possibilities" implies an intense concern for the playwright; we shall therefore look for manifestations of such an implied figure in the text. The notion of "humanity" will be treated here as the particular audience of a Beckett production. Both playwright and audience will be found in the dramatic and theatrical "vehicle", namely the text and the presentation of a play, as implied figures. Naturally, in a play the playwright is relatively more present, whereas in a production the audience constitutes a necessary condition. Concern for the "vehicle" deals with Beckett's awareness for the medium of art and the devices in which the work is presented; namely, the specifically theatrical, or radiophonic, modes of expression in which self-reference manifests itself in these performed acts.

Hans Georg Gadamer says that if self-consciousness is to become true self-consciousness it must find "another self-consciousness that is willing to be for it."[8] Gadamer's comment on self-consciousness also holds true, in a uniquely theatrical way, in Beckett's plays. Characteristically, the basic situation is that of appealing to "another self-consciousness". It is through the speaker – the dramatic character, the situation, and the whole theatrical vehicle – that Beckett appeals to the audience to give him "the impression he exists". The dialogue between characters in the plays is often a double-monologue; monologues sometimes tend to be a dialogue between two phases of the same self (Krapp in *Krapp's Last Tape*, for example). In either case the attempt is made to "reach out" for the necessary self-consciousness of another. The dialogue on stage (i.e., the dialogue that takes place in the "vehicle") reflects a *desired* dialogue between playwright and audience, and hence expresses a concern for humanity. Because the playwright has already done his share by the very act of writing and presenting the play, it is now up to the audience and the individual people that constitute it to do their share. The invitation, as it will be shown, is extended.

Beckett's self-consciousness reveals itself in his plays through self-referential utterances, in patterns of behaviour (both verbal and non-verbal), and through elements such as sets, lights, etc. All these elements are found in the dramatic text, in the dialogue and in the stage directions.

Beckett's highly self-conscious writing belongs to an old tradition that goes back as far as "the bard within the epic of the Odyssey and Euripides' parody of the conventions of Greek tragedy".[9] Whereas literature "practices" self-consciousness, philosophy has been trying for a long time to cope with some of the problems linked with the paradoxicality entangled in self-consciousness and its characteristic self-referential or reflexive manifestations. Although belonging primarily to the literary tradition, Beckett nevertheless makes constant and deliberate use of philosophical notions concerning self-reference.

The Cartesian *cogito ergo sum*, an important step in the development of modern epistemology and human consciousness, can be seen as a psycho-philosophical Copernican revolution, in which the self is now required to face his own boundaries. As an artist who primarily uses (and often deliberately abuses) philosophy, rather than simply obeying its discursive rules, Beckett refuses to accept the exclusiveness of the philosophical approach, although he does not renounce it altogether. The Cartesian dictum must not be understood in Beckett's texts as an inference or a syllogism, but as a performative act. *Cogito, ergo sum* "serves to express the performatory character of Descartes' insight . . . The function of the cogito is to call our attention to something everyone of us can ascertain when he gazes within himself". When interpreted in terms of Hintikka, the Finnish philosopher's "performative" version, Descartes' cogito represents a double fascination for Beckett: it reflects the well-known problem of body and soul, matter and spirit (Beckett ridiculizes the "conatus" . . .); Descartes can also be regarded as the cornerstone of modern self-reference. Whereas in previous generations, literary and dramatic self-reference served as a device to flaunt the artifice, it has, since Molière, Shakespeare, Rembrandt, Cervantes, Bach and Descartes become its very subject matter. In the twenty-first century self-reference is certainly both a device and a focus of interest.

As Ruby Cohn and Hugh Kenner have shown, there are many, particularly ironic, allusions to Descartes in Beckett's works. The reason for Beckett's fascination with Descartes is not merely the well-known split between body and soul,[10] but mainly with Descartes' interest in reflectiveness. Both Beckett and Descartes are, each in his own way, obsessed with self-reflectiveness. But whereas Descartes finds philosophical refuge in the ontological proof of the existence of God, for Beckett doubt is not only a method, but an inescapable reality from which a non-existent God cannot relieve man. Beckett's doubt is not methodical in the Cartesian sense; rather, it is both the method and the subject matter, as any rigorous self-reflective proposition is. Beckett never tries to evade ever-increasing indulgence in self-reflectiveness.[11] In her article on Beckett and philosophy, Ruby Cohn writes:

> Both logical Positivism and Existentialism – perhaps the two dominant contemporary philosophies – attempt to resolve Cartesian dualism by rejecting classical metaphysics . . . Heidegger declares that Aristotle's rational animal is necessarily a meta-physical animal as well, because reason and meta-physics both lead me away from Being, which is or should be the central concern of philosophy. The Positivists, on the other hand . . . reduce common language to elementary propositions that reflect

atomic facts. Since the forms of language cloak the structure of the world, the propositional ladder must be used in order to reach the simplest statement of experience, whereupon the ladder may be thrown away.[12]

Not committed to either logical positivism or existentialism, Beckett's reflexiveness can be partially explained by both. A third approach is advocated by Jaako Hintikka who maintains that the function of the word Cogito in Descartes' dictum is to refer to the thought-act through which the existential self-verifiability of 'I exist' manifests itself. Hintikka explains that the existential inconsistency of sentences "serves to express the performatory character of Descartes' insight . . . The function of the Cogito . . . is to call our attention to something everyone of us can ascertain when he gazes within himself".[13] Descartes' *Cogito*-insight therefore depends on "knowing oneself" in the same literal sense in which the insight into the self-defeating character of the statement "De Gaulle does not exist" when uttered by De Gaulle depends on De Gaulle's knowing De Gaulle. Beckett's self-reflective sentences are totally aware of their performatory character. Thus, Beckett's implied or explicit self-reflective sentences (emotionally charged self-reflective utterances such as I cry, I suffer, etc. – ergo I am; or medium-aware utterances such as I speak on radio – ergo I am; or I mime – ergo I am) are also of performatory quality rather than proofs, or inferences, of existence. They are merely attempts at *showing* the nonsensicality of the very attempt at proving existence. No adjective or verbal construction could make existence more "existing" than it is. Such performative utterances do not *describe* a situation: they create a situation.[14] And it is in this sense that one ought to relate to Beckett's line "It is not about something, it is that something itself" as a statement related to his own work.

The indubitability of the *Cogito*, the "I express" (for Beckett is an artist, not a philosopher) is due to the thought-act each man has to "perform himself" after having witnessed such an act being *performed* by an actor.

Descartes could replace the word *Cogito* by other words in the *Cogito, Ergo Sum*, but he could not replace the performance which for him revealed the indubitability of any such sentence. This performance could be described only by a "verb of intellection" like *Cogitare*.[15]

Cogito, ergo sum, as Hintikka points out, is expressed in the first person singular. Beckett, on the other hand, is interested in the reflexive aspects of the I, and can therefore replace "I think" with almost any other activity ascribably to the I. Furthermore, his attitude to the intellect contains far fewer demands for exclusivity than Descartes', for whom it was crucial not to err logically in his methodical doubt. Beckett's deliberate, almost methodical, lack of method uses self-reflective sentences in order to show the inaccessibility of language to emotion.[16] He uses the Cartesian doubt as a conclusion, rather than as a method to overcome doubt.

Another approach to reflexiveness can be found in Sartre's works. In his article on Descartes, he emphasizes human freedom in connection with the *Cogito*; Sartre believes that Descartes wishes to save Man's autonomy in his Encounter, and that his spontaneous response is to assert man's responsibility in face of the True.[17] With Beckett, again, we find a gap between the tautology of the thought thinking itself,[18] and the emotion and experiential weight that causes its intensity. In irony, says Sartre, "A man annihilates what he posits within one and the same act; he leads us to believe in order not to believe; he affirms to deny and denies to affirm . . . "[19]

Sartre's words refer to reflexiveness inasmuch as they apply to irony. Absolute consciousness, Sartre concludes, being purified of the self, contains nothing of the subject any more. No more is it a collection of images; it is, very simply, a first condition and an absolute source of existence. Beckett's protagonists are, in fact, such "purified of the subject" beings or, rather, people (albeit fictitious) who are reduced to a constant attempt at avoiding self-deceit: "That which affects itself with self-deception must be conscious of its self-deception since the being of consciousness is consciousness of being."[20] Here too an affinity between Sartre's philosophical theory and Beckett's literary practice can be clearly seen, together with the links between reflexiveness, paradox and literary creation. Beckett uses self-reflectiveness as a main tool to avoid self-deception, but because this reflexive process is of a solipsistic nature, and thus likely to be self-nourishing, the very use of literary self-reflectiveness is paradoxical.

Beckett moves between what Sartre calls "*conscience positionelle*" and "*conscience réfléchie*". But because pure reflexiveness is empty, he is in constant search of something to be reflected. It is the act of performance that extricates Beckett from complete silence or empty self-relfectiveness, the latter being like two mirrors with nothing in the middle to serve as the object of reflection.

In attempting to answer the questions "What does reflection signify? What does the self of self-reflection signify?" Paul Ricoeur presents reflection as a positing of the self:

> The positing of the self is a truth which posits itself; it can be neither verified nor deduced; it is at once the positing of a being and of an act; the positing of an existence and of an operation of thought: *I am, I think*; to exist, for me, is to think; exist inasmuch as I think. Since this truth cannot be verified like a fact, nor deduced like a conclusion, it has to posit itself in reflection.[21]

The second trait of reflection is the effort to recapture the Ego of the *Ego*

Cogito in the mirror of its objects, its works, its *acts*. Ricoeur especially emphasizes that which has previously been claimed about Beckett, that the positing of the Ego must be recaptured through its acts. Hence, one can treat Beckett's "obligation" to express in a Ricoeurian way: reflection is a task, an *Aufgabe* – the task of making my concrete experience equal to the positing of "I am". If there is any author who takes this notion of reflection as a task seriously, it is Beckett.[22]

Beckett's equivocal language, mainly paradoxes and tautologies (ensuing from contradictions and repetitions), is the expression of reflection in the sense that reflection is the "appropriation of our effort to exist . . . I cannot grasp the act of existing except in signs scattered in the world".[23] Beckett encounters what Ricoeur calls "the factual existence of symbolic logic" together with the "indigence of reflection which calls for interpretation. In positing itself, *reflection understands its own inability to transcend* to vain and empty abstraction of the *I think* and the necessity to recover itself by deciphering its own signs lost in the world of culture" (emphasis added).[24]

Beckett's supply of grist to the reflective mill is his attempt to exist – an attempt not belittled by the fact that it is the only one he can make.

The "signs" Beckett picks up in his cultural environment – from the two thieves of the New Testament (in *Waiting for Godot*) to ironical allusions to Spinoza's *conarium* (in *Endgame*) – are not only an accumulation of worn-out semi-truths to be inserted in plays about "nothingness in action". The act of writing fiction is a mode of existing by *creating* existence that is not less real than any other everyday reality. In putting plays on stage, reality becomes even more intense. Reflection then, is not just an achievement (and, hence, a tautological or paradoxical petrification of mental activity), but a positive series of acts, a process, an effort to do rather than to indulge in self-pity; it is a desire for knowledge and love for people. It is, finally, a (performative) creation of an act rather than a description of one.

As a task, and as a process, Beckett uses self-reflectiveness *against* solipsism because there is a constant demand to equate experience with the affirmation "I am".

Beckett's sophisticated technique of flaunting his artifice while remaining absolutely faithful to intellectual and emotional integrity involves resorting to tautologies, paradoxes, contradictions and metaphors, all of which are self-reflective in nature. And all of which contain a double meaning. On an everyday level a tautology repeats the same thing twice; intuitively the speaker intends to emphasize the identity of the object in question, yet probably from a slightly different point of view (such as "A rose is a rose", "Even nostalgia is not what it used to be", etc.). Sometimes the two similar objects are metaphorically linked, whereby the first "rose" is the vehicle of the second rose's "tenor". In a contradiction the opposite happens: two objects are presented as mutually exclusive. Logically, tautologies and contradictions are "senseless".

Contradiction leads to paradox in the same way that tautology may lead to metaphor. Two elements "yoked by violence" are presented in either a mutually exclusive structure or a seemingly complementary one. Only if a circumstance non-reducible to logic is added does one understand what a speaker can possibly mean when he says, for example, "A day is a day". The logical attempt to guarantee the non-ambiguity of arguments is likely to be proven empty, though it may be true according to that given logic's truth value table.[25]

Beckett's self-reflective phrases make logic clash with itself, mocking it by dialectically affirming and negating the same thing at the same time. This ensues from a tension between what Beckett calls the inability to express and the self-imposed obligation to do so.[26] Philosophers who try to solve the logical difficulty of self-reflective phrases may succeed in their task, yet fail in releasing the motivating *emotional* reason in the first place. When read in the proper context a statement such as "What shall I do, what should I do, in my situation, how proceed? By aporia pure and simple? Or by affirmations and negations invalidated as uttered or sooner or later?"[27] cannot be answered by logic alone (though the question is obviously a rhetorical one). Ricoeur suggests to "seek in the very nature of reflective thought the principle of a logic of double, a logic that is complex but not arbitrary, rigorous in its articulation but irreducible to the linearity of symbolic logic".[28] Although Ricoeur developed his arguments with regard to "transcendental reflection", his conclusions are valid as far as Beckett is concerned even without resorting to "transcendence".[29]

Beckett's self-reflective, self-referring utterances – as expressed by tautology, metaphor, contradiction and paradox – ought to be regarded as sheer nonsense when considered by rigorous, formal and symbolic logic. Roland Barthes, who is closer to literature than symbolic logic, says that "in tautology, there is a double murder: one kills rationality because it resists one; one kills language because it betrays one".[30] This is definitely true for Beckett, whose uncompromising integrity does not allow him *not* to define "like by like". In his attack on tautology, Barthes sees the intrinsic self-sufficiency and reflexiveness of tautology,

> as a magical act ashamed of itself which verbally makes the gesture of rationality, but immediately abandons the latter, and believe itself to be even with causality because it has uttered the word which introduces it. Tautology testifies to a profound distrust of language, which is rejected because it has failed.[31]

This again holds true for Beckett, who does not refuse language in the strict sense. Although writing against it Beckett does keep writing *in* language. And he does so by playing the two similar elements of tautology very dynamically against each other. This structure of tautology is similar to that of self-reflecting utterances in which the "I" plays itself against itself.

With regard to paradoxes, or "extended contradictions", two major paradoxes can be detected, both of which are paradoxically interlinked: (1) the paradox of expression ("there is nothing to express"), and (2) the very attempt at expressing paradox. Beckett's self-consciousness uses both, and does so not only in order to prove two members of a contradiction to be mutually exclusive and logically incongruous, but also in order to indicate that the very *use* of a self-reflective paradox is in itself paradoxical and reflexive. How, then, is one to escape this seemingly hermetic and perhaps nonsensical circle? Raymond Federman provides a clue:

> Too often we are guilty of reading paradoxes into Beckett's fiction because we cannot accept that which destroys itself as it creates itself – that which is contrary to common sense, or that which points to itself, even though ironically, as paradoxical. And yet, the primary meaning of the paradox is, as defined by the most basic dictionary: "a tenet contrary to received opinion: . . . an assertion or sentiment seemingly contradictory, or opposed to common sense, but yet may be true in fact". This definition can indeed apply to the whole Beckett canon . . . [32]

Maintaining that "Beckett's fiction becomes a denunciation of the illusory aspect of fiction – stories which pretend to pass as reality,"[33] Federman does perhaps not go far enough. Beckett writes fiction telling about fiction, thus creating a different kind of reality, such that fiction is denunciated through its own means, but finally, and paradoxically, becomes real through the process of the audience's active participation. When an act of self-consciousness is externalized and expressed in a play it can itself be the object of expression. This occurs in Beckett's self-reflective statements, which are utterly sincere and constantly yearning to be empty (in order to remain sincere). Sincerity and emptiness are inseparably linked. Because the self-reflective author makes his own consciousness the object of his writing, he usually avoids making clear-cut statements about the situation of Man, society or the world. Those are to be supplied by the audience. The work itself makes no clear "commitment" and avoids evaluation, except of itself. And because truth-value can be ascribed only to arguments, the work and its implied author remains sincere in the sense of having neither lied nor said the truth. If a statement is made, it is immediately put to the torture test of constant doubting reflexiveness that does nothing short of rendering it empty – because basically nothing has been affirmed. In Beckett's plays constant shifts between affirmation and negation are performed and with an asymptotic zig-yes-zag-no plunge into yet another layer of his self-reflective consciousness. The contradictory, tautological and para-doxical nature of statements is:

(a) an attempt at achieving solipsism, while
(b) knowing that this is impossible because
(c) he is trying to communicate his solipsism, otherwise he would not be a playwright who presents his works.[34]

Self-reference is the sharpest tool a self-conscious artist has in his attempt to make his "telling" coincide with his "showing". Through reflexiveness Beckett brings the two aspects of the described and the description to their closest, mutual proximity: "Philosophy and literary language both refer to the world, but are themselves the world they refer to."[35]

Susan Langer says that it is in the inaccessibility of the emotional to the formal field of logic and language that "the real nature of feeling is something language as such – as discursive symbolism – cannot render". The emotive aspect is much more closely linked with the literary than with the philosophical. Few sensitive people would doubt the passion (though in itself an extra-philosophical drive) with which Wittgenstein, for one, pursued the writing of his tractate. On the other hand, a number of critics noticed the use Beckett makes of philosophy, whether an ironic use or not. But a logical solution of an emotionally charged self-reflexive statement in Beckett's works, even though intel-lectually rewarding when successful, still leaves the recipient (readers or audience) with an odd sense of frustration: the existential malaise that brought a self-referring paradox in the first place is not yet solved. Self-reference and paradoxicality are hence both the means and the end of stating that "the form of language does not reflect the natural form of feeling".[36]

It is beyond the power of language, according to Beckett's incessant self-referential statements, to reflect anything but the inability to reflect, thus reflecting inability in a very able way and indulging in yet another paradox in an escalation of reflexiveness *ad infinitum*. Finally, it must be asked how the form of language in the theatre actually refers to itself. Beckett and his implied and "built-in" audience must seek odd conso-lation in the knowledge that this is "all he could manage, more than he could".[37]

Reflection in Beckett's texts is characterized by sincerity and empti-ness. Wayne Booth says: "Nobody seems to read these empty works without an intense emotional and intellectual response and it may be that without too much absurdity, we can make for ourselves a small opening into interpretation by looking at the response."[38] Iser explains this emptiness. In developing Roman Ingarden's ideas of *Unbestimmtheitsstellen*, he claims that a large degree of indeterminancy of a text calls for a similar participation on behalf of a reader who is invited to fill in the gaps:

> The indeterminate elements of literary prose – perhaps even of all litera-ture – presents the most important link between text and reader. It is the switch that activates the reader in using his own ideas in order to fulfil the intention of the text. This means that it is the basis of a textual structure in which the reader's part is already incorporated.[39]

Iser too says that, "The works of Beckett are among those whose inde-terminancy content is so high that they are often equated with a massive allegorization."[40] This remark is well proven by Iser's own analysis of some of Beckett's works, as well as by an ever-increasing number of critics who attempt to fill in what was not definitely set down.[41] "Every favourable critic implies that somehow Beckett has found in *him* a rare kindred spirit," says Wayne Booth (emphasis added). Indeed, this is hardly possible if one accepts that it depends on the uniquely theatrical way in which an audience, rather than a reader, is invited to fill them in.

The high degree of indeterminancy in Beckett's works is enhanced by the self-referential elements of the text and other theatrical means. Such self-referential manifestations may seem to exclude the audience because they happen to and between fictitious dramatic characters. Yet, the very act of performing them in front of an audience is in itself an implicit invitation for the audience to participate, at least vicariously, in someone else's reflection and self-reference. The strong inclination of turning inwards, of self-sufficiency – a trait rightly felt in Beckett's works – is a double-edged sword. Such a development in modern theatre suggests: "Leave me alone. I (the particular character or an entire play) am perfectly self-contained." Yet it is doing it *in public*, and hence, by its very mode of existence, implies: "I need you, the other, the audi-ence," in order to assert, as Gadamer says, the self-consciousness of the self through the self-consciousness of the other.

This need for the "other" is the connection between the self-reflective manifestations in Beckett's works and the many indeterminate gaps in them. The actual, always-present and performed-alive acts of self-consciousness invite the audience to "impose consistency, purpose and meaning . . . But in doing so, the spectator becomes the only person in the play".[42] This is true not only in regard to Iser's original idea about indeterminancy, due to its paradoxical nature, but also in regard to the self-reflective patterns that often *create* indeterminancy. By plunging with his or her real self into the fictitious self of a character, a member of an audience extracts the play from its theatricality and makes it *real*.

Despite all his lame and blind protagonists, despite his "crippled" language and constant reference to impotence in every possible sense of the word, Becket is still, in at least some minimal sense, a *doer*, a performer. Strangely, perhaps paradoxically, it is the very utterance of a reflexive paradox that, in a psychological–artistic way, is a momentary relief from the violent yoke of the rigid illogicality of paradox itself. It is the link between the performing, in the general sense of doing, and the *performatory*,[43] that is the only way out of negative self-reflexiveness. As far as Beckett is concerned, in order to accept his work the individual spectators must internalize it and "perform" it, all on their own.

2 The Message of the Medium – Theatrical Techniques

Nearly every one of Beckett's plays has at least one dramatic element as part of its subject matter, or focuses reflexively on an important component of a theatrical event. Often his plays revolve around various aspects of the theatrical situation itself, creating their own fictitious yet highly authentic reality. The plays are not "about something" – they are that something itself. Because they are their own subject matter the plays turn the means of their expressiveness into the very content of expression. Therefore stage space, movement and lights, stage properties, costumes, exits and entrances, dialogues and asides, notions on acting and directing, and of stage instructions and critics – are not just dramatic and theatrical devices in the service of some overall message. Rather, and especially in Beckett's *self*-referential plays, meaning must first be looked for in the actual components of drama as a genre, and in theatre as a medium. Because Beckett's technique is self-referential – in a way similar to the red colour in a Mark Rothko painting or a musical sequence in a Stockhausen piece – he deals with dramaturgical principles as well as with theatrical technique: the "meaning" lies *in*, rather than hovering above or beyond the components.

Following a tradition of scepticism, Beckett examines the validity of his expressive means while tentatively using them – having, obviously, no *other* means to use. In strictly conforming to the external framework of the black-box stage, Beckett systematically exposes the self-reference of the elements of which the organic whole of the play is composed. His form and theatrical technique create content, expressing the vision of a bleak, absurd, yet playful life to which we stubbornly cling: "To find a form that accommodates the mess, that is the task of the artist now."[1]

Waiting for Godot combines a wide range of theatrical means and devices – characters, props, movement – than do any of the later plays. It is, perhaps, Beckett's most accessible play. As it is about waiting or even "waiting for . . . waiting", the play enlists a wide spectrum of *theatrical means* to reinforce the sense of the futility of activity. Later plays, however, demand of the audience greater concentration on single theatrical devices. From this play on, Beckett proves to be more and more economic in his use of stage-technical means – less light, less space, less props, etc. Only "offstage" becomes *more*. Having drawn attention to themselves, the means of expression commit theatrical suicide by merging into the almost impossible; they dwindle into the active and very present void of offstage, the only way non-being can actually be presented in a theatre.

It is the actual performance of a play that extricates Beckett from the intrinsic paradox of self-reference: if indeed the plays are exclusively self-referential, why (and how) do they mean anything to "non"-selves? Theatre does not necessarily have to conform to the rules of formal logic, and the answer lies on the experiential level. Beckett does not describe a human situation on stage, he creates one in front of an audience and, implicitly at least, demands full and real partnership and cooperation from the audience. It is the real individual self of any member of the audience that has to substitute for the self of the character. From the point of view of the *medium*, this can be done only if all the components of the medium are enlisted in the same self-referential way.

Typical theatrical elements – such as space, movement, props, light and offstage – are each given what can be called a *leading* part in Beckett's plays. At the same time, these elements are carefully balanced and orchestrated in the individual play. Jindrich Honzl says: "We are discovering that stage 'space' need not be spatial but that sound can be a stage and music can be a dramatic event and scenery can be a text."[2]

One can see the plays' texts, and certainly the playwright's directions concerning non-textual theatrical elements, as a transposition from one semiotic system ("text") to another ("production" or "performance"). In theatre, such transposition is projected into stage-space, and constitutes the dramatic space, a set of immaterial relations that constantly change in time as the relations themselves change. Beckett, however, succeeds both in allotting a central role to each theatrical device, and in orchestrating them so that they are still well-harmonized. From a semiological point of view, text and stage directions can be viewed almost as systems in opposition: because of frequent textual references to non-textual elements, they serve as mutually corrective systems. They often annotate and comment on each other, maintain the tension and support each other. The theatrical devices, individually and together, draw attention to themselves, to the medium of which they are part, and to their author. And all this is done before an audience.

Space

In a play "you have definite space and people in this space. That's relaxing".[3] But the actual locations Beckett chooses for his characters and for the actors who play them is anything but relaxing. In the first plays there is at least something an actor can relate to spatially – a country road and a tree; an empty room with two windows, two ashbins and a wheelchair; a mound in the middle of a *"trompe l'oeil"* desert. In later plays the actors find urns, a narrow-lit strip to pace on, a hole in the backdrop to stick a head or a mouth through. In some plays pieces of furniture are deliberately detached from the room to which they might have belonged – a bench, a table, a rocking chair. The rest of the stage space is referred to in words, lights, gestures and movements. Some of the characters dwell on the very edge of the stage, suggesting that their existence is psychologically interior and real rather than exterior and fictitious.

Beckett characters are well aware of their spaces and stage locations; they go through precise routines of examining their whereabouts. In most plays they refer to their location first and foremost as to a *stage* in a theatre; only then might they make other suggestions to where they are. There exists a whole range of unease between a Beckett character and his or her space – from slight discomfort to excruciating suffering. In actually referring space to themselves, or describing it as a space of themselves, the plays manage to turn the public event of a theatre performance into a highly private matter. Lack of specificity on stage naturally avoids the realistic fallacy; rather, it calls for a process of "gap filling". Indeterminacies in the text, as Ingarden, Booth and Iser have shown, can here be seen in theatrical-performative and actual terms rather than as just "reading" into lines. In presenting a stage full with emptiness, Beckett activates the audience's imagination and involvement, and extends an invitation to make this stage space their own: a well-furnished fully decorated stage is perhaps more appealing at first sight. Yet, as Peter Brooke emphasized, it cannot compete with the suggestiveness of an empty space.

In *Waiting for Godot*, Beckett delineates the outline for many of the sophisticated but simple uses he makes of stage in his later plays. The three conventional spatial dimensions, or axes of movement, on any stage, are (1) the sideways, left–right axis, (2) the up and down stage axis, and (3) the vertical axis of ground to top. Here they are all thoroughly employed. Each axis can be regarded as a spatial metaphor to the main motif of the play: "Let's go . . . we can't, we are waiting for Godot."

The sideways direction along the "country road" is the most frequent in the play, reinforcing the sense of a world devoid of centre and focus. Lucky's rope, for example, is "long enough to allow him to reach the middle of the stage before Pozzo appears" (WFG, 21), in this way emphasizing that the road stretches way beyond stage left and right. The spectators thus see a rather arbitrary fragment of a much longer road. Change and development are expected to appear from the wings, but as soon as potential action is dragged toward centre stage, it dissipates into sheer aimless activity of passing time. Waiting is performed in the centre where the three axes meet; in spatial terms this suggests that there is "nothing to be done".

Conversely, the upstage–downstage axis represents enclosure, entrapment between the back wall and the auditorium, a confinement of sorts: "Imbecile! There is no way out there." The vertical direction, a combination of the sideways openness and the frontal finality, suggests the quest for redemption, debasement of fellow characters and a mock-metaphysical solution for the entire play. All characters frequently raise their eyes to the sky, wondering if night will ever come. All of them mould stage space and shape it with every conceivable movement of their bodies – they roll, walk, jump, sit, lie and slouch – trying to do something to their much too weakly-defined location. Still, there is one thing they know for sure – they are on stage in a theatre. Notwithstanding all else that space can be (they call it "the midst of nothingness"), they also tell each other where the toilet is in the theatre – "second door to the left". "(Estragon moves to centre, halts with his back to the auditorium). Charming spot. (He turns, advances to the front, halts, facing auditorium). Inspiring prospects. (He turns to Vladimir). Let's go" (WFG, 14).

Whereas the stage in *Waiting for Godot* is exposed as theatrical mostly through text and movement, the stage directions of *Happy Days* call for maximal simplicity and symmetry. The *en face* view of the set and the actress is a direct, frontal appeal to the audience, making no pretense at verisimilitude. Indeed, the *"pompier trompe l'oeil"* backcloth is there to represent a theatre set, exposing the artificiality of the device in a self-referential manner. It emphasizes the theatricality of the foreground and the overall effect. As in many other Beckett's plays, it is a declaration of the stage and its space *as* theatrical.

Within this large expanse Winnie's playing area is deliberately and strikingly limited. In the blazing light her situation in the mound is made protruding in contrast to the background. An unblinking face-to-face position is established between Winnie and the audience; a unique diagonal direction between her and Willie; and a vertical relationship within herself between being metaphorically and literally "sucked down" by the earth while constantly yearning upward. "I would simply float up into the blue . . . Don't you ever have that feeling, Willie, of being sucked up?" (*HD*, 152). Being sucked down and yet feeling sucked-up is the subject of the play; space and movement represent metaphoric embodiments of an existential predicament.

Krapp, like Winnie, Vladimir and Clov, goes through a long process of orientation on stage in order to establish his stage existence, both as actor and as a dramatic persona. He is seen fumbling, standing, stooping, advancing to the edge of the stage, staring vacuously before him, and so on. Beckett introduces the actor as well as the audience to stage space before the first words are spoken: "(Table, and immediately adjacent area in strong light, rest of stage in darkness.)" Having remained motionless for a moment, Krapp then thoroughly checks the small spaces of his pockets and the table drawers, and the large stage space around him. By first pushing the banana peel into the pit it is suggested that he is conscious of the spectators, despises them, and has decided to turn in on himself. He paces to and fro, testing the right–left axis movement. He will return to this axis three times in the play, to the exclusion of almost all other directional movement. Only a small section of Krapp's assumed room is presented, and a possible reason is supplied:

> With all this darkness around me I feel less alone (pause). In a way (pause) I love to get up and move about in it, then back to . . . (hesitates) . . . me (pause) Krapp. (*KLT*, 217)

Krapp is uniquely identified with his space. Hence the exits into darkness represent an escape from the self, dramatized through visual and spatial means, and more conventionally by bringing the ledger and having a drink.

Play goes yet one step further in Beckett's exploration of stage space. What might previously have seemed even faintly "realistic" is replaced with three figures in urns. As in *Krapp's Last Tape*, the contours of the stage itself disappear, perhaps in the attempt to prefer the undefined space *of* the play to the more defined space *in* the play. *Play* seems to extend the auditorium onto the stage, where the audience sees impassive faces "undeviatingly front throughout". The reduction of stage size and playing area coincides with less light and movement, yet with a growing intensity of focus.

Confinement in space moves from a road to a room, a kitchen, an ashbin, a wheelchair, a tiny area of light, a mound – and now, to an urn. Except for the light and the figures' lips, nothing moves. Textual references to the distant past, to the outside and to space and movement, replace actual movement or a sense of space on stage. Space here is not just diminished, it is fictionalized through the characters' speeches. The treatment of space in *Play* foreshadows that of *That Time* and *Not I*, where it is treated almost as a non-performing medium – it is talked about. In *Come and Go*, as opposed to *Play*, the figures are able to move quite freely and suffer no apparent physical pain. Characteristically though, since they are able to move, Beckett denies them the ability to verbally express themselves freely, working toward an increasingly radical separation between text and movement. Hence, if *Play* is a stylized orchestration of dialogue, *Come and Go* is a stylized arrangement of movement on stage – in and out of its space.

In *Play*, Beckett temporarily eliminates the non-speaking figure by denying it the eliciting light. In *Come and Go*, however, a single figure must consciously and theatrically perform an exit. Emotional tensions among characters are explored through metaphorized stage space, which, as the name *Come and Go* suggests, is a play of exits and entrances.

Beckett deliberately uses all four main directions on the stage: front, back, left and right. Each direction recurs three times, returning at the end to the initial position, facing front. More than in any of the other plays, the characters do not play a role, but rather *play at playing*. Their existences are limited to their stage existence. They do not have enough substance – dramatic, philosophical or otherwise – to symbolize anything but their own existence as characters in the play. While their main role is to occupy stage space, paradoxically their absence from stage is as effective as their presence, if not more so. Stage space becomes a participant in the play.

The spatial relationship between Mouth and Auditor in *Not I* is diagonal – just as it is between Winnie and Willie in *Happy Days* (though Willie is on Winnie's right and to the back). *Not I* may therefore be conceived as a late third act of *Happy Days*. Winnie has sunk so far into her mound that only her mouth remains, and Willie has become the Auditor. The mound has moved from its upright position to a horizontal one, with only its edge turned toward the audience.

In *Not I*, Beckett delicately balances between both sides of the metaphoric equation of the world as a stage: "Out . . . into this world . . . tiny little thing" (*NI*, 376). The frame of reference for the opening words is at once "the world", a womb out of which the little girl emerges, and the stage onto which Mouth spills her first words. Hence the first word could only be "out". Space in *Not I* is conceived in terms of outward movement. Through manipulating stage space Beckett shows how difficult it is for anyone to move out of his inner space.

Not I is Beckett's first play located off centre. Unlike Winnie in *Happy Days*, Mouth is situated upstage audience right. In subsequent plays Beckett continues to move the action from the centre to either left or right. Since all directions or axes are lost and inner space takes over, there is no point in centring the action. In *Not I, That Time* and *Footfalls* the concept of space is internal, like a sock turned inside out. Whereas the previous plays attempted to see inside from the outside, here one is already inside. Centreed action is often associated, as in *Endgame* and *Happy Days*, with deliberate theatrical consciousness in the self-reflective context of "now I am acting". *Not I* is self-reflective through its reference to inner space, which cannot be spoken of in terms of directions at all since inner space is what *Not I* tries to get "out" into this world in an excruciating attempt to pour it on stage. Whereas Winnie speaks of Mildred or Milly as the subject of her story, Mouth is herself an embodied story; Mouth is inseparable from her story.

In *That Time* a whole head, rather than only a mouth, performs the listening part done by the Auditor in *Not I*. He listens to three of his own inner voices distributed and broadcast from three electronic speakers as inner voices of three phases in his life. Nothing but the head is seen and the audience must now combine and synthesize the minimal visual stage space with a relatively complex, three-fold auditive and conjured-up "space" of the voice(s).

Footfalls marks another variation of inner space. Space is linked with subjectivity of point of view, since one does not know whether May is an evocation of V's voice (as in *That Time*), or whether V's voice is a projection of what happens in the mind of the pacing May.

The play most concerned with space is *Endgame*, where the stage is presented as the only still barely living place on earth. The main motif of waiting in *Waiting for Godot* is here replaced with "I'll leave you – you can't", justified by the "objective" statement "there's nowhere else". Waiting is associated mainly with time; location is of lesser importance. Perhaps the meeting with Godot is to take place somewhere else on the open-ended road. Accordingly, the activity in a "waiting for ... waiting" play is a centrifugal pressure toward the outside. With all its variations of inner and outer places, psychological spaces and many "voids in enclosure" (which serve as spatial metonyms), *Endgame* examines the confinements of a location "finished, it's finished, nearly finished, it must be nearly finished".

The characters in *Endgame* embody three stages of immobility, each governed by a corresponding limitation of space. Clov confines himself to his relatively large kitchen space (3×3 m); Hamm is confined to his armchair on castors but can be moved; Nagg and Nell can only raise their heads out of the ashbins. In addition, the characters are all closed in by the stage; actors and audience are closed in by the theatre, and so on, *ad infinitum*; mentally, no one can escape, though actors and audience can (and some do) walk out.

Clov's opening moves in the play establish stage space by examining it. Stiffly staggering through the room, Clov defines the shape and size of the playing area; he moves sideways and downstage–upstage, and climbs up to the windows. His moves are related to the inside and outside worlds, and to the various "lids" and curtains that lie between them. He completes his trip in stage space by dryly commenting: "Nice dimensions, nice proportions" (*EG*, 93).

The outside is said to include "earth", "sea", "hills", "nature", "flora", "pomona". Inner or closed space is represented by covers, and by closed and covered props and objects – ashbins, windows, the handkerchief on Hamm's face, the sheets over the bins – and in the dialogue: "here we're in a hole" or "put me in my coffin". Significantly, body and heart are also described in terms of closed space: "last night I saw the inside of my breast" and "the bigger a man is, the fuller he is . . . and the emptier" (*EG*, 93).

It soon becomes clear that the concept of outer space and the possibility of escaping there are illusory. "Outside of here it's dead", says Hamm. Morbid imagery dominates references to the outside: "corpsed", "extinguished", "zero", "ashes" and "grey". Reversing the picture of Creation, in which Light, Earth and Water were the beginning of life, Beckett here reduces life to a blood-stained "old stancher". The room, grim as it is, remains the last source of life. In order to avoid a new beginning, a re-creation of the world, the rat will die outside and the little boy will not be allowed in. The colourful and lively scene of fishing on open seas dissipates into "there is no more nature". Nature exists, but only as a negative force: "We lose our hair, our teeth! Our bloom! Our ideals!"

In designing his stage spaces, Beckett implies that spatial relationships and structures on stage correspond to the relationship between stage and audience. The characters are provided with various "lids" which reveal or unveil: a telescope, glasses, sheets, curtains. Through the curtains, however, one sees only death, the telescope detects nothing but extinction, and the sheets, once removed, reveal the pitiful sight of Hamm. All are momentary glimpses into closed and open spaces. Inasmuch as Clov brings Hamm information from the outside, he brings the same information to the audience. Opening lids, uncovering sheets and drawing back curtains suggest a person looking inside himself, and a stage being opened and exposed to the audience. The audience is drawn into the act of looking out, but the audience is on the "outside" and so ends up, as it were, viewing itself. Relationships among the characters mirror their spatial arrangement on stage. Clov's yearning to leave Hamm is counteracted by Hamm's paralysis and lack of will; Nagg and Nell echo this oppressive bond. The outer space for which Clov supposedly longs is suggested on stage by the two windows facing away from the audience. But the audience is also on the outside. Thus a third parallel is implied in the relationship between audience and actors, whereby the audience's yearning for freedom is counteracted by the actor's entrapment, or vice versa. Nagg and Nell, confined to their bins, often fantasize about far and open places. They speak of the Ardennes, the road to Sedan and Lake Como. Hamm, just a little more mobile than his parents, is interested in his immediate surroundings rather than in distant places. Clov, the most mobile character, is obsessed with his closed-in kitchen space. He says: "I love order. It's my dream. A world where all would be silent and still and each thing in its last place, under the last dust." Beckett endows his most stationary characters with memory and imagination that can compensate them for their immobility, while his more mobile characters yearn for close and closed spaces.

Ultimately, the stage in *Endgame* is a self-reflective metaphor of internal or inner space. Because Hamm is blind, his perception of space is already interior, he can indeed look only inside his breast. Throughout the play, Hamm's gaze is directed inwards, whereas Clov looks outwards – sometimes with the help of a telescope – and mutters vague remarks as to what he observes. Neither the audience nor Hamm is convinced that the objects he describes exist in reality. Does he invent them? Does he speak of them in order to aggravate Hamm, console him, or both? The audience, with Hamm, is forced to depend on Clov's eyes, on his repeated walks to the windows, and on his reports about "offstage".

In *Waiting for Godot*, Pozzo remarks, "The blind have no notion of time. The things of time are hidden from them too." But do the blind have a sense of space? By referring to its own use of space, *Endgame* brings us closer to the concept of internal or inner space. In the later plays these inner spaces receive a radical theatrical treatment, in which space is gradually internalized, becoming inner and offstage space at one and the same time.

Movement

Space and movement are closely linked on stage. It is through movement, and its gradual stripping to an almost absolute standstill, that Beckett's characters relate to themselves and to their surroundings. Many of these characters are invalids – blind, paralyzed, old and weak – who, bitterly and courageously, yearn for the ideal condition where they would not have to move at all. For them, movement, including that of their still flickering consciousness, is superfluous and unwanted – a primary difficulty. It must never be taken for granted that a Beckett character moves.

The stylized, hectic, incessant music-hall, and pantomime-like movement of *Waiting for Godot* is gradually reduced in the next plays; it is made stiffer, more obsessive, slower and painful. In *Happy Days*, the two characters are set up to contrast and mirror one another's spatial situation. "What a curse, mobility," Winnie says. And when Willie, as usual, does not answer, she tells him, "Well I don't blame you, no, it would ill become me, who cannot move, to blame my Willie because he cannot speak." Winnie is not just stuck; she speaks it, acts it out, knows it, knows that others know, that they know she knows, and so on.

Willie is also boxed in, but to a lesser extent. He is sprawled out and free to move in and out of his hole. "Weary of your hole dear?" Winnie asks him, adding self-consciously, "Well I can understand that." Krapp is free to move in and out of his narrowly lit desk area, but the three figures in *Play* can only move their mouths. In *Not I*, only one mouth is seen; it moves vehemently. Its contortions are well orchestrated and juxtaposed with the gradually reduced forehand gestures of the Auditor. In *That Time*, only breathing and eye movement is a sign of life, and in *Breath* nothing at all moves – at least not visually. Here movement is delivered to the light and the sound. The figure in *A Piece of Monologue* seems to be able to move but chooses not to. *Footfalls*, *Come and Go*, *Rockaby*, *What Where* and Ohio *Impromptu* present movement patterns that are stylized, rigid, compulsive and often deliberately mechanical. Even in *Theatre I* and *Theatre II*, special attention is given to a man in a wheelchair and to C who neither moves nor talks. *Catastrophe* shows clearly how movement is used and abused for the sake of theatrical effect – a director tells his assistant how a protagonist ought to pose.

Becket demands a unique treatment of movement so as to draw special attention not only to the kind of movement but rather to the very phenomenon. In an early interview he said:

> Producers don't seem to have any sense of form in movement. This kind of form one finds in music, for instance, where themes keep recurring. When, in a text, actions are repeated; they ought to be made unusual the first time, so that when they happen again – in exactly the same way – an audience will recognize them from before.[4]

Beckett also wrote three plays dedicated almost only to movement, in which he eliminated the use of words altogether: *Act Without Words I*, *Act Without Words II* and *Quad*.

> As in *Waiting for Godot* stage business summarizes our lives. When the character in *Act Without Words I* is flung back from the wings, he turns his attention to the stage to which he is condemned and he explores its space.[5]

In *Act Without Words II*, falling is replaced by rhythmic movements. John Spurling sees both pantomimes in terms of "punishments from the underworld".[6] He identifies the pantomimes with the myths of Tantalus and Sisyphus.

Eugene Webb, in a commentary on the two pantomimes, says that "Beckett presents in very simple stylized form, pictures of certain aspects of the human condition."[7] In Webb's view, *Act Without Words I* emphasizes the relation of man to the external world which frustrates him, whereas *Act Without Words II* focuses on man's relation to the internal forces within his reach or in his control. In *Act Without Words I*, man is not even tempted to hope, having learnt from experience that his hopes are futile and barren. Webb, referring to Martin Heidegger, discusses this state of *Geworfenheit* as an extension of man's basic existential situation. For him, the dominant theme is the consciousness that follows the state of being "thrown".

Ruby Cohn finds in the pantomimes a statement on the spiritual aspect of man's "stage-like" surroundings. There is no escape from despair in *Act Without Words I*, despite the character's suicide attempt.

John Fletcher claims that *Act Without Words I* is embarrassingly obvious, particularly the attempted suicide. He admits, however, that the two pantomimes shed light on the author's plays, for the Beckettian hero is closely linked with "circus clownery, music hall, cross talk and dramatic mime".[8] And yet the implications inherent in Beckett's choice of the pantomime form are not followed through. Fletcher, along with other critics, restricts his interpretation to thematic analysis, adding that "unlike the real clown [Beckett's clown] seeks not to amuse others, but to cheat his own boredom; he is acting, but for himself".[9] This may be so, but to overlook the means and medium by which Beckett demonstrates this process is to disregard one of the most essential aspects of his artistry. Some critics fail to draw a distinction between conventional pantomime and Beckett's significantly different use of the form.

Traditional pantomime relies almost entirely on convention; its essence is style, which is the attempt to mould a set of movements into a meaningful continuum. Behavioural patterns are crystalized through precise stylization. The shrug of a shoulder or the nod of a head on the part of good mime can unify an entire series of movements. Classical pantomime, developed in the French schools of Decroux, Lecoque, Marceau and Jean-Louis Berrault is familiar to Beckett: in this type of pantomime the stage is empty and the mime is generally alone, creating his own world by means of pose and movement. The glass in Marcel Marceau's "Cocktail Party" exists only in the spectator's imagination but is suggested by the contours of the player's hand; the spectator is invited to fill in the imaginary glass. There is no ambiguity in the meaning behind each movement or in the imaginary world, which the spectator is called upon to join. In Beckett's pantomime, however, objects do actually exist on stage and it is up to the audience to determine or guess at their significance. The classical mime artist calls attention to how he can create an entire world with his body; Beckett's pantomime questions the validity of this very assumption, asking whether anything can be communicated without words. It is, basically, a language of movement in a process of disintegration, of calling attention to itself and not to the world it could possibly describe. While using some of the conventions of pantomime, Beckett mocks the need for such conventions of communication. From this perspective, one can discern a relationship between the way Beckett uses words (*"il n'y a rien d'autre, monsieur"*), and the way he presents movement and action. Both are underscored by a sense that there is simply no better alternative. It is just another theatrical technique which will soon implode into its own ruins.

The pantomimes represent a step in the search for pure minimalist modes of expression. Whereas Beckett's radioplays deprive the audience of the security of visual images, the pantomimes deprive us of the relative security of words. In both cases the omission is an integral part of what the play is trying to convey. The overall picture must be completed in the minds of the listeners and spectators.

Critics of Beckett's pantomimes who add to the movements the same verbal interpretations disregard the author's manipulation of the medium for its reductive quality. Jan Kott's description of *Act Without Words I* as a Book of Job without the happy ending, various references to Tantalus and Sisyphus, and Barnard's suggestion of the subtitle, "As flies to wanton boys are we to the gods," link Beckett to a cultural background shared by critic and author. As such, these critics relate to Beckett's *Act Without Words* primarily on the conventional level, whereby an invitation is extended to replace actions and movement by verbal paraphrase. A position on stage and the arrangement of stage props are perceived as symbolizing a given human condition. Yet, in the same way that Beckett explores the function of words, so in his pantomimes he makes a statement about the *absence* of words. Beckett, rather, uses space and movement as tentatively as he does dialogue and words. The "act" of attempted suicide in *Act Without Words I* is therefore not "embarrassing in its banality", but doubly impressive, because Beckett consciously works with, and comments on, banality.

Beckett's first pantomime for one player takes place in the desert, under dazzling light. *Act Without Words* has indeed more elements of classical pantomime – "reflections," "dusting," "body poses" – than *Act Without Words II*. But rather than create objects through movement, the pantomime plays with the objects themselves, just as Vladimir and Estragon play with words in *Waiting for Godot*.

The first pantomime is a pseudo-metaphysical comment on man's conditioning or automatic action and reaction. Since automatic response does not require the intervention of words, the absence of words is essential to the pantomime's central theme, for the pantomime forces the audience to rely on its conditioning, eliciting from the spectator a series of automatic associations. This "statement" is acted out through the audience's reaction or response to the play. The pantomime technique becomes a self-reflective comment on that very technique; the theme is not only presented but dramatized through the actual theatrical event.

Offstage in *Act Without Words I* takes on the role of the goad of the second pantomime, sending the player hints and objects, and whistling to him. After being thrown onto the desert-stage twice the player tries to exit; but both times he is thrown back. He learns that he had better not attempt to flee. The player's stage-life consists mainly of falling and reflecting. He continues to rise from his falls until the very end, when he lays himself down in resignation. His reflections serve as intervals between the actions.

The player in *Act Without Words I* is a combination of the passive and active players in *Act Without Words II*. The first series of "acts" ends in reflection, which, like an aside, conventionally indicates introversion. Then the tree descends and casts its shadow in the desert. The whistle goads the player, drawing his attention to the tree; he sits in its shadow looking at his hands. It is to his hands that he returns at the close of the mime.

The next series of events does not seem to be logically cohesive; any sense of continuity depends on the spectators' efforts to ascribe intentions to the backstage forces. A pair of scissors descends, the palms of the tree close, a pitcher labeled "water" descends and the player reaches for it. The spectator, together with the stage figure, does not succeed in discovering any causality in the events, which are interrelated only by a time sequence. Presumably, *propter hoc* should not be derived from *post hoc*; the act of ascribing significance arises from a need to ascribe meaning rather than from the objective (or arbitrary) development of events.

A similar lack of causality and significance marks the descent of three blocks, which the player diligently proceeds to organize. He toils in arranging the blocks properly (as in his attempt to reach the pitcher), but his labor may be futile, since the "water pitcher" may turn out to be the name of the label, bearing no connection to the contents of the pitcher. This action is not cyclical, as in the second pantomime, but linear, ending with the look the player casts at his hands. This look signifies man's ultimate acceptance of "being there", in the same way that the descending props can finally be understood only in the sense of "being there". It is the same motion that freezes Vladimir and Estragon at the end of *Waiting for Godot*, Winnie and Willie at the end of *Happy Days*, Krapp at the end of *Krapp;s Last Tape*, and the "freeze" at the end of *Theatre II*. The word-less movement, establishing a connection between man and his objects, also fails, and movement becomes dead still.

Unable to live without the help of external objects, one can at least try to commit suicide with them. Through mime and the use of movement Beckett demonstrates that movement too is unnecessary. The player's last act, turning to his hands, suggests a resignation of movement; the act without words ends as an act without movement, as though negating the very principle on which it is based. In both pantomimes the subject matter of movement is movement itself.

Beckett's second pantomime calls for two players, A and B. A is slow, strange and distracted. B is brisk, fast and precise. The pantomime also includes a goad, a non-human participant, a personified object of movement. At the opening of the pantomime the two sacks and the small goad enter, the goad spurs A into action. The goad is active, pushing forward, retreating, and coming on again. Pointing up A's non-reactiveness, the goad serves as an indirect characterization of A and B, measuring their movement against its own unchanging rhythm. Essentially, the goad is a catalyst for action, a spur for "external powers", consciousness, nature or God. Significantly, the two players never see the goad; it disappears before they emerge from their sacks. They remain unaware of who or what woke them from their inactive state of sleep, pre-birth or death. As soon as the goad achieves its purpose – to create movement – it disappears. The series of actions then undertaken by the two human characters are performed independently of the goad. The "intention" suggested by the goad's actions is thus illusory. Its actions are as arbitrary as the series of actions performed by A and B.

The differences between the two characters become immediately evident, but ultimately the differences are superficial. A only wakes up after being prodded twice by the goad. His actions are slow, interspersed with periods of reflection. In order to deal with his life (or a new day), he relies on pills and prayers. Even in eating his carrot he demonstrates lethargy. B, on the other hand, awakens at the first spur of the goad. He checks his watch ten times during the play, exercises instead of praying and brushes his teeth instead of popping a pill. He takes good care of himself and consumes carrots with relish. He turns to the compass and map, orienting himself in time and space. Yet, like A, at the end of the day (or perhaps his life) he returns to the sack.

The contrast between these two behavioural patterns turns the pantomime into a dramatic affair, but neither of the two characters is defined as morally or spiritually superior to the other. B's compulsion to expend energy – to do, to act – may be interpreted either as a courageous, though objectively unjustified, challenge to life; or, on the other hand, as much ado about nothing. A's lethargy and lack of will may be as valid a response to the situation as B's activity. The two characters are, in a sense, Beckettian archetypes, recalling Vladimir and Estragon, Hamm and Clov, Winnie and Willie, and other active/passive couples.

The neutral, detached goad reveals both A and B as characters who are mechanically conditioned to respond to stimuli, each according to his pre-conditioned nature. Similarly, each spectator in the audience will evaluate the characters according to his conditioning. The gap-filling process, which is intensified in pantomime, allows the audience to re-enact the theme of the play, through the relationships between themselves and the stage, and through their understanding of movement pure and simple. The absence of words forces the spectator to rely even more than usual on his or her interpretative faculties. Movement in the pantomime falls into three categories: (1) motions of the goad in place, (2) the human response to the goad in place, and (3) movement of both from right to left. In Beckett's original chart the goad enters first without wheels, then on one wheel, then on two. In the pantomime, linear time clashes with cyclical time. Linear time is expressed by the movement from left to the right; whereby left indicates beginning and right indicates end. Cyclical time is signified by A's second awakening, suggesting that the entire pantomime is meant to be performed again and again. Like *Waiting for Godot*, *Act Without Words II* concentrates on sideways movement, but here repetition is not conceived in terms of time or waiting but in terms of space. The two players appear from offstage-left and will soon disappear offstage-right, presumably going through the same motions forever, on stage as well as off.

Act Without Words II includes in its spatial conception closed inner spaces. The sacks, as both womb and tomb, recall Nagg and Nell's ashbins. While in *Endgame* three degrees of mobility are distributed among four characters, both characters in *Act Without Words* incorporate Clov's imperfect mobility, Hamm's stationary mobility, and Nagg and Nell's complete immobility. Although A is more lethargic than B, both begin and end like Nagg and Nell, and in their movements are confined, like Clov and Hamm, to a series of trite, repetitive actions. The absence of words, like Hamm's sightlessness, directs the attention to internal existence; muteness, like blindness, cuts one off from the external world. Deprived of words, movement is stripped of meaning and becomes banal. *Act Without Words I* and *II* are not banal plays, they are about the banality that ensues when acts are not covered by a veil of words to give us the illusion of content, meaning and depth in human existence. One may also argue that the illusion of content is equally banal . . .

The goad, perhaps, is the inside interpreter of the pantomime. Its neutrality puts an end to any other attempts at interpretation. The characters simply act their parts and the goad merely awakens them for a while before pushing them to stage-right.

Quad (1980) was described by Martin Esslin as "a dynamic, witty yet terrifying attempt to compress eternity as endless recurrence into a single dramatic image, a poem without words".[9] The piece – a mime for dancers – is a square dance in which the performers–characters are doomed to an internal, perpetual ritual of self-referential movement. The movement seems to be yearning for some external significance, perhaps suggested by the colours used and by the musical instruments played. The constant, persistent avoidance of the centre is perhaps indicative of what Beckett often does with words; even bodily expression revolves only around its empty self-centredness.

Light

Lighting in all Beckett plays is either darker or brighter than one finds in conventional theatre. The unnaturalness of light draws attention to light itself rather than just to the stage lit by it. "If there were only darkness, all would be clear. It is because there is not only darkness but also light that our situation becomes inexplicable."[10] Light can be a symbol of life, and its absence a symbol of death.[11] Excessive light is associated with intense heat and often with bareness. Light can represent sight, insight and understanding. Between the practical inexistence of total darkness and the equally excruciating impossibility of absolute light, Beckett explores shades of stage lighting, most of them in various intensities of grey. While giving precise instructions concerning the size, colour and angle of the lit areas on stage, light in the plays is always conspicuously and deliberately unsettling and ambivalent. It draws attention to itself not only because of the highly sparse use made of it, but because it is used "non-realistically". Also, there are many verbal comments interspersed in the text which note the technical as well as metaphoric functions of light as life. Usually spots or small areas of stage are focused on, only rarely is a whole stage lit up. Perhaps, if it were a physical possibility, Beckett would use spotlights that shed black beams.

The unconventional manipulation of lighting in the form of the two light shifts in *Waiting for Godot* – "The light suddenly falls . . . In a moment it is night . . . The moon rises at back" – is anticipated in the text. "Will night never come", "night doesn't fall", and "waiting for night"

are phrases repeated continually by most of the characters. Pozzo fore-
sees how night will fall:

> Tirelessly, torrents of red and white light it begins to lose its effulgence, to
> grow pale . . . pale, even a little paler until . . . ppfff! Finished. It comes to
> rest . . . but behind this veil of gentleness and peace night is charging . . .
> and will burst upon us . . . pop! Like that . . . just when we least expect it
> . . . That's how it is on this bitch of an earth. (*WFG*, 36)

Vladimir and Estragon wait for night because then they can stop waiting
for Godot. They often scrutinize the sky when they want to know the
time or identify the place. Dusk light, half way between day and night,
does not help them either: it indicates uncertainty in time and space.

The central association of light is its contrast with night. "The light
gleams an instant then it's night once more." The sudden though clearly
expected fall of the light suggests sudden death. The tramps emerge
again at twilight on the following day. Absolute darkness suggests
absolute lack of life; the "moon" replaces the light of the evening sun,
and sustains the characters until the next day. Although "the sun will
set, the moon will rise and we away . . . from here", on stage it is neither
evening nor night, nor morning or day; it is an extended dusk where the
lighting conditions represent insecurity and expectation. Godot can be
linked either with light or with darkness. The sudden sunset and the
immediate rising of the moon is deliberately theatrical and neutralizes
any sentimentality the sudden darkness might create.

In *Endgame*, there is no escape from the grey, decayed light inside or
from the grey desolation outside. Hamm's inner self and his surroundings are equally barren. Clov reminds Hamm that old Mother Pegg died
of darkness because Hamm did not give her oil for her lamp. Hamm
craves for a ray of sunlight; he claims to feel it on his head, but Clov
assures him that the sensation is illusory, a result of wishful thinking.

In *Act Without Words I* the light is dazzling, but not more comforting.
Light does not necessarily signify life, or even goodness. Krapp feels less
alone "with all this darkness round me". Light represents an encounter
with himself; a return from the darkness into the lit centre is a return
"back here to . . . me, Krapp". He sings in the dark backstage area:

> How the day is over
> Night is drawing nigh-igh
> Shadows . . .
> (*KLT*, 222)

Night and absence of light are associated with silence. In *Endgame*,
light is supposed to filter in through one window and sound through
the other; but neither light nor sound actually comes in because "the
earth might be uninhabited". The grey light of *Endgame* and the fast light

shifts of *Waiting for Godot* become "the blaze of hellish light" in *Happy Days*.

> I speak of when I . . . could seek out a shady place, like you, when I was
> tired of the sun, or a sunny place when I was tired of the shade, like you.
> (*HD*, 153)

Beckett develops the notion of "evil" light: "Don't lie sprawling there in this hellish sun," Winnie tells Willie. Throughout her happy day, Winnie is preparing for night. "It is", she says, "a little soon – to make ready – for the night"; being the optimist she is, she still prefers the scorching heat to night. She is afraid of a black night without end because it (obviously) connotes death. "Hail holy light" are Winnie's opening words in Act II, when she has no protection whatsoever from light. But she is also aware of the deadening effect of heat and light: "Shall I myself not melt perhaps in the end – little by little charred to a black cinder – On the other hand, did I ever know a temperate time?" Final darkness comes both through the gradual fading of light and through a great burst of light that will "melt" the "flesh". "Fear no more", Winnie says, quoting a Psalm that speaks of fear of day and fear of night, in order to encourage herself.

In *Come and Go*, the lighting is "soft, from above only and concentrated on playing area, rest of stage as dark as possible". Here light draws least attention to itself, rather it serves to light the costumes of the characters. It is also one of the rare occasions where light is described as "soft". The text itself comments on the dim lighting:

> *Vi*: How do you think Ru is looking?
> *Flo*: One sees little in this light. (*CG*, 89)

In *Breath*, light and sound are directly associated with life; darkness and silence with death. The gradual increase of sound and light may indicate that there also exists some prime of life, when light is greatest.

Mouth in *Not I* speaks "about all that light" and "about all the time this ray or beam . . . like moon beam". This ray or beam is, first and foremost, the very projector that cast light on Mouth in the play. The light mentioned is metaphorically united with the light lighting the play.

In *Footfalls*, the light is "dim, strongest at foot level, less on body, least on head". May refers to it as "a faint tangle of pale grey tatters". The visual effect created by her trailing corresponds to the lighting system.

The play that offers the most insight into the function of light is *Play*, which is "about" light and lighting:

> speech is provoked by a spotlight projected on faces alone . . . The transfer
> of light from one face to another is immediate. Not blackout . . . the
> response to light is not quite immediate . . . (*PL*, 307)

The only moving element in the play is light itself. The perceiver, the audience – the other – becomes identified with the searching theatrical spotlight.

Light is the activating force of the play, its primary structural element, and the thing to and about which the three characters speak. As an active force, the spotlight moves rapidly from one face to another, soliciting the characters' short speeches. As a structural device, the light blacks out about half way through the play and becomes weaker, about half its previous strength, along with a dramatic shift in speech.

In *Play*, Beckett turns from the perceived to the perceiver. The mobile element in the play is not a character or a "goad" but light, which represents an activating perception of a sort. The characters respond accordingly, speaking when the light falls on them. Whether the spotlight stands for God's providence, the audience's scrutinizing eye, an eye of "the other", a voice of conscience, or simply for what it is, a spotlight, it is always a perceiver rather than that which is perceived: "And now that you are . . . mere eye. Just looking. At my face. On and off . . . Looking for something. In my face. Some truth. In my eyes. Not even" (*PL*, 317).

The urns are arranged so that they are "touching one another". The light replaces any movement the figures may be expected to perform. By avoiding sideways movement, and at the same time having the characters so close to one another, *Play* creates an effect of utter solitude and isolation. The love-triangle in which the three players are involved is the direct textual reason for this image of mutual solitude. The contrast between the spatial arrangement (in which the characters face front at all times, as though oblivious to each others' presence), and the dialogue (through which they are programmed to function with each other), has a powerful impact, in which a three-in-one or one-in-three unit is presented.

The various functions of light in *Play* are mentioned by all three characters, each in his or her particular way. M is mainly concerned with "being seen"; he is the first to realize that they are all in a different situation. He describes the experience as "down, all going down, into the dark, peace is coming at last". He wonders whether he is "hiding something". Addressing the light he says, "Lost the thing you want?" He does not want to be abandoned: "Why not keep on glaring? I might bring it up for you." M is not sure whether he can ascribe any meaning to light, perhaps it is "mere eye. No mind?" M finally understands that "as much as being seen" is the only sure thing in his situation. But before getting a chance to find the answer to this question, he, together with his two ladies, is made to repeat the entire play again.

The attitude of W1 to light differs. She begins by asking for mercy – "tongue still hanging out for mercy". But her most vehement and consistent line is "Get off me". She suggests the possibility that the light might be weary of her. Like Winnie, she calls it "Hellish half-light", and like M, she asks, "Is it that I do not tell the truth . . . and then no more light at last, for truth?"

Referring to the times when the light is not on her and she is not made to talk, she says: "Silence and darkness were all I craved. Well, I get a certain amount of both. They being one." She expresses Beckett's ambivalence in using light: "Dying for dark – and the darker the worse." She knows the light is playing with her, just as M thinks he is being seen.

For W2, the present situation is confusing, but she prefers "this to . . . the other thing. Definitely. There are endurable moments." The "other thing" is complete darkness, and she wonders whether the light might blaze her "clean out of my wits, but it would not be like you". Like the other two, she makes the mistake of "looking for sense where possibly there is none". She wonders what the light does when it goes out: "Sift?"

All three characters play with the possibility that the light just plays with them. They shift, together with the scenic shifts, from responding to the light by speaking of their love triangle, to wondering about the inquisition itself. It is as though they enquire in the second part about the logic and validity of the confessions made in the first part. The light in the first part is therefore only a means, which, in the second part, is asked to account for its action. In the first part it is a device; in part two it is the object, a means that has become a theme, the subject matter.

M, W1 and W2 all want to know what the light stands for, to explain it and make sense of it. Each character regards the light in terms of his or her situation in the love affair. W2, the "other" woman, is about to go mad. Woman 1 wants the light off her, while Man finally starts to realize that he is "as much being seen". The secrecy with which he tried to handle his affair is no longer there. It is now out in the light. The two women address the light as though it were M. The man wants peace and quiet, both from the women and from the light. All characters project psychologically onto the light what the light makes them project by physically projecting on them.

In *Play*, light is the protagonist. The shift is from a rather banal story to that of questioning the inquisitive "solicitor" of the story. In the second part of the play, light is drawn into the action, and is as much a subject of interrogation as that which interrogates, shifting between implied self-reflectiveness and explicit self-reflectiveness. The second part moves from the inquiring light to the inquiring characters. Neither the light nor the people can transcend the theatrical situation. Yet Beckett succeeds in rendering this tautology in the refreshing light of self-reflexiveness. He unites the "content" of the story in *Play* with its modes of presentation – a lively dialogue between a projector and his projected actors on stage.

Stage Properties

Things give us the feeling that they have been in the world before us. Perhaps not only on the theatre stage are we invited to use them only temporarily.[12] Since early times certain objects, other than their obvious materiality, are supposed to be imbued with holiness, namely spiritual qualities. On a theatre stage, however, props, "theatre things" (and properties) are often a material bridge between images and ideas, animated with whatever the playwright, director and actors infuse into them.[13]

Sustenance props, such as biscuits and "pap", run short in *Endgame*; Krapp has a craving for bananas and alcoholic drinks; the water in *Act Without Words I* remains unattainable. Many medical props appear in the plays: Pozzo uses a vaporizer; Hamm misses his painkiller; Krapp relies on drink as his remedy; and the lethargic man in *Act Without Words II* uses pills. Winnie has a bottle of red medicine that she throws at Willie, injuring him, while Willie forgets his Vaseline outside his hole. In contrast, Beckett also introduces murderous instruments, though, characteristically, their potential is never actualized. The rope in *Waiting for Godot* snaps, Clov does not kill Hamm with the axe in *Endgame* (though he considers the possibility), and Winnie never uses her revolver. The rope and scissors in *Act Without Words I* are useless as instruments of suicide. Visual aid props are also common. Pozzo, Hamm and Winnie have spectacles; Clov uses a telescope; Winnie uses a magnifying glass. Krapp is deliberately described as needing a pair of glasses, being very near-sighted. Hamm and Pozzo (in Act II) are blind and yet wear dark glasses in order to emphasize their misfortune.

The general tendency is to endow props with life, and then to cast them away and show their uselessness. Like words and movement, props appear as an immaterial layer to that which is really human. They are only a means – in life and theatre alike. Props are presented as super-fluous, dysfunctional extensions of human needs or abilities – they are gradually peeled off.

A revealing remark concerning stage properties and their role in Beckett's plays is expressed by Winnie in *Happy Days*: "Ah yes, things have their life, that is what I always say, things have a life. Take my looking glass, it does not need me" (*HD*, 40). In many of the other plays too, characters demonstrate a remarkable self-consciousness in opposi-tion to dependency on existing things. Things don't have a life of their own, but they become very lively "spokesmen" to characters who cannot or will not use words.

Most of the props in Beckett's plays are simple, everyday objects in natural realistic surroundings. With few exceptions, they are things people wear, carry, or have around the house; the context of the play transforms them into significant objects. Usually there are very few props on an almost empty stage, and an economic use is made of what *is* there. In *Waiting for Godot*, the tramps carry with them all they need. The tree and the mound emphasize the bareness of the stage, which encourages a closer viewing of the props.

Stage properties characterize the figures. By constantly activating the little they have, each time in a slightly different way and according to a musical principle of motif and variation, the figures succeed in creating a feeling of abundance and variety (of poverty), as well as exposing their idiosyncrasies. Rather than having all they need, they need what they have, to the extent that they are rendered as (almost) self-contained. Vladimir repeatedly looks into his hat, puts it on and takes it off; Vladimir and Estragon exchange hats in a long procedure; Lucky can't think without his hat on. Exchange of hats implies an exchange of personality; hats serve to characterize each player as an individual. The chicken serves a similar purpose. Pozzo, indifferent to the other three, gnaws the meat enthusiastically; Lucky and Estragon watch enviously, and Vladimir considers it scandalous. The prop not only provides a non-textual, indirect indication of the characters' different roles, but also identifies Estragon with Lucky.

Use of a rope reveals the characters' relationship with one another more clearly than any of the other props: it is the rope that ties them together, figuratively and literally. Pozzo and Lucky lead each other with a rope; Vladimir and Estragon are tied by a common pact to hang themselves together. Here the rope serves a more ambiguous and subtle purpose. Whereas a master lashes his slave, one presumably does not commit suicide with one's pants off. The two ropes are presented so as to comment on each other and underline the motif of bondage. In Act II, Pozzo uses Lucky as a blindman's dog, and the same rope becomes a sign of his dependency rather than his dominance.

The more common a prop is, the more suspicion and trouble it causes. Things cannot be trusted. The boots never fit, but the whip is used quite casually. Pozzo's pipe raises more comment ("Puffs like a grampus") than his vaporizer. Pozzo's watch (which he then loses) appears about a third of the way through the play; thereafter no new props are introduced and the old ones are used again and again, and become part of a routine. The only prop in the play that is used just once is Vladimir's coat: Vladimir covers Estragon's shoulders with it. Because it is not part of a familiar routine, the gesture is truly affectionate, and provides for a rare moment of true intimacy.

Props in the play are juxtaposed with the characters: they often relate both to themselves and to each other as objects. At one point the stage instructions suggest marionettes: "They remain motionless, arms dangling, heads sunk, sagging at the knees." Physical contact between Vladimir and Estragon is generally a result not of warm feelings but of clownery. In clownery the performer develops a personal relationship with objects, struggling with their resistance to his manipulations; conversely, he treats humans (including himself) as though they were objects. This is evident when Pozzo indulges in self-pity after having declared that he was taking Lucky to the market to be sold.

Props are often used as "mini-spaces". Pockets, shoes, hats and bags are all small closed-in spaces. By having his characters fumble, poke and draw out the "wrong" items from their small personal spaces, Beckett comments on the elusiveness of the larger stage space. Vladimir must always check whether his hat is really empty before putting it on. Estragon cannot get his shoes off and Vladimir remarks: "There's a man all over for you, blaming on his boots the faults of his feet" (*WFG*, 12).

In casting away a prop, or just not having one, Beckett emphasizes utter self-reliance, perhaps not so much as an act of willpower but as an inevitable adaptation to life itself.

In *Endgame*, props are unavailable or insufficient. Existence can go on, it is implied, even without minimal assistance from objects: the characters are gradually stripped of their worldly possessions, meager as they already are, leaving nothing but the unaccommodated self. There are no bicycle wheels, no pap, no painkiller and no sawdust for Nagg and Nell. Hamm notes with his typical black humor that there are "no phone calls" and in the end there are not even coffins. Surely, this is a definite sign of creeping death, an object-language counterpoint that complements the major elements in the play. Like the overcoat in *Waiting for Godot*, Hamm's picture, which faces the wall, is used only once. It is a textual joke, since the audience never gets a chance to see the picture. Clov puts the alarm clock instead of the picture on the wall, adding that he is "winding up," thereby figuratively comparing himself to a prop.

Hamm treats Clov as an object. He whistles to him, orders him about and only rarely acknowledges Clov as an other. When Clov suggests putting an end to "playing", Hamm says: "Never". In a game one is allowed to treat the other as object; perhaps Clov wants to achieve a more humane relationship by dropping the "game". The most strikingly self-reflective reference to the use of props occurs in the story about the tailor and the pair of trousers. The story is a humorous metaphor for the gradual diminution of materials or objects in the play. Nagg further comments that even Hamm's way of telling that story is getting "worse and worse".

In *Act Without Words I*, objects are arbitrary, descending on stage without a reasonable coherence. The attempt on the part of the audience, the characters and the critics to grasp the significance or purpose of the objects is but the exercise of that prerogative.

Despite many attempts at manipulating objects, the player discovers that objects do not help him either to live or to die. Ultimately, he is isolated from the objects surrounding him and there is nothing left for him but to look at his hands, for it is by means of his hands that he "handles" (or doesn't handle) the world of objects or his own life.

He learns (or is conditioned) not to respond to the temptations of props, apparently manipulated by some cruel fate operating from backstage. Props are "flung to the stage" as is the actor. He decides not to reach out for them or to endow them with significance: he cannot apply his abstract laws of "here" to the concrete existence of what is sent from "there". If the world functions properly, one may assume no more than a happy coincidence between man and object. Beckett effectively dramatizes the courage of resisting temptation. His player, in need of water, lies quietly and gazes at the audience. When he perceives that there is no salvation to be found in the audience either, his gaze returns to the stage and rests on his own hands.

Act Without Words I examines how props play with people. It is therefore less important to note what objects descend on stage, than that objects do descend and that man is first tempted by them, then conditioned to mistrust them, and finally rejects them in an act of defiance. The play begins and ends without any props at all, suggesting that objects are in themselves lifeless and senseless.

In *Krapp's Last Tape*, the relationship between the live Krapp and the recorded Krapp is reflected in the use of props. Krapp's past self resides in the reel-box, while his present self is in the small circle of light on stage, undeed another "box". Eating the banana passes without comment from live Krapp, but recorded Krapp speaks of eating a fourth banana. The black ball is a prop that never appears on stage. Especially in the later plays, there is an increase of objects whose mode of existence is auditory-temporal rather than spatial-visual. These imaginary props point to a further internalization of the "plot".

The banana – one of the more conspicuous props in the play – has a number of functions. It is a phallic symbol ("Plans for a less . . . [hesitates] . . . engrossing sexual life"); it suggests exploitation in throwing away the peel after having consumed the content; and probably most important, like Krapp's two (or more) selves, the banana has an inside and an outside. Only at the end do we discover which of the selves is the peel and which is the content. The banana establishes Krapp's contemptuous attitude to the audience, but at the same time it evokes a sense of sympathy for the pathos and humor of weakness. Live Krapp does not treat his recorded self as an object, although, in a sense, it is a self that is preserved mechanically-electronically. Still, he decides not to yearn for the old years: "Not with the fire in me now!" Whatever this fire may be, it is more alive than the past, mechanized self; no matter how lifeless the human self, it is still preferable to the "objectified" self.

In *Act Without Words II*, the significance of the props lies in their function as a substitute for words. The absence of speech reinforces the impression that the actors behave like mechanized dolls, and are themselves props. The goad's action, arbitrary as it may be, has more purpose than the activity of the two characters; it pushes them from one side of the stage to the other, while their movements seem to exist in a vacuum.

Breath is a play in which Beckett seems to have collected props (perhaps from all of his own other plays . . .), testing whether they can visually lie there in their own right and power. They are arranged horizontally on stage, as garbage, yet even here they are given meaning by the human vagitus. They represent what man will leave behind when he dies: a heap of garbage.

An intricate pattern of using props is revealed in *Happy Days*. Winnie needs Willie simply to be here, so that she will know she is not talking to herself: "Just to know that in theory you can hear me though in fact you don't." Willie, until the end, is seen only in bits and pieces of hat, newspaper or hand. He is, in a way, nothing more than a prop. Winnie feels almost equal affection toward her real props and toward Willie. As an old couple they are used to treating each other more as objects than as people. Only in the end, when Willie crawls out of the mound, is his human selfhood really asserted. He may have transformed from prop to person. Albeit too late.

Winnie relies on the bag the way one relies on one's soul, memory or imagination:

> Could I enumerate its contents? . . . Could I, if some kind person were to come along and ask, "what all have you got in that very big black bag Winnie?" Give an exhaustive answer? . . . No . . . the depths in particular, who knows what treasures. (*HD*, 151)

The bag connotes self-reliance, activity, variety and depth; like Winnie, it is an unmoving object. There is always something in the bag, like in Winnie's soul, to take out, think about and play with before sinking further down.

Because Winnie is an incurable optimist, props in *Happy Days* become supportive objects; the very opposite is true of *Endgame*. Both plays are concerned with "what remains", but Hamm treats the progressive deterioration of props with grim, self-conscious pessimism, whereas Winnie is happy with the slightest attention or minimal sign of life she can produce. Glass instruments – Winnie's glasses, the magnifying glass, the mirror and the bottle – point to Winnie's interest in "seeing herself" and the world around her, although her range of vision is extremely limited.

In *Happy Days*, props form an intricate pattern of associations. Almost all the props are actively related to one another. After thoroughly examining her toothbrush, Winnie looks at it with her glasses and then with the magnifying glass. She wipes it with the handkerchief, and comments on the "hog's setae" and on the handle. The handkerchief is used in turn for wiping eyes and glasses. Winnie takes out the revolver, a red bottle of medicine and a red lipstick; but instead of killing Willie with the revolver, she throws the bottle and it hits Willie, whose red bloodstained head appears for an instant. A series of props are arranged so that they form a continuum of life and death, yoked together by the colour red (blood, love, health) into a superb little "prop-scene", a brilliant non-verbal conversation of things, finally summed-up by the words "ensign crimson". The revolver stands for death, the bottle for health and the lipstick for love. Ironically, Winnie "shoots" her beloved Willie with medicine and wounds him, like the toy dog in *Endgame* that becomes a substitute gaff.

In the second act, new objects are no longer introduced and the familiar ones have accumulated a series of associations. The revolver, for instance, has by now acquired the necessary charge of potential threat and, like the rope in *Waiting for Godot*, of a possible way out for Winnie. The dirty postcard is a comic comment on the impossibility of lovemaking between Winnie and Willie – a point in their relationship which is verbally referred to later: "There was a time when I could have given you a hand."

By the end of Act I, Winnie has returned her props to her bag. Act II opens with the revolver, the bag and the parasol, all of which lie next to her. She relates to her props – now untouchables – in words, activating them as before, but verbally. Having previously fumbled with them so much, the relationships between herself and her objects have already been established, and Winnie's situation is made to look even worse. Even the trifling, though intense, use of objects is denied her. Thus, attention ought to be paid both to her and to her objects, though separately. Winnie will sink, her props stay.

Like Winnie, the props in *Happy Days* move along the sky–earth axis. The parasol is supposed to protect her from heat and light, but is not as heat-resistant as Winnie herself: it catches fire. Her bag is an earth image from which objects emerge.

Although Winnie is almost completely immobile, she is one of the most lively and active characters in Beckett's plays, constantly talking, fidgeting and fumbling. Winnie checks her existence not only against the presupposed self-consciousness of another self (Willie), but also against the absence of self in objects. She finds relief and consolation in the words she utters incessantly, as well as in the contents of her bag.

Playing with props is more significant to the play's dramatic structure than the dialogue. Winnie's activity convinces the spectator that something is really "happening" in the play. She talks about and to objects, saying, "So much to be thankful for. There will always be the bag." With Winnie, words become objects, and she turns them about as she does the pistol or the toothbrush. She uses words, examines them and then abandons them, just as she returns objects to her bag. She fondles words as she does the mirror and the comb, trying to endow them with the concreteness of objects. Through Winnie the relationship between words and objects in the theatre is dramatized:

> Is not that so Willie? When even words fail at times? (Pause, back. Front) What is one to do then, until they come again? Brush and comb the hair . . . (HD, 147)

Or:

> Cast your mind forward, Winnie, to the time when words must fail. (She closes eyes. Pause. Opens eyes) And do not overdo the bag. (HD, 149)

Winnie makes words of objects and objects of words. Even the pistol turns from object to a mere name, a word:

> You'd think that the weight of this thing would bring it down among the . . . last round. But no. It doesn't. Ever uppermost, like Browning. (Pause) Brownie . . . (turning a little towards Willie) Remember brownie, Willie? (HD, 151)

Words and movement and objects continually mirror and reflect one another.

> Fortunately I'm in tongue again. (Pause) That is what I find so wonderful, my two lamps. When one goes out, the other burns brighter. (HD, 153)

The two "lamps" – props and words – are interchangeable; when she can't use one, she uses the other.

Dressed to Kill

Although not props in the strict sense, costumes can often function as props. At the same time, other theatrical elements too can be a part of everyday life. When Beckett's tramps appear in bowler hats, the effect is both comic and pathetic, but also realistic. Krapp's costume is not entirely unfeasible for an old lonely man who dresses like a dandy. The black and white colour arrangement is also appropriate in view of the lighting and Krapp's exits and entrances from darkness to light.

In *Happy Days*, the contrast between Winnie's costume and her position in the mound is even more striking. Her arms and shoulders are exposed, she wears a pearl necklace and is "well preserved"; she might well be tanning at leisure. Willie wears fancy hats and is "dressed to kill". Clov changes at the end of *Endgame* from his indoor clothes to a "Panama hat, tweed coat, raincoat over his arm, umbrella, bag." Yet he does not leave. In the same way that he announces "This is what we call making an exit" so his costume change refers directly to his role as actor. It is as though Clov had finished his role and returned as the actor playing Clov, reading to leave the theatre but politely waiting for the actor playing Hamm to finish his role. The costume change identifies Clov with the audience; like the audience he is "impassive and motion-less, his eyes fixed on Hamm, till the end". He has become a spectator, watching the end of the game.

The same device is used in *Act Without Words II*. The two players step out of the sacks wearing shirts. Outside B's sack lies "a little pile of clothes neatly folded (coat and trousers surmounted by boots and hat)". The pile of clothes is referred to in the stage instructions as C. Player A comes out of the sack, puts the clothes on, goes through a set of motions, undresses and returns to the sack with his shirt. Then B emerges, puts on the same clothes, enacts his routine and undresses, folds the clothes, and returns to the sack with his shirt. The clothes become both the char-acters' articles and the *actors'* costumes. As theatrical costume, the clothes are there to be used by any player playing the part. Costumes are often used to reflect back to the audience. Like Nagg and Nell, who have lost their legs, their house and all their possessions, who live in trash bins, and have managed to cling to their night caps, A and B in *Act Without Words II* have only their shirts to keep them from betraying their complete vulnerability. As Winnie says, "Go back into your hole now, Willie, you've exposed yourself enough."

The costumes of the three women in *Come and Go* are situated at the focus of attention in this play. The slight difference between the dull violet (Ru), dull red (Vi) and dull yellow (Flo), as well as the similarity in "Full length coats, buttoned high" (*CG*, 356), suggests that costume here works to both cover and discover. The short text (121 words) and the stylized movement draw attention to the stage clothing: the external, visual aspects are emphasized over the potentially more revealing textual aspect. Exits and entrances, equally, are woven into a theatrical grammar, almost as a joke at the expense of the convention of talking "behind one's back". The text can therefore be regarded as illus-trating an action, the visual centre of which is the costumes. Faces, usually the main instrument of expression, are shaded with "drab nondescript" broad-brimmed hats, a mask of sorts. The colours – yellow, red and violet – suggest, together with the text, that even nostalgia is not what is used to be: the usually warm and lively colours[14] are here dull and juxtaposed against the formalized action on stage and the hushed atmosphere.

The women walk in and out as though they were in a fashion show, but, ironically, the costumes do not change. Costume is what the women have become; their abstract formulaic language is only dimly suggestive of character. Since their movement on stage is equally devoid of expression, costume alone defines their existence. Like stage space, costumes finally become another form of entrapment; like props, they isolate the characters both from their surroundings and from themselves.

3 The Poetics of Offstage

Offstage has been given insufficient critical acclaim; its immense potential is on the whole as yet unrevealed. Offstage should be regarded as the link between drama and theatre, and in this particular context - between the "dramatic practices" and "theatrical techniques" of the previous chapter. In many modern plays and productions it is both a technique and a "content", a medium and a message alike. Since theatre deals with "presences" in time, in space and in actual three-dimensional human beings who are really there, the feeling for the *not here, not now,* and *not I* has always been very strong. The shadowy *Doppelgänger* of the theatre, offstage, has developed side by side with drama and theatre alike.

In varying degrees of consciousness, technical expertise and elegance, many playwrights and directors have used offstage as an active, sometimes dominant element in their plays. From the drama of Pirandello to Beckett, Stoppard and Handke; and in parallel in the theatre from Stanislavski to Apia and Kraig, and to Grotowski and Brook, theatre has acquired more and more the sense of being a *mode* of existence rather than a fictitious substitute for reality. In a counter Parmenidean way we can say that in modern drama and theatre, Nothingness exists.

In the theatre the stage is the area of occurrences. An area unseen by the audience, a specific spacing from which the stage action is activated, further envelops every stage. Offstage is the area from which the actors come and into which they disappear after and between their stage presentations; set and stage properties are shifted there and back; voices ensue from there. The character, function, location, and modes of activation of stage activity are mutually conditioned by what "happens" on stage. Offstage is the black aura of stage, it is the specific emptiness that hovers around the stage, sometimes serving as the padding between outer reality and inner theatrical reality, or illusion.[1]

Offstage is as old as the stage itself. The reason not to pluck out Oedipus' eyes in front of Greek audiences was probably not only technical, there were also aesthetic reasons linked to the modes of activating spectators' imagination. On-stage reports of offstage events is a well-known technique to "presentify" unpresented events, times, spaces and characters, thus enriching the plot and its complications. Shakespeare was the great master in suspending audience disbelief through a balanced use of offstage and allowing on-stage events to serve as tips of offstage icebergs (occurrences).

Chekhov forcefully dragged offstage on stage. Once the classical structure of a play was shattered, dramatic action became sheer activity. Accordingly, in medium-oriented theatrical terms (rather than dramatic-generic notions), the offstage elements gained relative significance in the entire play.[2] One can hardly imagine Ionesco's *Rhinoceros*, O'Neil's *Before Breakfast*, Bond's *Help*, Coquetau's *La Voix Humaine*, Sartre's *Huis Clos*, Synge's *Riders to the Sea*, Handke's *Der Ritt uber den Bodensee*, Maeterllinck's *Les Avaugles*, and a large number of other modern plays, without the intensive use of offstage.

No other writer has succeeded in theatrically presenting the unpresentable like Samuel Beckett. All the theatrical elements so meticulously examined by Beckett should be considered self-referentially in terms of the attitude to the "non-being" off-stage – Beckett's most important tool as well as most important metaphor in his plays. What Beckett has in fact done is push his protagonists further and further backstage, exploring what can and what ought to be said on the very threshold of offstage. Beckett manipulates offstage as a theatrical device. Thus any study of space and movement in Beckett's plays leads inevitably – as the characters themselves are led – to the space offstage. Through the activation of offstage, Beckett emphasizes the self-reference of space, movement, light and props, but at the same time strips them of their conventional power to signify. It is as though he endows these expressive theatrical techniques with the negative gravity of a black hole. Offstage – dramatically *and* theatrically – sucks us all in.

The circle is the original stage form, as it encloses the inside and shuts off the outside. In the mythological–ritualistic sense, the theatrical circle is the architectronic embodiment of the participants' *Imago Mundi*. Naturally, the structure of stage space influences the extent to which an audience will participate in the theatrical illusion.

Within the frame of a "black box", Beckett's stages are often lit to appear round, or at least elliptic. This creates the sense of a world that is both enclosed and revealed, as though the privacy of the characters' acts were being deliberately disturbed by onlookers, the audience. Beckett's self-reflective use of stage space reinforces the concept of theatre as a reactive art. Over the years Beckett has progressively condensed his message to a bare minimum; stripping the medium brings the medium itself into focus as the subject matter of the play.

Inasmuch as Beckett fights language with anti-language, or stretches his characters between being seen and being unseen, so too he does not simply accept the mere theatricality of his *dramatis personae*: all his plays reveal the constant, sometimes ominous presence of anti-theatre, the ever-growing nothingness of offstage.[3] "If there is only darkness, all would be clear. It is because there is not only darkness but also light that our situation becomes inexplicable."[4] It is the polarity between the "is" and "is not" that is inexplicable, though it is showable, presentable, and shockingly immediate in the theatre.

In theatre, offstage is "anti-space". As a concept and as a technical device it is closely related to stage space. Alain Robbe-Grillet was among the first to emphasize the notion of *being there* in Beckett's drama and the first to contrast the stage as *Dasein*, with offstage as non-being: "Everything that is, is here, off the stage there is nothing, non-being."[5] Movement, props, costumes, make-up and lighting define and are defined by stage space, but they are also manifestations of external intentions or powers outside the stage. Beckett incorporates the phenomenon of offstage into his plays by manipulating it as a theatrical device. His use of offstage is a further modification of the stage/world metaphor. If both stage and show-time are supposed to mirror man's life, then offstage – the area beyond the stage in spatial terms, or before the show and after the show in a temporal sense – stands for external intentions or powers outside the stage. The notions of *there* (beyond) and *then* (future and past) influence the here and now in different ways. They can assume the form of any "other" times, other places, other people, hopes for the future, regrets or nostalgia for the past, eternal life or death, inner space or external space.

Krapp's Last Tape can be viewed as a dialogue between the visual, spatial presence of a live Krapp on stage and the recorded, auditory and temporal presence of a long-past offstage Krapp. Different periods in Krapp's life are juxtaposed in the ever-present stage space. The play takes place on a "late evening in the future" and includes two periods in the past; all three time-levels are present on stage. Whenever the live Krapp exits from the stage his recorded self is also switched off. Thus his identity becomes tentative and uncertain. The relatively long exits leave the stage empty and exposed to the audience's scrutiny, drawing attention to the emptied-by-Krapp space. The last scene is a "freeze"; suggesting an offstage meeting between visual Krapp's gaze and auditive-taped Krapp's empty spools of memory. Similar dialogues between stage activity and a possible offstage meaning appear in many of Beckett's plays.

Technically, offstage is the space stretching beyond the visually perceptible three dimensions of stage: length, width and height. Traced from *Waiting for Godot* to *Footfalls*, Beckett's theatrical technique reveals a constant narrowing of stage space. Offstage, consequently, looms larger and becomes more imposing, more ominous. Sideways movement, which translates time into spatial terms, is central in *Waiting for Godot*, *Act Without Words II* and *Footfalls*. The vertical axis of movement is used in *Waiting for Godot*, in *Happy Days* and in *That Time*. The most definite development, however, is that of upstage–downstage movement and positioning. The more a Beckett character faces the audience, the less his or her body is seen. The bodies of the actors dwindle into offstage until finally only a mouth remains visible.

Offstage is a dynamic mode of "non-being" for whom or which the characters wait. Godot is the hoped-for and feared entity; indeed, he is essentially the very embodiment of offstage. He presumably sends a live messenger, a little boy. In *Endgame*, offstage is the death outside, the silent sea and the deserted earth. In *Act Without Words I*, Godot "rides again" and plays a prominent role, tempting the actor with a number of (pseudo-?) significant props such as a tree, water, ropes. The entire mime can be regarded as a dialogue in movement (instead of words), which the stage character conducts with unknown offstage forces in the flies. The player's most common position is with his back to the audience; only in the end does he turn toward the audience, yearning perhaps for a more fruitful outcome, giving-up offstage to face "what there is" in the auditorium. In *Act Without Words II*, offstage is represented by a goad.

In *Play* and *Come and Go*, offstage is brought closer and resides, so to speak, on stage. The women in *Come and Go* do not actually exit, they disappear in the dark, into offstage. In the same way the absence of light in *Play* casts the characters momentarily into offstage. In *Breath*, birth and death take place offstage, in this way effecting an inversion of stage space. In *Not I*, Mouth is sucked into offstage. In *That Time*, the voices come from offstage. In *Footfalls*, because of the interplay between stage M and offstage V, one no longer knows who resides in whose head. Offstage can therefore be viewed both as the inner self and as an active external force.

Beckett populates his offstage with many characters, including a whole class of little boys and girls ("as if the sex matters"). Only one of them – the boy in *Waiting for Godot* – is allowed on stage. In *Endgame*, the boy is likely to be killed if he enters Hamm's room. Hamm refuses to give corn to the little boy's father or to take in the child. Hamm was once a "tiny boy . . . frightened in the dark", whose parents let him cry so they could sleep in peace; thus Hamm himself was an offstage boy both spatially (in darkness) and temporally (in the past). In *Happy Days*, Willie, in one of his rare speeches, reads aloud: "Wanted a little boy."

Winnie imagines herself, or her real daughter or an imaginary daughter, as "a Mildred . . . she will have memories, of the womb, before she dies, the mother's womb (pause). She is now four or five already."

In *Not I*, there is a deliberate confusion between giving birth and being born "out . . . into this world". With the womb as a metaphor for offstage, the confusion suggests that offstage envelops the stage and is, at the same time, a constituent element of it. Another unseen offstage baby is the one born (and who dies) in *Breath*. In *Come and Go*, the characters remember Miss Wade's playground. Beckett moves gradually from positing offstage children, who are not allowed on stage, to presenting characters, who remember their own childhood (a temporal aspect of offstage). Images of childhood are evoked in *That Time* – the boy in the garden on the stone – and in *Footfalls*, in which mother and daughter recall the past.

In *Play*, offstage and auditorium are set up as extensions of the stage. As the borderlines of stage cannot be seen, the darkness surrounding the characters is intended to include the audience. The only reference in the text to direction is to downward movement, associated with the darkness brought on by the Man's "change":

> Down, all going down, into the dark, peace is coming, I thought, after all, at last, I was right, after all, thank God, when first this change. (PL, 312)

In Beckett's earlier plays offstage seems both distant and distinct from the stage, though it is always present. In the later plays, offstage sucks the characters in and creeps out to replace stage space. A number of characters on stage seem to live on the verge of offstage. Whenever Vladimir or Estragon enter, it is as though they had been away for a long while: "Where were you? I thought you were gone forever." The exaggerated reaction is comical, but at the same time suggesting that offstage kills identity. Offstage follows other rules of continuity and memory (or perhaps there are no rules at all). When Pozzo and Lucky return for the second time they are taken for what they are in a second "now" rather than for what they used to be in Act I. Whoever comes back from the "over there" of offstage must be remoulded into the "here" of stage. Exits and entrances in *Waiting for Godot*, as well as in *Endgame* and *Come and Go*, are charged with a sense of momentary but complete elimination of previous identity or even existence. In *Endgame*, Clov lives on the verge of offstage, and leaves for his kitchen whenever he can. His exits are counterbalanced by Hamm's obsession with always being there, on stage and right in the centre. Nagg and Nell, too, live in a semi-offstage area, concealed but present on stage. In *Act Without Words I*, offstage is exceptionally active; the character is not allowed the forgetfulness and partial luxury of occasional theatrical and spiritual non-existence, as are Clov, Nagg and Nell. Whenever the player tries to escape offstage, he is flung back. In *Happy Days*, Willie lives on the edge of offstage, sending only occasional visual or verbal signs of life. From *Play* onwards, the protagonists, rather than the secondary characters, dwell on the borders of offstage. Parts of their bodies are already "there", leaving only a face or mouth "here".

The later plays bring offstage to the stage by increasing references to other times and places. In *Waiting for Godot*, there are relatively few remarks about anything that lies beyond the immediate stage reality. The tramps mention the Eiffel Tower, Mâcon country and the river Rhône. In *Endgame*, Nagg and Nell speak of the Ardennes and Lake Como, and Hamm refers to a place called Kov "beyond the gulf". *Krapp's Last Tape* contains numerable references to other times, as the play juxtaposes past and present; and to other places, such as wine houses, the house on the canal, the seaside, lovemaking in the punt (three times), the Baltic, a railway station and cities, towns and streets with names like Connogh, Croghan and Kedar. In *Endgame*, offstage is associated with death or sterility. The places mentioned are linked with an accident (Nagg and Nell lost their legs in the Ardennes); the little offstage boy is left without corn (a symbol of life).

In *Happy Days* Winnie returns for a moment to her past. The more the position of the characters on stage is closed and limited, the more they refer to other times and spaces, while simultaneously reflecting on their present reality. This is especially the case in *Not I* and *That Time*. Mouth, being verbally born, and giving verbal birth to words on stage, goes back, first to the womb, then to "buttoned up breeches", home, an orphanage, a field, the space into which he stares, an interrogation in a shopping centre, and a place called Croker's Acres – "a little mound there". These spaces are all figuratively united by the spot from which Mouth delivers the speech – on stage behind the curtain: a "god forsaken hole . . . called . . . no matter". *That Time*, despite its title, takes place in this time. *That Time*, and the places mentioned by the three voices, are evoked in the present. There is no "that time": the past exists only in the present, on stage. In both *Not I* and *That Time*, Beckett is very precise in his naming of other places. But it is not the reality of the places or events that is important, it is their verbalization on stage at the present moment. It is the utter enclosure in some undefined space – the stage – that brings about the need to recall other places.

Offstage participates in the plays not only through visual signs and textual references, but also through sounds. There is a terrible cry in *Waiting for Godot*, a whistle in *Act Without Words I*, a bell in *Happy Days*, a chime in *Footfalls*, breathing and a *vagitus* in *Breath* and, finally, a full voice in *Footfalls* and three voices in *That Time*. These auditory signs are, in a sense, emanations of Godot, the "God" of offstage. But the human offstage voices belong to a different category than the bell, chime and whistle, which are impersonal, domineering and arbitrary. Human voices appear as the culmination of a process of disintegration; Beckett sends parts of a character offstage and allows them to talk to the parts of their selves that remain on stage. Eventually all will be pulled into offstage. The "terrible cry" in *Waiting for Godot* first calls out "mister" and then enters. In *Breath*, the offstage voice is a vagitus, a breath, a death rattle. When the voices are cast off the stage, breathing remains. In *That Time*, the player's slow breathing functions in the same way as the Auditor's movements in *Not I*. In *Footfalls* which includes both human offstage voices and non-human sound effects, the mother's voice has left the stage. In a characteristically dialectical way, Beckett brings together two seemingly contradictory offstage auditory signs. The first group, of human voices, speaks for the quintessential interiority – or "inner" space – that can be expressed on any "outside" space of stage; the second group, of non-human voices, represents the most extreme form of *non-here* and *not-now* that the stage can produce.

Rockaby takes place on the physical verge of offstage. The woman on the chair sways back and forth in and out of light – on stage and offstage. Whereas "she" is still on stage, her voice is mostly offstage. The dialogue between on stage and offstage here is more intimate and more intense because it takes place inside one and the same person. Whereas in *Footfalls* such a dialogue occurs between two (albeit) indistinct figures, in *Rockaby* the figure, not having "another living soul", becomes "her own other" – a distinct split between the stage and the beyond.

A Piece of Monologue treats offstage in a highly original and sophisticated way. The whole play can be regarded as a series of poetic mock-technical stage directions. The speaker stands well off centre, down stage audience left, and is given no instruction to move at all. Here, the obvious is stated: the drama ensues from the tension created between the immobility of the set and the almost purely auditive dynamic of the words spoken. All the action has left the stage; the action that remains is evoked by words that ought to conjure it up in the audience's imagination only. *A Piece of Monologue* can be regarded as a series of verbalized stage instructions otherwise and usually left to be performed in action. Another variation on the offstage motif can be seen in *Ohio Impromptu*, where the words "little is left to tell" occur many times. Here too a clear impression is given; the essential is unutterable and the stage has been chosen to represent that which is only a faint sign of what ought yet cannot be said. In a situation of reading (a play?) aloud, Beckett turns the two characters into veritable icons of author and audience, or audience and actor, or rather any two people engaged in performing sombre texts offstage.

In *Catastrophe*, Beckett extends offstage in the opposite direction. Other than the relatively obvious political interpretation of the play (dedicated to the Vaclav Havel who was imprisoned at the time of Beckett writing the play), on the basic theatrical level this is a play in which theatre-direction is sharply exposed and self-referentially criticized. Whereby people, actors and characters dwindle into offstage in *Happy Days*, *Not I*, *Rockaby* and other plays, in *Catastrophe* Beckett as director fades himself out into offstage. (He does something similar in *Ohio Impromptu*, as a writer talking to his other self as "character".) In *Catastrophe*, the fade-out effect leaves a vice-exister on stage in the form of an assistant director. In a highly ironic way Beckett criticizes himself and his manipulations of actors, and finally retreats into the audience's side of offstage.

Perhaps the most "offstagy" play is *What Where*, in which four characters and a voice inhabit the stage for short spurts of tortured expression. The characters seem to finish each other off, offstage, leaving on stage only a voice, which is visually not there anyway. If offstage is to supply a meaning that is not there on stage, Beckett refuses to say. He ends the play with, "Make sense who may. I switch off" (*WW*, 476).

Offstage is that point in infinity where two parallel lines are said to meet. In Beckett's plays, offstage is usually located on the upstage–downstage axis. The theatrical effect of his later plays is such that the audience is forcibly drawn onto the stage. If offstage is a metaphor for the space from which the playwright operates, then the audience is invited "inside" the author himself. The invisible author is associated with the audience, as both exist offstage; the audience thus becomes a part of this inaccessibleness or inexhaustibility of reality.

Theatre uses the stage and its space as its main means of expression. For Beckett, however, complete expression is, and must be, impossible. Offstage offers a means of communicating the sense of imperfect communication. It is both concrete and unseen; it is "space" that bodies forth man's internal being and his external surroundings. It can send signs and provoke a response, but by definition it must remain inaccessible. Offstage, in Beckett's plays, is, finally, a most precise mode of overcoming the paradox of existing nothingness.

"I" on the Threshold of Offstage

In Beckett's novel *The Unnamable* (1949–50), the character says, "It is myself I hear, howling behind my dissertation." In *Stirrings Still* (1989) a "self so-called" is mentioned, an expression that only a fully self-conscious, self-evading first person singular can logically and psychologically use. Beckett's writings are laden with various notions of the self, its dubious identity, its relations with the author, with the particular medium, with other characters and with potential readers. The self, Beckett once said, "exists by proxy" and the "so-called self" conceals "a presence, embryonic, undeveloped, of a self that might have been but never got born, an *être manqué*".

In Beckett's prose and poetry a constant quest for the embryonic presence of a self, perhaps as proxy for his own self, can easily be detected; but in his dramatic works the characters need actors as actual "proxies" to provide the necessary vehicle to carry the self. Whereas theatrical texts are delivered (in the sense of "born" and "rendered") on stage and not "directed" in the readers' minds, a theatrical presentation of a play-text necessitates an "other", namely the real self of an actor, to substitute for the fictitious selves of the characters. In Beckett's highly self-referential drama the actor cannot be a "good" proxy unless he/she fills in the character's self with his/her own. Theatre also demands an actual space for the self to be in. While this is true for all plays, Beckett's *self-referential* drama requires the actors to posit their selves in front of a live audience in order for the reference to happen at all. Only if the actors refer their Beckettian texts to themselves, and not only to their roles, does the play really "work", at least as far as the self-referential aspects are concerned.

Many Beckett characters express in both words and movement their awareness of their theatricality, i.e. that they are "there" in a deliberately artificial, artistic situation. Lines that acknowledge this theatrical situation are often delivered from the straits of agonized spaces from which the actors/characters often call into doubt the authenticity of "a self", be it the character's self, the implied author's self or perhaps even the actor's. The characters are thereby paradoxically negating and confirming "selfhood" at one and the same time. Whereas the character may or may not refer to his or her self "so-called", the actor playing the role must ascribe at least a minimal quality of selfhood to particular lines. These lines often refer to the acting situation itself.

"The true essence of the "I" is independent of anything external; therefore nothing external can call it by the name 'I' . . . this [the 'I'] is the 'hidden Sanctum' of the soul . . . Only an entity equal to the soul may enter there . . . " (Steiner). The word *sanctum* is explicitly used by Beckett, too, in this particular context, in his television play . . . *but the clouds* . . . (415), and an unbiased reading of his treatment of the self indeed shows a consistent reverence toward that *être manqué*, the self. A number of Beckett scholars have dealt with the uniqueness of "acting-out" his roles. Jonathan Kalb rightly emphasizes that:

> Beckett requires a "holy" actor no less than Artaud and Grotowski . . .
> Thus, acting effectively involves a kind of quest for an indescribable grail
> inside the author's stage directions and the music of his words . . . a

process, long and torturous to some, of learning to trust the text with a unanimity of spirit rarely found outside ensembles such as Grotowski's or Brecht's. Beckett's actors come away from productions with enormous trust in the author's theatrical sense, even when he is not present as director, and even when the directors who are present do not, as frequently happens, share in the performers' acclaim for him.[6]

Connor goes further in describing the typical Beckett voice:

> Beckett hears in these performers the voice that speaks to him when he is writing. The metaphor of voice here sinks to a deeper and more mystical level; the actors' voices are no longer repetitions of Beckett's own voice, but rather of that deeper more authentic voice that speaks through him and his writing.[7] (192)

However, it is in the performative act of self-creation in Beckett's texts, when it is indeed self-referentially performed, that the true self-reference of an actor really expresses individually the self of the author and thus extends an invitation to the audience to posit their selves too. Alan Schneider, from a director's point of view as well as a friend's, tells how "without sounding mystical or psychotic, I've felt that he [Becket, in absence . . .] was indeed there."[8]

In discussing "acting selves" in Beckett's plays, I deliberately refrain from using the documented material supplied by the many Beckett actors who have warmly pronounced their appreciation for his humour, sincerity, depth, intelligence and courage, and have related how this world became their in a very personal way.[9] I prefer, instead, to show how the texts themselves suggest that acting Beckett roles necessitates an unprecedented placing of the actor's real and complete self in order to mediate between the author's self and the selves of the audience. In this way I hope to shed some unmystical light on the evasive self of Beckettian characters and suggest that they definitely strive to what may be called the spiritual.

If Baron von Münchhausen were a Beckett actor, his horse could be regarded as the medium of theatre itself. When stuck in the mud (of life, of the play, of the role . . .), he pulls himself and his horse up by his own hair. Physically, Beckett actors cannot extricate themselves from their piteous stage-trapped situations; external leverage is needed for that. Psychologically, Beckett sometimes endows his proxy selves with other partners on stage, to share their agony. "Pity me, pity me!" shout Didi and Gogo, and Hamm self-ironically says, "Can there be misery – loftier than mine?" Spiritually, however, Beckett actors, in their character roles, are expected to use their totally exposed and stripped-to-a-bare-minimum selves as the hair by which they raise themselves. Many of the characters remain with little but their barely flickering consciousness, in fact creating themselves through speech acts. Beckett implicitly demands of his actors to do what must actually ensue from within: they must be themselves while being stuck in space on stage, between the author's text and the response – hopefully sympathetic – of an audience. They have hardly anything at their disposal with which to achieve this, other than "self" materials.

Presented with characters bereft of personal (even genetic) histories or recognizable social influences, often maimed, blinded and half-insane, those Beckett actors who choose to play such difficult roles cannot rely on Stanislavskian theories of sensory memories or fictitious biographies. There is very little in the way of characterization for the actors to draw from, other than minimal text and the inseparable stage instruction concerning movement in stage-space, make-up and costume. They must "drag up the past" (*Not I*) and make it present in and for the here and now of the stage. They are conditioned to learn about their roles from the physically immediate, often painful and confining whereabouts on stage, such as an open country road, a closed room, a burial urn. The actors must make the best and exploit the inconvenience of being strapped so that head or mouth does not move, as in *Not I* and in *That Time*, or stand fully exposed, humiliated and silent, as in *Catastrophe*, until they are finally given the privilege of casting the last look towards the real as well as fictitious audience.

The manipulated, tortured, puppet-like protagonist at the beginning of *Catastrophe* is an almost redeemed actor by the end. The play is a double-edged metaphor of director's theatre as a political manipulation. In no other play does Beckett concentrate so intensively on the actor as a subdued puppet in the beginning, and as free human being in the end. It is, finally, the fixed look of the actor that stays with the audience rather than the oppressive directions given to him by the director and his assistant. It is, I assume, the real self of the actor and the fictitious self of the role that constitute the final beat of the play.

Endgame begins with "Me – to play" after a series of theatrical openings of window curtains, sheets and lids to reveal the inner spaces of small-scale stages on a now discovered main stage. In *Happy Days* the actress delivers a text that can equally apply to the character and to the actress playing her, as is the case in so many other Beckett plays. "Someone is looking at me still . . . Caring for me still" (160). Live Krapp, albeit alone, is confronted with his younger (or past) recorded selves. "With all this darkness round me I feel less alone," says the actor, both for the character and for himself.

"Am I as much as being seen?" asks the man in *Play* in which visual exposure to a light-source (the eyes of the actual audience) is the main motivation as well as technique for advancing the plot.

In *That Time* a head, to which the audience may naturally ascribe a "self", is seen but never speaks. It just listens to three of "his own" voices, former selves from three periods in his life, theatrically functioning as "vice-selves". Voice B tells the head, "Could you ever say I to yourself in your life turning point that was a great word with you . . . " (390).

Footfalls includes a line explicitly addressed to a live audience: "How could you possibly have said Amen if, as you claim, you were not there?" (403). Between the symbiotically attached double *you*'s of the piece, the audience will never really know whether walking and talking M "is" inside V's unseen head, or vice versa, or whether either one or both figures exist at all or are merely ghostly apparitions of one another or of the audience. The characters try to replace each other's "I" with their own: "I walk here now . . . Rather I come and stand" (401). The mother and daughter in *Footfalls* are perhaps the same person.

In *A Piece of Monologue*, the unmoving Speaker shifts yet one step further away from his self and delivers a speech in the third person ("he") in a text that hovers between stage instruction and a "mono"-dialogue addressed to himself. Like *Not I*, this play too takes the audience from "birth" to "gone", replacing the I with "he", as though the three selves are the listener's, who synthesizes them in silence. *Rockaby* is a dialogue between a woman on a rocking chair and her recorded voice. The live, mostly quiet figure joins "her recorded voice" four times with the word "more", "a little softer each time" (434) until the "coming to rest of rock", the falling of her head and a "slow fade out". She "was her own other . . . " (441)

In Beckett's last play, *What Where*, four players, "as alike as possible" (469), seem like a four headed, four-bodied quadruple self, wearing the same grey gowns and long grey hair. They enter and exit in an interrogation and torture-like situation, in the presence of a V – Bam's voice. Bam is both in and somehow out of the situation, "obviously the boss or overlord". These four figures may represent the four seasons or ages in human development, from spring to winter, thus emphasizing that they are not really separate selves. *Quad*, in this respect, is more extreme in effacing selfhood, because it does so through movement and music, but without any speech. *Not I* was Beckett's first explicit dramatic attempt to portray a self avoiding its self, as not only the name but the entire play makes clear. Although Mouth is not aware of the other, the presence of the auditor, who expresses helpless compassion through four progressively feebler movements of arms raising and falling, is nonetheless necessary as a witness. One may ask whether the real "I" in *Not I* could possibly be ascribed to Beckett, the author. Probably not, since the actress refers to a "She" when she vehemently avoids the first person singular. Is the circumscribed and denied "I" the "self" of the actress? Again, logically, it is not, because the actress is not "She" (as in

"What? . . . Who? . . . No! . . . She! . . . "), therefore she, the actress, can say so without lying. However, the "I" cannot be determined as the "I" of any given member of the audience either. Yet tentatively, illusorily, or artistically it is indeed the "I" of whoever posits his or her "I" for the fictitious character's, be it author, director, actor, or audience. In order to initiate such a hermeneutical search for real and/or fictitious selves in the theatre, it must be the "I" of the actress who starts the cycle in a live performance.

Rudolf Steiner discussed the Cartesian *cogito ergo sum* in terms of a self-creating basis for a free human being: "My investigation touches firm ground only when I find an object which exists in a sense which I can derive from the object itself. But I am myself such an object in that *I think* . . . [emphasis added]. The object of observation is qualitatively identical with the activity directed upon it."[10] A similar argument can be made for acting. In his analysis of the famous dictum, Jaako Hintikka also argues that the thinking activity maintains itself as long as it follows the necessary conditions of being uttered by a first person singular in the present tense. It is then, as shown in **chapter 1**, a performative act rather than a syllogism.[11]

Whereas Steiner and Hintikka treat the "I" philosophically, Beckett as a playwright is not obliged to remain in the limits of discursive logics alone. Indeed, his numerous allusions and references to philosophers such as Descartes, Geulincx, and others are well known. However, as a dramatist, his main concern – at least for the self – is expressed in spatial terms. There exists a fascinating correlation between Beckett's treatment of the self and placing that self-maintaining self at the brink of theatrical existence – the very edge of offstage. His self-doubting, double, triple, or quadruple selves are quite often playing them-selves in the twilight zones of the lit areas of the stage.

In *Not I* the audience sees the mouth only. The speaking parts of the figure in *That Time* are recorded on tape, as is most of the text in *Rockaby*. May one assume that the Beckettian self is often no other than the body-less voice?

The Indian term *kamaloka* refers to a situation in which the soul looks back on life after death as soon as the body stops functioning physically. The situation in Dante's *Inferno* is similar, quite in line with Christian beliefs in the afterlife. In many of Beckett's plays too this threshold can be said to be expressed in the correlation between text and situation of the character in space. Thresholds of selfhood and stage/offstage-hood are mutually complementary. In *Footfalls*, as one particularly significant example, M walks on the threshold until she decides? is compelled? to cross toward the "beyond". In *Play* the three are stuck in what has often been called limbo.

Both texts and spaces in Beckett's (especially later) plays are presented in a way that is no longer material, only halfway mental, and often in a tone suggesting a yearning for the beyond. As a sceptic, Beckett does not enable his critics to come up with firm conclusion on this spiritual (?), ghostly (?) nature of his plays. Nevertheless, without being "there" in the beyond, he brings us as close to "there" as possible. His actors and interpreters are given lines, spaces, and situations that must by definition be in the spatial–temporal present of a theatre performance. In order to be truly self-referential, they must, in fact, be themselves.

On and Offstage – Spiritual Performatives

> "(No) danger of the spiritual thing."
> (*Play*, CDW, 309)

Beckett's works reveal a unique brinkmanship between accepting and rejecting religion, the Divine, or even a more general spiritual perspective. I shall not focus on "religious notions" in Beckett's works, or on his admittedly problematic attitude to God.[12] However, his lucidly intellectual approach, his merciless scepticism, and his frequently ridiculing attitude towards sentimental and simplistic notions of "the spiritual thing" (*Eh, Joe*, CDW, 365) must be juxtaposed with his intensive quest for a "beyond". "Spiritual" has often been manipulated by institutionalized religions and innumerable sects alike, and harnessed to endless political, financial, and psychological utterly non-spiritual purposes. Consequently, I treat a wider aspect in Beckett's "sceptic spirituality" and refer to "spiritual" characters and situations, albeit within the framework of dramatic analysis and performance theory. Beckett uses the term "spiritual" in various ways, deriding and longing on different occasions, perhaps because he too realized that the term itself as well as many of its implications and associations has undergone severe degradation by excessive use, misuse, and abuse.

Notions of a "beyond" hover in and above Beckett's drama like a restlessly re-appearing deconstructed Godot. Though the word "ghost" is sparingly used in his drama, the plays are replete with ghost lights, ghostly characters, and ghost-like situations.[13] The frequent appearances of these literal and metaphorical threshold phenomena, no less than their quality, have driven me to explore the possible existence of a spiritual perception in Beckett's plays from a predominantly theatrical perspective, rather than a religious or psychoanalytical one. Most of Beckett's dramatic works manifest a quest for an unattainable "beyond" that may indeed be "out there", or, and equally unattainable, "inside" the dramatic personae. (Doubting, it may be added, keeps spirituality alive, and Beckett seems to manifest an asymptotic tendency towards the divine.) In their often-heightened reflexivity, Beckett's characters try to reach an indefinable but intensely looked-for "other" state of consciousness or reality, in realizing the situation: "All my lousy life I've crawled about in the mud! And you talk to me about scenery. (*Looking wildly about him.*) Look at this muckheap! I've never stirred from it!" (*WFG*, 56).

This manifested quest for a "beyond" is expressed, primarily, in this playwright's revolutionary usage of offstage. Beckett's offstage is not only the "relevant to the stage" unseen space, but has developed into a theatrical "entity", always "there" as a present, exclusively theatrical void, a black halo, over (and sometimes on) each and every stage.

Allusions to some higher forces are constantly employed, both playfully and seriously, in *Waiting for Godot*: "We're not tied?" (*WFG*, 19). In *Happy Days* Winnie, perhaps naively, opens her day with "Hail Holy Light". In *Endgame*, on the other hand, God is bitterly discarded as "The bastard! He doesn't exist!" The response, however ironic, is "Not yet". In the later dramatic works the perception of issues "not from here and now", is more refined. An ominous being roams in the offstage flies of *Act Without Words I*. In *Cascando*, significantly, the light, unseen by radio listeners, is spoken about in a serious tone: "He need only . . . turn over . . . he'd see them . . . shine on him . . . ." (*CAS*, 303), suggesting that the character shuns the light. W1, M and W2 in *Play* are forced to respond to an inquisitive light, the nature of which is left for them and for the audience to reflect. Is it "mere eye" or "another" consciousness? The female voice in *Eh Joe*, whether inside Joe's head or really there ("He really hears her", Beckett said), alludes to known prayers, and asks "How's your Lord these days?", and quotes the threatening line "Thou fool thy soul", as an anticipation realized at the very moment of utterance. Mouth in *Not I* laughs wildly on mentioning "a merciful . . . God" (*NI*, 377), nevertheless she also says, "God is love".

The "beyond", explicitly demonstrated in Beckett's drama, is expressed by specific medium-accommodating means. It is naturally always hidden, on or offstage, while the characters try theatrically (or cinematographically or radiophonically), to reach it. Moreover, whatever the medium used, it tries to break its own expressive as well as technical limitations, and reach beyond itself. Though not rigid, Beckett was, mediumally speaking, a purist.[14] At the same time, since, unlike MacLuhan, Beckett's medium is not only the message, his various expressive means can be regarded as a component of the message and a metaphor of the characters' conditions. Characters like Didi and Gogo, Hamm and Winnie, the man in *Act Without Words I* or M in *Footfalls*, constantly attempt to reach "beyond". Being "here" onstage rather than "there" and off it, they do not and cannot know what is "there".

Logically, they are not entitled to call it "spiritual" either. But their author may (and does) create a series of discrepancies between the dialogical text of what they say, and the authorial text (alias "stage instructions") of what they must do.[15] Whereas the characters' texts tend more often than not to the sceptical or "secular" trend, their stage instructions are (equally often) "Holy".

If "Holy" means a numinous attitude towards divine beings in specially consecrated times, spaces and plots (or events), Beckett's drama is not holy. If, however, the notion of "Holy" is allowed to mean an (artistic) attempt to reach essences that are neither only physical nor even mental, then Beckett's plays come as close as possible to it. In some religious beliefs, the yearning for the divine is perfectly "kosher", and some theologies are willing to accept "The Road" (e.g. the Jesuit "El Camino") without conditioning Paradise on reaching the target-line. "Holiness", like "spirituality", has become a cliché, and is often treated accordingly by Beckett. Notwithstanding, the plays still reveal an astounding degree of reverence toward an inexplicable "out there", beyond the stage, off the screen, in the silences of radio-plays. As a rational sceptic, Beckett is as explicit as the intellect can account for. As an artist not always committed to discursive thinking, he nevertheless points out a direction towards other-than-physical and mental possibilities. Under the notion of the present *in absentia* "being" of offstage, the following section discusses ritual elements, creation motifs, and the "unsaid" as three active manifestations of offstage.

Secular Rituals as Surrogate Religiosity

Beckett's dramatic works reveal an intensive use of rituals. In this exploration of spiritual tendencies in his drama, it does not suffice to maintain that theatre, as a whole, is a kind of ritual in any case (following the historical or anthropological methodologies of Huizinga, Van Gennep, Goffman, Berne; or theatre oriented ones of Turner, Schechner, Carlson and others). As long as theatre reflects social orders and systems of faith where the Divine is tolerated, if not taken for granted, as constituting a value-system, ritualistic theatrical patterns too are more likely to accommodate the message, rebellious as they may be. The Greek gods, for instance, may have been presented as cruel, lascivious or downright unjust in Classical drama, but they were nevertheless believed by their spectators to exist.

Characters in Beckett's intensively liminal and ritualistic plays certainly do not take the existence of a God for granted. They do, however, perform personal rituals, individualized derivations of *rites de passage*, of birth and death primarily, and the various modes along which the characters spend their time in between the two.[16] These modes are created verbally as well as designed through costumes, movement, lighting and props, in a manner both formal and free. Beckett imposes ritualised behavioural patterns upon his characters, while denying them the relative comfort of believing in the objective, absolute and obligating value-system on which those very same ritual systems rely. The intensive ritualization, expressed by repetitive words and actions,[17] can be experienced as a conscious, ironically pathetic attempt to impose meaning upon desolate spaces and human situations where perhaps there isn't any. Moreover, rituals can be characterized as deliberate quantifiers of qualitative elements, translating the "unspeakable" into a "liveable", at least "bearable" situation.

Beckett's stage-designs, suggestive, metaphoric or symbolic as they are often interpreted, do not volunteer significance all by themselves. Many Beckett characters are avid ritualizers. Realizing their locations and situations and reacting to them, they must consequently guess, allude to, find or create some sense for the spaces and situations in which they are stuck. As in the core of many religious rituals they do so performatively, in doing rather than describing things. But in the absence of an accepted value-system, even the mini-rituals in the early plays constantly collapse, and are exposed by their performers as merely a crutch: "We always find something, eh, Didi, to give us the impression that we exist?" (WFG, 63).

In the later plays, the very performance of the rituals replaces the externally given meaning-and-order. This does not mean that the rituals are rendered completely empty. In their explicit theatrical and often meta-theatrical framework, they become self-supportive and self-referential. Not only "song must come from the heart" but rituals too give us the impression that they "pour out from the inmost, like a thrush" (HD, 155). They are functional in combining "meaningful" cyclical time with "meaningless" linear time, and they are a consciously tentative attempt to endow space too with some sense. Beckett's theatrical rituals constitute an independent, indigenous "meaning", valid for as long as the character ascribes the ritual with some personal meaning, minimal as it is. Attempting to endow sheer time and space with an imposed quasi-meaningful plot, some Beckettian rituals are designed, predominantly, to subvert the passage of time, as in Waiting for Godot, and to encapsulate linear time with cyclical patterns. They may also be more space-oriented and fight or fill-in the claustrophobic space, as in Endgame and Act Without Words I + II, which represent time in spatial terms through movement that connects the two. In Act Without Words I the character is an obsessively orderly man, who returns the cubes to the place from which they had descended, as though acknowledging the higher order that placed them there to begin with. The effect, I believe, is caustically humorous. In *Act Without Words II* the players are either slow, awkward and absent, or brisk, rapid and precise. Both live their lives as an imposed ritual, performing similar series of actions. In *Happy Days* Winnie's ritualised activity is counter-balanced with the vertical axis, as an answer to the scorching "holy" light. Through her fiddling with her bag, her comb and toothbrush etc., she feels "sucked up" when, in fact, she is being sucked down. Rituals may indeed have an uplifting effect.

Some rituals help Beckett's characters cope with their crippled bodies, and their emotional and mental difficulties, thus serving as a painful corset, a frame to sustain a soul torn with grief and loneliness. The orderly (by definition) rituals complement the disorderly flux of emotions and create a delicately chaotic pattern of a higher level. The more obsessive they are, the more they tend to underline the vacuity of offstage. A good example for this is the speech pattern of Mouth in *Not I*. Bereft of any stage properties, and sunk yet another step into offstage, her whole being indeed is "hanging on its words" alone (CDW, 379). The performance of on-stage rituals, moreover, may have a liberating effect on the actors, not only on the characters. In meticulously following Beckett's precise and "ritual" stage instructions, the actors are nevertheless invited to enlist their creative freedom from within.[18] Unlike traditional religious and theatrical rituals, usually beastly respectful, some of Beckett's are at least humorous, if not downright funny. It helps pass the time. Hamm, for one, often tends to flaunt his own ritualistic (story-telling, play-within-a-play) artifice: "I'll soon have finished with this story. [Pause.] Unless I bring in other characters" (*EG*, 118).

Rituals are intended to give us the impression that we exist, as in *Waiting for Godot*, and some of them must be filled-in by the audience. Having experienced compulsive unchanging movement patterns in *What Where* or in *Quad*, for example, the audience is practically forced to supply their own meaning to it, spiritual or any other. Finally, rituals are commensurate with Beckett's substituting a rejected theocentric providence with an anthropocentric, fully endorsed human spirituality. Devoid of an external initiatory significance, Beckett's rituals can be seen as an auxiliary and tentative initiation of the self by her- or himself.

Creators

Regarded from a theatrical perspective, God is a director who creates images and characters ("Personae"), who are supposed to be and act in the newly created world. Nevertheless, the new human creatures have not yet been given any precise stage instructions, except that they should "be fruitful and multiply"; and must not eat from "the tree of knowledge of good and evil . . . for in the day that you eat of it you shall die." The biblical narrator presents God as a frustrated director, dissatisfied with his actors who do not properly perform their roles, yet not seeming to know in advance how the play should finally shape. The right play in the Bible is not only that humankind should keep God's rules – but that humankind must become God's image.[19]

In many of his works, Beckett follows one of the most fundamental creation stories in Western culture, and like Adam, who follows God, he begets characters who create other creating characters "in his own likeness, after his own image" (*Genesis* 5:3). As often physically passive and crippled, but mentally conscious and self-referential, many Beckett characters revolve versions of creation stories in their minds, inventing characters and selves for themselves in a godlike manner. Malone creates Macmann; the Unnamable creates Mahood, to mention but two of Beckett's prose works. Godot could be an invented creation by and common to his two waiters. Clov sees, or does he invent?, a boy who, unlike the boy in *Waiting for Godot* is not allowed to enter and is left offstage in his already dubious onto-theatrical situation. Winnie tells her Mildred story – it could be her own childhood memory. Maddie Rooney in *All That Fall* creates a daughter (or exorcises a younger self) in a similar vein. *Waiting for Godot* features a live child, angelic as he may be. Jerry and the Lynch twins appear as live children in *All That Fall*, but Addie in *Embers* is even more of a vocal phantom than her phantom-like mother Ada. The only live child in Beckett's film and TV scripts is the boy in *Ghost Trio*, perhaps another younger self of the man in the grey room. In his later dramatic works Beckett seems to shift from procreation to mental creation, of children at least, but the "progeny" are almost always creative creatures.

"The fable of one fabling of one with you in the dark" (Beckett, *Company*, 1996:46) is a good example. Different from their appearance in prose, an onstage character is truly a Golem, in whose creation the actors too take part, as theatrically self-referential creation fables. Even the Old Testament God needed company and therefore talks (to himself or to the angels?) in the plural: "Let *us* make man . . . " (*Genesis* 1:26, italics added). In theatre, the audience is a *sine qua non*.

Beckett's stage characters are sometimes forced creators. The woman in *Rockaby*, "all eyes," is looking "for another, another living soul" and finding none, she creates, or realizes that she "was her own other/ own other living soul" (CDW, 441). The relationships between the (still) living, looking, listening, and rocking woman and her recorded voice are reminiscent of Krapp and his exorcised voice, his old self. The woman's mouth in *Not I* gives birth to herself with the word "out" – a word of birth, also the birth of the first clearly audible word in the play. Similarly, the man in *A Piece of Monologue* opens with "Birth was the death of him." In *Ohio Impromptu* the reader can be interpreted as the younger self of the listener. Despite a rigorous attempt to present P as subdued, the true (?) self of P is made quite obvious at the end of *Catastrophe*.[20]

In art, and especially in modern art, Man creates (by) him/her-self. Observed from the performative as well as performance oriented perspective, there is a direct link between the divine "image", and that with which humans wish to create, as a continuation of, or a rebellion against a divine creator. From a theocentric point of view, the biblical God created Man in His own image. It can also be argued that it has always been Man who created his god(s) in his own image, much as Xenophanes maintained in the sixth century BCE that horses would create their gods in equestrian shape. In Beckett's theatre, we are invited to unwillingly suspend our belief in the created personae.

Beckett characters represent an ancient (artistic) desire to continue the human "self", and expand it and the creator's self with a creature as much alike the creator as possible. Of special interest is the moment when a Beckett creature says (or deliberately does not say) "I" to itself, and traces the (fictitious?) humanity involved in saying "I". According to numerous religious traditions, the "I" is nothing short of the divine element in Man. There is a vast gap between himself and the divine creator ("All my life I've compared myself to him"). The self, according to Beckett, exists by proxy and is always an *êtremanque*.[21] In counter-distinction to the *Genesis* myth, a self creates another self, for company, perhaps like God, yet in the obvious "image" of both the narrator and the author. "At me too someone is looking . . . " we are reminded.

Offstage Messengers: Bodies, Characters, Sights and Voices

Dramatic manifestations of spirits, ghosts, inner voices and such-like "Schwankende Gestalten" (Goethe, *Faust*) can relatively easily be treated as theatrical images in other playwrights' works. Their accumulation in Beckett's works adds up to a quality beyond quantity and creates a coherent pantheon of liminal vice-existers, as well as a "spiritual" kind of dramatic syntax.

Godot "Himself" can conveniently be called the Father of modern offstage characters. "[The boy] is after all a messenger, coming from a totally different sphere", he is "from a totally different dimension" as Beckett told the Buettners.[22] Whether coming from angelic spheres or from some mytho-poetic other realm, in theatrical terms at least the boy certainly comes from offstage. The flies in *Act Without Words I* are inhabited by a good God or another evil power, perhaps one of Godot's cousins. Whereas Godot is almost passive in the play, in *Act Without*

Words I the offstage power is not just active, but the sole motivating element. In *Endgame*, a boy is conspicuously denied an entrance. There is ample evidence for the existence of a whole class of Beckett children who dwell offstage, although it is not always clear if they are remembered as independently "real", or as the characters' younger selves. Nevertheless they are vigorously exorcised and after *Waiting for Godot*, they do not set foot onstage, except, perhaps, for the reader in *Ohio Impromptu*.

An astounding number of Beckett characters are located on the verge of offstage, gradually dwindling into the "not-here" black area out there. Nag and Nell live in dustbins and die there, out of sight, in an onstage "offstage". Winnie, likewise, sinks vertically into her mound. Mouth in *Not I* is virtually sucked into blackness with a long fade-out. Krapp's recorded voice is private vocal exorcising ritual of an old (younger) self from the past, presented as an evening in the future, and dragged into the necessarily eternal present of any theatre show. C in *Theatre II* stands back to the audience, about to jump from a sixth floor, upstage. The figures in *Play*, up to their necks in urns, are located in a limbo-like dramatic space, indeed a purgatory[23] and most of their bodies are offstage. The exits of Vi, Flo + Ru create a fascinating pattern of disappearing acts. Similar to *Krapp's Last Tape* and *Waiting for Godot*, short exits and entrances emphasize the borderlines between stage and offstage. Moreover, offstage in *Waiting for Godot* functions as an identity eraser, and when Didi and Gogo return onstage they must relocate themselves, space and time-wise. The baby in *Breath* is vocally born onto the stage, and re-born into offstage at the end of its 35-second long life. *A Piece of Monologue* is replete with ghosts. In a homeopathic way, the ghosts mentioned in the text play an ontological game with the ghost-like figure who speaks about them: authorial (stage-instruction text) and dialogical text ghost one another. V, "in the shape of a small megaphone at head level" (*WW*, 469) in *What Where* is a voice, never seen.

Are these vocal and visual apparitions only psychological projections? Offstage, as the only clearly close yet "not-here" theatrical space, a constantly present non-being that surrounds each and every stage, often sends various specific vocal and visual messengers to Beckett's onstage characters. A strange attractor, to quote Lorenz, an evasive Him is also constantly there on stage. The "Him" may be interpreted in different ways. It could be God ("*Esse est Percipi*"), without whose providence the world will not exist. It might be Beckett himself, the implied author, as an obvious option. It can also be another "witnessing" character on stage (according to a medium-oriented approach). Finally, the "Him" may indicate the actual audience, to whose "I" the text appeals, in a need to replace the fictive selves of the characters with the real ones of living people who share the same space for as long as the performance lasts.

"Beyond" and the (Stage) Instructions on How to Get There

Beckett's theatrical endings can be divided into "never-ending ends", "freezing ends", and "fading ends". The theatrical endings are well supported dramatically, from a structural perspective. Some of the plays are peculiarly open-ended, or designed as an extraordinary freeze, a dramatic *aporia*, or else as a "dissolve" of the characters stuck halfway between on- and offstage. Open-ended final-beats are an implicit demand for an existential choice regarding "The Holy".

Estragon and Vladimir "do not move" at the end of the play, and are likely to continue not moving in the next act, following the second, which should, in fact be played one evening following the first act. Hamm re-shrouds himself while Clov freezes on the threshold of offstage, at the end of *Endgame*. In *Happy Days* Willie's hand reaches toward Winnie and freezes before the light goes down. "[They look at each other. Long pause.]" Another "hand-oriented" ending is *Act Without Words I*: "He looks at his hands". *Act Without Words II* ends with A's prayer. Krapp's last tape keeps turning on in silence. In *Theatre I* wrenches the pole from B's grasp. In *Theatre II* A raises his handkerchief timidly towards C's face, whose back is to the audience. A Freeze? The end of *Play* suggests that W1, W2 and M will continue forever. Any actual theatrical show of their lighted relationships is but a fraction of their eternal dramatic situation. *Come and Go* ends with silence. *Breath* ends like it started, with a *vagitus*, indicating a birth into another realm. In some of the later plays the freezes become a dwindling into offstage. Mouth in *Not I* is sucked into offstage, but goes on talking, beyond the fade-out of the light. In *That Time* the head keeps a toothless smile for five seconds, then fades out. The entire act IV of *Footfalls* presents an empty stage from which M was sucked out. Fade out. In *A Piece of Monologue*: "Thirty seconds before end of speech lamplight begins to fail. Lamp out. Silence. SPEAKER, globe, foot of pallet, barely visible in diffuse light. Ten seconds. Curtain." In *Rockaby* the woman dies on stage – "(Together: echo of 'rock her off', coming to rest of rock, slow fade out.)." A rare event, since even Nag and Nell die out of sight in *Happy Days* and the other characters' deaths are "only" suggested. *Ohio Improptu* ends with a textually "explained" freeze: Listener and Reader have turned to stone. Fade out. Catastrophe ends with a long fade-out. Finally, in *What Where*: "I switch off. [*Light off p. Pause. Light off v.*]" Many of these liminal endings are highly suggestive of another "realm" – the realm of offstage, on the verge of which these endings happen.

Beckett's later drama is pervaded by "repetitive formulas and ritual acts, disembodied voices and sounds, ghostly visitations, prayers, strange rites carried on in the dark of night".[24] *Footfalls* is one of the most explicit dramatic attempts Beckett made in indicating the threshold between the stage and a theatrical "beyond", primarily through the stage instructions. M paces along a nine-step long lit path, precisely limited by darkness. Whenever reaching the border, she either turns back or stops. In the end she stops again, and does not reappear in the final 10 seconds long "act IV". Katharine Worth notes that the theatre in *Footfalls* "became a kind of a church"; and finally May's restless soul departed.[25] Semiotically, however, May touches upon the *limes* of (this particular) theatre. Moreover, one may ask whether M is a visual projection of V; or is V a vocal projection of M, as a voice inside or outside of her? Rather than V appearing onstage, M joins (?) V offstage. Like Mouth in *Not I*, and P in *Catastrophe*, she is gradually sucked into the offstage beyond. In fact, it is "offstage", the active absence, that finally dominates a disappearing stage. The complete dialogue and stage directions text suggests a sceptical brinkmanship between "secular" text and "holy" stage directions – from and towards "A Divine"?

The yearning for the beyond in Beckett's plays is relatively clear. Its nature, nevertheless, is definitely not and not supposed to be. Meaning, like Winnie's song, must come from within. Jean-Michel Rabaté, halfway between textuality and psychoanalysis, mentions "A paradoxical positivity is granted to life *in extremis*, the happiness of living, of seeing and breathing are asserted precisely at the moment of their fading away."[26] If spirituality for Beckett is freedom (not bliss, God forbid!), the likely conclusion is that he can only point out a way there, rather than tell us what it is, and actors and audiences alike must choose whether and how to walk it. I contend that "make sense who may" (*What Where*), the last words in Beckett's last play, is a piece of spiritually responsible and serious advice rather than a tongue-in-cheek evasion. With exquisite spiritual tact, free of any charge or religious blackmail, Beckett offers an alternative spirituality. Keir Elam uses the image of the ferryboat on the Acheron to say that the boat returns him (Beckett) "to the hell of his own making on *this* side of the divide" (in Pilling, CCB, 1994: 162). I suggest that Beckett rather subtly points out a tentative approach which may replace the dubious, unreliable, cruel (if existing) divine consciousness with the human one. Lacan explains that ghosts arise from "the gap left by omission of a significant rite".[27] On Beckett's stages and off them, the characters and their ghosts try to make up for this Lacanian omission. In many of his plays, the body is lamed and tortured, the feelings and emotions, familiar as they are, are observed from afar. But the self-conscious thinking process, ghostly on and offstage, is always here and now and individual, and in focus. Perhaps a real spirit but always offstage, or inside the unseen of the human being.

The Unseen . . . and "Unsaid"

Many of Beckett's plays contain a secret; not the often strange onstage position of the characters, but a secret regarding something apparently quite essential, yet conspicuously left unsaid. Hamm and Clov have an intensive repartee concerning "what's happened" out there, and why all is dead (CDW, 128–9). The recorded storm-scene in *Krapp's Last Tape* is cut off by Krapp just before reaching its explicit peak: "Spiritually a year of profound gloom and indigence until that memorable night in March (. . .) never to be forgotten, when suddenly I saw the whole thing. The vision at last (. . .) This I fancy is what I have chiefly to record this evening, against the day when my work will be done and perhaps no place left in my memory, warm or cold, for the miracle that . . . (hesitates) . . . for the fire that set it alight. What I suddenly saw then was this, that the belief I had been going on all my life, namely – (Krapp switches off impatiently . . .)". A little later yet another "essential" is hidden, skipped over: " . . . the dark I have always struggled to keep under is in reality my most – " and again Krapp switches off, cursing (CDW, 220). Krapp does not want to confront what he once thought to be "his most" – I assume – meaningful moment, and so the audience too is denied it. In *Come and Go* the three women tell about each other secrets that the audience, again, is not allowed to hear. They elicit three "oh"s', which are "Three very different sounds" (CDW, 357), unlike most of this short text which is supposed to be spoken as "low" and "colourless".

Theatre II seems to offer an entire play dedicated to evading the essentials, which I understand as the implied author's ironical, indirect and self-critical confession. A and B encounter the phrase "morbidly sensitive to the opinions of others" – repeated nine times in the play, thus drawing a great deal of attention. This hilarious repetition explains why A and B cannot "make out" C, and the phrase serves as an intra-textual reason why Beckett evades the "essential". In a much more sombre "inquiry" play, *What Where*, the characters are given "the works" until they confess. But the audience never learns what the "what" or the "where" are and where it all happens.

4 The Radioplays

Critics often apply dramatic or literary criteria to Beckett's radioplays instead of using medium-oriented approaches. The progression from *All That Fall* (1956) to *Radio II* (in the early sixties), as well as the significance of the radioplays in the context of Beckett's art as a whole, is likely to become clearer through analysis of particular radiophonic modes of expression. The radioplays reveal the originality and rich auditive imagination of their author; they also constitute the purely auditive aspect in Beckett's quest for self-reference.

Beckett's radioplays were written within a short period of six years (1956–62) and present an intensive search in the art of "meaningful noises". His radiophonic sensitivity invites focusing on a number of elements that prove to be not just "technique" but uniquely medium-oriented components, and indeed metaphors to the meaning of the piece as a whole. Moreover, Beckett's radioplays are auditive milestones in a search dedicated to finding significance, if any, in the exclusive world of silence, voices, music, and sound effects.

Radio is a "poor" medium[1] because it engages only the sense of hearing, and a "hot" medium because of its power "to involve people in depth".[2] The listener is asked to add to the audio-data projected from the receiver his or her own tastes, odours, visual images, and tactile equivalents. The auditory stimuli of radio serve not only as verbal or musical messages *per se*, but as hooks and catalysts for the listener's imagination. In Dylan Thomas' *Under Milkwood* this aspect of radio-technique merges with poetic vision:

> Only you can hear and see, behind the eyes of the sleepers, the movement and countries and images and colours and dismays and rainbows and tunes and wishes and flight and fall and despair and big seas of their dreams.[3]

A radioplay is projected from the radio-receiver, but takes place in the listener's head. Metaphorically, radio is a theatre within the skull. Because the listener must provide the visual (and other sensory comple- ments) counterpart and "design the picture", he or she becomes an active participant in the performance. In this sense, the manipulation of space becomes the subject matter of many radioplays. Radio's "space- lessness", its capacity for illusion, its intimacy, and the invitation it extends to the listener to co-create the play, are central to Beckett's radio- phonic technique. Through a process of continual reflection these characteristics become the underlying themes.

In Beckett's radioplays, as well as in any conceivable radioplay, one may discern between radiophonic silence and the three main types of noises – sound effects, music, and words. Silence, on radio, is an acting "space":

> having no point of favoured focus . . . it is a sphere without fixed bound- aries, space made by the thing itself . . . creating its own dimensions moment by moment . . . the ear favours sound from any direction . . . The essential feature of sound, however, is not its location but that it be, that it fill space.[4]

Particularly in Beckett's radioplays, silence, because of its unperceived, neutral, limitless and unknown "emptiness," is given an active part; sometimes it is even made a dramatic pesona. Like an empty stage or a movie screen, radiophonic silence is specified and contextualized in a radioplay so as to embody nothingness – like offstage does to stage – thus creating a significant if not central thematic effect.

All radiophonic sounds are born from silence and die into that silence. Silence can therefore be compared with a pre-natal or post-death entity. Yet, and so long as there is no absolute silence on radio, one is bound to hear, even in a totally non-echoing room, the obligatorily non-silent intruders of the listener to silence, namely the sound of the nervous system and the sound of the blood circulating. Naturally, radiophonic silence depends also on electronic and conceptual aspects, which limit the quality, etc., of the kinds of silence listeners experience. Silent sound- space is formed with the "five determinants: frequency at pitch, amplitude of loudness, overtone, structure or timbre, duration and morphology".[5]

Beckett proceeds from relatively affluent "sound-and-gimmick" radio in *All That Fall* to the highly economic and minimalist *Radio I* and *Radio II*. Self-reference is found both in the sequence of the pieces for radio and in the radiophonic elements. Since radio, as a basically dramatic medium relies on characterization, structure, entries and exists, etc., it is possible on occasion to borrow certain criteria from music, theatre, or literature. In a similar way that *Waiting for Godot* can be described to include many of the elements that appear in the plays that follow, so too does *All That Fall* contain elements to be developed in the later radioplays. However, it does so in a much more sharpened, self-referential and medium-oriented manner, where the radiophonic elements are combined to create a world that questions the function, validity and ultimate purpose of those very means. Self-reference, in the radioplays too, is not only a technique but a subject-matter, which reveals itself in each one of the artistic components. In examining whether the radioplays "mean" the same as the theatre plays, or whether due to their different *mode* of expression they also mean different things, the medium will not be regarded here as "the message", but as a realization of a metaphor to life living in it as well as outside of it.

All That Fall

Beckett's first radioplay, *All That Fall* (1956), was immediately received as a radio classic. The story, which involves old Mrs Rooney's walk to the railway station to meet her husband and their return home, takes place in a small Irish town. Plot-time corresponds to broadcasting-time, and "surprisingly, Beckett returns in this radioplay to traditional dramaturgy".[6] While on the surface this radioplay seems to keep the unities of time, the consideration of classical criteria fails to take into account radiophonic technique as the major carrier of the "message". It is time itself and not the "unity of time" that is the key factor. Time is not only the exclusive dimension in which all radioplays function, but also the subject matter and theme of *All That Fall*. As with music, time in radioplays is active not only in terms of one sound following another, but as a happening, an "event".[7] *All That Fall* is not only the name of the radioplay, but also a metaphor that describes a "lingering dissolution" dependent upon time. Even allusions to a "country road" or "railway station" are temporal–tonal by nature; they exist in the imagination of the listener, who is invited to translate the audio–temporal language into a visual-spatial one of his own.

Unity of plot is a more complex matter. Plot involves both structure and story. Beckett's radioplays are wordy, radiophonic "stories" in a special sense: he seems to be haunted by the inability to tell a story along with the urgent need to do so. There is a "story" in the most traditional sense: Mrs Rooney goes to pick up her husband, meets him, returns home with him, and finds out why he was delayed. There is also an added element of intrigue or mystery: did Mr Rooney murder the boy by pushing him under the wheels? The structure of the piece, however, departs from the criteria of classical drama and relies, instead, on

musical phrasing techniques. Donald McWhinnie describes his interpretation of the piece in terms of musical structures:

> The author specifies four animals; this corresponds exactly to the four in
> the bar metre of Mrs Rooney's walk . . . which is the percussive accom-
> paniment to the play and which, in its larger stages becomes charged with
> emotional significance in itself.

In order to achieve the required rhythmical effect, McWhinnie suggests
stylized sound effects rather than realistic ones. In this way he can
"Consolidate the underlying rhythm . . . and merge imperceptibly the
musical and realistic elements of the play."[8] McWhinnie's medium-
oriented   approach   is   radiophonic–musical   rather   than
literary–dramatic.

   Plot, time, and space in radioplays are dealt with through sequences
of silence interspersed with words, music and effects. "Radio dialogue
is obliged to compensate for the missing visual dimension . . . "[9] Beckett
develops the idea of space in radio in a pseudo-Cartesian manner,
implying "I emit noises ergo I am." This lies as the hypothesis of both
the content and the mode of the Beckettian radioplay. The absence of a
visual dimension means that the main character, Maddy Rooney, is
spatially non-existent for the listener as soon as she stops talking. But,
as she says, "Do not imagine, because I am silent, that I am not present
and alive" (*ATF*, 185). While characterizing her in a straightforward
desperate wish to assert herself, Beckett also makes a major, self-referential point on the nature of radio. In order to come closer to the
radiophonic mode we should relinquish a purely dramatic analysis and
elicit help from the organization of auditory stimuli. Mrs Rooney's
mock-Cartesian proof of existence can serve as a motto for most of
Beckett's radiophonic protagonists: in order to exist on the air they must
make noises with words, or music or sound effects. On radio their
silence equals non-being, except in rare cases where a mute character (!)
is placed before a microphone and is brought to radiophonic existence
through the conjuring-up voices of his partners. The very act of emit-
ting voices stands closer not only to the listener's ear but also to the
importance traditionally allocated to *what* is being said: radiophonic
reality lies primarily in sounding and not in sense.

   All That Fall begins with an explicit exposition of the four radiophonic
elements. "Rural sounds . . . silence . . . faint music . . . " only then come
the first words – "poor woman" (*ATF*, 172). This polyphony generates
the dynamics of the radiophonic elements, which are orchestrated so as
to evoke the sense of "all that fall", of sickness, fatigue and despair,
along with the feeling that despite all this, one is alive. These elements
reappear together, at the dramatic rhythmical and melodic peak in the
middle of the play, when the train arrives at the station:

Tommy: (excitedly, in the distance) – She's coming (pause, nearer). She's at the level crossing! immediately exaggerated station sounds. Falling signals. Bells, Whistles. Crescendo of train whistle approaching. Sound of train rushing through station). (*ATF*, 187)

In McWhinnie's version the noise is surrealistic, very loud and almost chaotic. As Mrs Rooney screams, "The upmail! The upmail!" one train disappears "off mike" while the train on which Dan Rooney is supposed to arrive comes in. The passengers disembark; Mrs Rooney roars, looking for her husband; the train leaves and then a Silence, which after the cascade of very loud and mixed noises seems "emptier", heavily charged, more terrible. Maddy and Dan meet first in silence, then in the sound effect of her shuffling feet and the thump of his stick, and only then in words, "Oh Dan, there you are!" At this point the third part of the radioplay begins with Dan and Maddy's way home, a slow and painful move toward the dénouement, a final disintegration. Although *All That Fall* still very much "refers" to a world around it, each of the three "noisy" components shows more or less explicit signs of medium self-awareness.

Words in a radioplay can represent actual speech or merely the thoughts of the radiophonic character (as with Henry in *Embers*, or Words in *Words and Music*, and Opener and Voice in *Cascando*). Since audio-space is defined only by sound, location can be established rather freely, and the listener can accept speech as referring to the speaker's inner thoughts. Furthermore, the sound is close to the listener's ear and creates a sense of intimacy; the listener feels he is listening in on the psyche of the speaker. Credibility will hence ensue from the *way* in which words are uttered, without hurting the sense of intimacy.

Mrs Rooney, like many other Beckettian characters, is an obsessive and conscious user of words. She usually talks to herself. Without stage space or other visual contexts to distract the listener, the effect is intense, almost claustrophobic: "I use none but the simplest words, I hope, and yet I sometimes find my way of speaking very . . . bizarre" (*ATF*, 173). Even stronger is the short repartee:

Mr Rooney: . . . sometimes one would think you were struggling with a dead language.
Mrs Rooney: Yes, indeed . . . I often have this feeling, it is unspeakable excruciating. (*ATF*, 194)

Mrs Rooney's attempts to communicate almost always result in estrangement, of which she is highly aware: "I estrange them all . . . a few words, simple words . . . from my heart . . . and I am all alone . . . once more . . . " (*ATF*, 182). Such words are more precise and self-refer-

ential on radio than in the theatre. Nobody talks with her, rather she is
talked to. Indeed, she herself is the only person with whom she can
really converse, at least in the first half of the radioplay. Her loneliness,
which is designed to appeal to the listener, becomes both the result and
the consequence of her obsessive monologues. In fact, the listener is the
closest person to Maddy, closer even than her husband. But like Dan,
the listener is blind in regard to her. A real and unconventional intimacy
is thus established since she is – or sounds – really alone, whereas an
actress on stage would have to use a stage convention of loneliness
because there is an actual audience to confront.

Dialogues as another form of "words" in this radioplay are fast,
broken and dynamic; they rarely succeed in clearly communicating
either feelings or information, as far as the words alone are concerned.
The characters are enclosed in their own worlds and find it extremely
difficult to enter the world of another. Language, even in conversation,
becomes self-conscious and tentative. The speakers lead each other by
means of sounding the words rather than by the "meaning of the very
utterances":

> *Maddy*: Why do you stop? Do you want to say something?
> *Dan*: No.
> *Maddy*: Then why do you stop?
> *Dan*: It is easier.
> *Maddy*: Are you very wet?
> *Dan*: To the buff.
> *Maddy*: The buff?
> *Dan*: The buff. From Buffalo.
> *Maddy*: Put your arm aro und me. (Pause) Be nice to me! (Pause.
> Gratefully) Ah, Dan . . . (*ATF*, 197)

Some other dialogues in *All That Fall* also work in accordance with
musical rules of motif, orchestration, counterpoint, etc. Walking is often
juxtaposed aurally with talking: "Once and for all, do not ask me to
speak and move at the same time." The author's technique of pairing
these two elements is taken one step further on the Rooney's way home
in the rain, when more sound effects, more nonsense talk, and longer
silences are added.

The function of music in a radioplay is particularly important because
music, like a radioplay, works its art through time. There is not only an
external similarity between the two in terms of tempo, melody, and
harmony – but these elements are also extended to an internal similarity.
One can therefore discuss music *in* the radioplay, and music as an art
form lending its rules *to* the radioplay. Music can also serve as a *model*
for the art form of the radioplay. The rules applicable to music can be
applied to the radioplay, notwithstanding that music is an element

within the play. Music is temporal art not in the barren and empty sense.

> that its tones succeed one another in time. It is temporal art in the concrete
> sense that it enlists the flux of time as a force to serve its ends . . . Time
> happens; time is an event.[10]

Music can provide atmosphere or background, or it can serve as a scene
divider. Apart from the illustrative or structural function of music, it
may acquire an independent role. In radioplays, music often functions
like sets in theatre. Background music relies heavily on conventional
forms: sweet music for lovers, ominous music for ghosts, and so on.

The musical motif "Death and the Maiden" serves as a thematic
subtext as well as a structural device. It plays at the beginning and at the
end, acting as timekeeper for broadcasting and fictional time, and as a
milestone on the Rooney's way home. When the musical phrase is first
heard Mrs Rooney remarks: " . . . poor woman, all alone in that ruinous
old house" (ATF, 172). When Dan and Maddy hear the same phrase
repeated on their way home, the music is charged with what has
happened to them during the play:

> (Silence but for music playing. Music dies). All day the same old record.
> All alone in that great empty old house. (ATF, 172)

Dan's barely audible identification of the tune "Death and the Maiden"
seems to be a direct comment on his wife and on the shadow of death
looming over both their lives. The low degree of semantic explicitness
that is traditionally ascribed to music is here compensated with the
actual utterance of the name of Schubert's well-known piece. In this way
not only is the intrinsic musical quality used as "mood" music but its
name also reflects the motif of dying.

In many radioplays music reinforces the sub-textual elements,
whereas sound effects help in establishing the con-textual, environ-
mental elements. Often sound effects are identifiable only in context.
Broadcasted independently, they would probably not sound real at all.

Sound effects are radiophonic sounds other than words or music,
such as atmospheric acoustics of "choked," "outdoors," "bedroom",
"echo." Atmospheric effects are usually slightly prolonged and serve as
background sound. Spot effects, like the slamming and creaking of
doors, police sirens and bells, usually refer to the immediate situation.
Sound effects can be compared to the sets, the costumes or even to the
lighting of theatre. They can be used, like words or music, realistically,
figuratively, metaphorically or symbolically, and can serve to indicate
scenic changes and shifts.[11]

Like the property motifs in Waiting for Godot, the sound effect motifs
of Maddy's dragging feet and Dan's blind tappings function as a basso
ostinato, a comment, a means of characterization, a time-and-rhythm

keeper. At the beginning the sound serves to describe Maddy's illness and old age; Maddy relates to it by complaining. Once the relation between the sound effect and the words is established, Beckett abandons its literal significance and plays it against Dan's blind tappings. The shuffling and the tapping create a sense of doom; groping blindly or stumbling along, Dan and Maddy Rooney move toward their final fall. But the effect is created through sound rather than through words. The "dialogue" between Maddy's dragging feet and Dan's tapping stick, to the background of pouring rain and wind, operates on an abstract level. Measuring their walk solely by their tedious and painful efforts provides a sense of time passing as no verbal dialogue could do.

Sound effects can also provide comic relief:

> *Mrs Rooney*: Well, you know, it will be dead in time, just like our old Gaelic, there is that to be said. (Urgent Baa)
> *Mr Rooney*: Good God! (*ATF*, 194)

Where stylized sound effects counteract lyricism in the dialogue, the effect is both ironic and pathetic:

> *Mrs Rooney*: All is still. No living soul in sight. There is no one to ask. The world is feeding. The wind . . . (brief wind) scarcely stirs the leaves, and the birds . . . (brief chirp). (*ATF*, 192)

Sound effects that startle both Maddy and the listener, such as the bicycle bell, work to emphasize the continual shifts between Mrs Rooney's inner world and an external reality.

The above examples illustrate how sound effects serve as the carriers of those meanings that the author prefers to express in non-verbal ways. In *All That Fall*, Beckett seems to be fascinated with sound effects and uses as many of them as possible. (There is a rapid decrease of sound effects in the later radioplays, as though Beckett were disposing, as in his stage plays, with décor). Yet their intrinsic value is more than merely illustrative. Rural sounds, steps, cars, wind, rain and trains are used both realistically and metaphorically; they gain metaphorical value through juxtaposition with other sound effects and with words; they substitute for words, do what words cannot do (or not as precisely), and shorten the way to an intuitive, direct and non-verbal understanding.

The sound effects, even in this first of Beckett's radioplays, show a tendency toward self-reference: for example, Maddy evokes the sound effects of wind and birds rather than reacts to them after they are sounded. In this way sound effects draw attention to themselves and to their "radiophoneness".

The radioplays that follow, however, gradually shed radiophonic paraphernalia and move toward a reductive stripping of the medium so that the medium itself becomes the focus of attention.

Embers

Whereas in *All That Fall* reality is conceived as objective and external, *Embers* presents an almost exclusively inner world. Maddy, an obsessive talker, is sick, old, often alone and sometimes pitifully aggressive, but she nevertheless manages to communicate fairly well with other people. Her thoughts and feelings are strongly linked with events outside of herself. In contrast, *Embers* relinquishes external circumstances and deliberately subjectifies words, music, sound effects and even silence itself, presenting the radiophonic elements as projections into and out of the mind of Henri, the only "live" human character in the radioplay. Neither Maddy Rooney nor Henri need the theatrical convention of the monologue (which works on radio as a direct appeal to the listener without the artificiality of the stage). However, the basic "point of hearing" in *Embers* is the inside of Henri's skull, while Maddy Rooney is still heard from the outside.

In a key line the voice of Ada, Henri's wife, tells him: "You will be quite alone with your voice, there will be no other voice in the world but yours" (*EM*, 262). When he is actually alone with his own voice, Henri conjures up the memory of Ada's words and realizes that the prophecy has come true. The apparent paradox of the line lies in the discrepancy between what the words say and the very fact that they are voiced at all. In his second radioplay, Beckett reduces the eleven and more independent characters of *All That Fall* to one speaker and four voices (of which the speaker seems to be partly in control). Similarly, the rich auditive weaving of bicycles, cars and trains, rain storm and animals, music and many human voices are made much simpler in *Embers*. Henri becomes not just the only auditive foothold of the piece, but the built-in director, sound effect manipulator and the listener of the radioplay of his own life. The real listener is hence invited to crawl through the radio receiver into the inside of Henri's theatre in the skull and co-create the visual counterparts of the story together with him. Martin Esslin suggests that this partnership is a unique feature of radio in general;[12] but in *Embers*, Beckett makes the listeners' participation a necessary condition and an almost explicit critical notion. When Henri says, "who is beside me now?" the line will, retroactively, refer to the evocation of the memory of his father, but at the particular moment of utterance it quite simply means nobody else but the actual listener.

Embers is not, as Tindall claims, a "dream play, perhaps too intricate, interior and obscure for radio".[13] Weaned, perhaps, on the understanding that radio is the autistically handicapped brother of theatre, such an approach fails to see the intricate, interior and obscure as advantages which turn the play into a radio classic.

In *Embers*, Beckett practices with radio an idea suggested in *The Unnamable* (a non-vocal medium): "All is a question of voices ... In all these words, all these strangers, this dust of words with no ground for their setting." The broadcasting event is in itself some kind of life in which the medium enacts the hypothesis: "I emit a noise, ergo I am." Henri says: "every syllable is a second gained," whereby "second" can mean both 1/60th of a minute and "a second syllable". Henri is engaged in a verbalized war against everlasting silence, in which sheer utterance is as important as any semantic significance of any given word. Every syllable is, at the same real and radiophonic time, a war launched against silence and death, and another step closer toward them. In this respect, too, the actual delivery of the radioplay is manifest of life – it refers to *itself* less than to the world around it.

The radioplay opens with an explanation for the noise of the sea and ends with the words "underneath all quiet. Like a grave. Not a sound. All day, all night not a sound." Not only is Henri doomed to prolong his existence with uttered radiophonic words, but the listener too, by listening consciously to these words, is an hour closer to the final (and not just radiophonic) silence. In his enclosure in his own world of noises and voices Henri's only real (unknown) partner is the listener, who is drawn closer and closer into Henri's skull. The quasi-Cartesian proof of existence in *All That Fall*, "Do not imagine, because I am silent, that I am not present and alive," becomes life itself.

Verbalizing in *Embers* has two main functions. Words are used in the conventional sense, as if they had a firm ontological basis and can be explained by means of ordinary literary analysis or a consideration of metaphors, themes, etc. Here, and in the other radioplays, one can almost hear the protagonist imploring words themselves to signify. On another level, words are used live through vocal utterance: they are identified with life itself. Esslin writes: "In fact his use of the dramatic medium shows that he has tried to find means of expressions beyond the language."[14] Not only is meaning transferable, but Beckett ultimately seems to question the signifying capacity of language. He uses language tentatively, consciously, perhaps as a default. The question still remains whether Henri's words are supposed to express real memories or only memories of other words. Perhaps there is no way of knowing; perhaps one can only respond to Beckett's words on a non-verbal level, and attempt to gain access to meaning by intuition.

The mere existence of voiced words has to be evaluated before one discusses their meaning. The almost constant tension between meaningful words and words-as-words makes *Embers* a masterpiece of radioplays, in which the main character is doomed to examine his story, his story-of-the-story (Bolton, Holloway), and finally the very sense of utterance altogether. The process thus draws attention to radio itself. As in the theatre, the use of a story-within-a-story, an *ars-poetic* device calls for attention to the medium. The "message" tends to dwindle into its own modes of expression in a constant process of interiorization. The "inside story" Henri tells about Holloway and Bolton relates to the story *of* Henri, also told by himself in a similar way that Henri's story "of himself" relates to the listener. Henri listens to himself in a way similar to the listener listening to him. The vocal Russian-doll effect focuses the listener's mind and ear on speech as an *act*.

The story-within-a-story device functions like words on words, or, according to Henri, it goes "around and around with a gramophone":

> What happened was this, I put them on and then I took them off again and then I put them on again and then I took them off again and then I put them on again and then I . . . (*EM*, 257)

The fictional space of *All That Fall* is the road to the railway and back, paved with many sound effects. In *Embers*, "space" is perceived by Henri alone, and in a more consciously artificial mode. In a precise sense, "a radio play does not exist in space but in time . . . but if the play is to mean anything, it must create an *illusion* of space".[15] The illusionary space of *Embers* is Henri's verbalized consciousness, in his inner world of personified memories, his regrets and ghosts from the past. They are dragged into the broadcasting-time and made present (temporarily) from the point of view of the medium, and visually (perhaps) from the point of view of the receivers.

The fictional space is a vague space, in which scenes shift according to their emotional impact on their radiophonic director. Henri elicits his images of Bolton and Holloway, of his daughter's riding and music lessons, of other scenes on the (same?) beach, etc. It is the intimacy of the medium that grants such scenes their verisimilitude, once their extreme subjectivity is accepted. The impact, naturally, also depends on complete subservience to Henri's self-reference. Distance, as one important aspect of radio, can easily be used to indicate different levels of reality, so that a remote voice (as Beckett notes for Ada's) means "less real" in these pseudo-spatial conventions.

Scenes slip into one another with no definite borders between them. One matter is never fully completed before the next one pushes the radioplay forward. This type of linear structural development, as another aspect of illusionary radiophonic space, reinforces its highly subjective, associative nature. In most of the sequences Beckett uses repetition, combined with a motif and variations, into which small vocal vignettes are woven. Henri's relation with his father, for instance, parallels the relationship with his daughter. Alternatively, Henri becomes father and son, husband and friend – and seems to be failing all.

The sea is the only vocal entity apparently outside of Henri's head.

"Radiophonically" it is explicitly referred to as an ominous, impersonal "sucking" murmur on the shores of which Henri is sitting, half-mesmerized and yet fighting. The sea drowned Henri's father and now Henri tries to drown the sound of the sea with the sound of his words. The sea may represent eternity, death, the outer world, but primarily it stands for objective time, which, as Beckett indicates, is audible whenever Henri pauses.

Words, then, may be regarded as keepers of time, *Embers* is a radioplay haunted with time and its various vocal manifestations. Sitting on the verge of sea and land, Henri makes time itself a self-referential notion in and of the radioplay. The sea, as an everlasting time symbol, threatens to drown Henri's private time and life. The word "time" appears frequently and the radioplay is replete with direct and indirect measurements of time.

Time is organized in two ways. The first is linear, single-directional and irreversible. Time, through tones, becomes concrete experiential content; the experience of musical rhythm is an experience of time made possible through tones, which explains part of Henri's compulsory talking. But time is also portrayed as pseudo-cyclical, synchronic, and reversible. Henri, in an effort to avoid the inevitable, jumps between past and present, mixing various points of time as though to camouflage them. Yet, even when he painfully remembers his daughter's music lesson so that he can avoid the inverted future, linear time laughs in his face in the form of the teacher beating time with a ruler. The final remark of this scene is almost farcical in its anti-sentimentalism. "It was not enough to drag her into the world, now she must play the piano" (*EM*, 259). The only music in this piece is undercut with this snide remark. Henri's past and present are closely interwoven, to the extent that he, as well as the listener, cannot tell them apart.

There are many other auditory timekeepers in the radioplay, and Beckett uses them here in a more intense way than in *All That Fall*. The sounds of hooves, pebbles, and the music-teacher's ruler all mark the passage of time. They are heard as sound effects, contextualized and juxtaposed with words and silences. An interesting allusion is made to Shakespeare, linking the timekeeping image of the horses' hooves with the "hour of glass" in a particularly radiophonic way by creating an ironic connection between King Henri IV and "Henri of Embers":

> Think, when we talk of horses that you see them
> Printing their proud hoofs because the receiving earth
> For 'tis your thoughts that now must deck our kings
> Carry them here and there, jumping o'er time
> Turning the accomplishment of many years
> Into an hour of glass.

Henri, in directing his own play in his head, and in using voice as a self-expressive as well as self-referential vehicle, occupies a peculiar location between life of words and radiophonic death. He hovers on the verge of "inside-land" and "outside-sea", between past and present, all the time screening slow-motion vocal-pictures inside his head.

Words and Music

Whereas every dramatic work must have, in varying proportions, elements of self-reference as well as elements of reference to the world outside of itself, *Words and Music*, compared with the earlier radioplays, almost exclusively refers to its own means. It is a close, nearly formal and abstract study of the way in which words, music and sound effect are made to *mean*. The radioplay is a short, highly economic quartet for the four elements of radio. Its structure is a clear and sophisticated case of serving as a metaphor to the self-referential meaning. The radioplay is built toward a cooperation between words and music in a song, in order to substitute and be more "expressive" than sound effects or even silence.

Words and Music is an allegory of art as a process of imaginative exploration. What it explores is the situation of an artist in relation to his life; it attempts to embody, in artistic form, in a fusion of emotion and thought, an adequate vision of the artist's reality.

The figures (the word "characters" is misleading) are Croak, Words and Music. Words (also called Joe), and Music (Bob), are Croak's two servants. Like other inseparable Beckett couples, these two are "cooped-up" together in the dark, living in mutual disharmony. When one of them is to "perform", the other voices discontent, as though doubting the rival's ability to express adequately anything at all. Words is more aggressive, intellectual and discursive, perhaps more masculine. Music is emotional, sentimental, more intuitive and submissive. The master of these two undisguised modes of expression is very explicitly called Croak, the characterization suggesting a death-groan, a neither verbal nor musical vocal expression, in fact, a sound effect. Croak emits only very laconic utterances throughout the play, although he is the "protagonist". Croak is associated with the "submissive" sound of his shuffling slippers and the aggressive thuds of his club. As a radiophonic motif, one observes here the development from Maddy's "dragging feet" and Dan's blind-stick taps, now merged into the "personality" of Croak.

Croak is a tyrannical master, unable to express himself without his two personified modes of expression, whom he nevertheless rebukes as "Dogs", imploring them to "be friends" and calling them "my comforts . . . my balms," all depending on the degree of success in which they "say" what he "feels". Croak needs his servants in order to overcome the gap between the need to express himself and the inability to do so properly or at all. Self-referentiality ensues from concentrating on the means of expression rather than on a particular content. Croak needs Words and Music to avoid silence, which is associated with death. In this he is similar to Henri and Maddy Rooney. Only here his weapons are given an explicit and active role. As befits a radioplay, Words and Music serve as radiophonic extensions, as semi-detached and external-ized means of expression, in the service of a frustrated master.

Both servants constantly address Croak, and thus his silence becomes the focus of their attention as well as the listener's – a subtle and effec-tive way of establishing presence. Beckett also uses this technique in *All That Fall* (Maddy addressing Mr Barrel) and in *Embers* (the evocation of characters), but here he exploits it fully. Croak is an embittered, gloomy and suffering master. He not only fights silence, he tyrannizes his modes of expression. As the radioplay proceeds one learns that there is some-thing – memory, an experience, some essential and very crucial issue and artistic message, or even life itself – that Croak wants to convey through his servants, to the outside world and, more probably, to himself.

Words, the more complex figure of the two, describes the dramatic situation for the listener. Words' duty is to deliver speeches on topics such as love, sloth, age, and the soul. At the beginning of the play we hear him rehearsing his lecture on sloth. It is as though the only func-tion of Words were to produce worn-out scholastic casuistries, reminiscent of Lucky's monologue in *Waiting for Godot*.

Words walks the tightrope between language as meaning and language as mere sound. He is a compulsive figure who must utter something, no matter what, in order to justify his existence. Beckett is sceptical about Words, but continues to use him (and them). Words tries to be logical, intellectual, discursive and meaningful, yet succeeds only in achieving parody of meaning. Beckett uses Croak, who uses Words (and Music), to express very eloquently how difficult (or impossible) it is to express anything adequately. The tension between what Words says and how he says it extricates Beckett from the danger of boring the audience by talking about boredom.

Music tries to convey the emotional, non-verbal message that weighs on Croak. Music is freed of the need to express himself discursively; he elicits memories through the power of association, by appealing directly to emotion. Music is less active than Words, but his role is far from being secondary. Since Music is not bound by rules of semantic explicitness, perhaps he can "say" more in less time. Words rejects Music, while Music seems to be more tolerant. When the two are required to join in a common effort, Words first refuses, then, when threatened by Croak, agrees reluctantly to cooperate. Music gains the upper hand in the quarrel and grows louder, drowning Words' words. Only at the very end does Words beseech Music to continue, perhaps because he recognizes his own inability to save Croak or, at least, to please him.

Words sometimes employs musical patterns of repetition or emphasis, while Music sometimes functions as though he were Words. Music has a real role to play; perhaps for the first time in the history of radioplays he tries "to speak". The inability of Music to talk can be compared with the inability of Words to penetrate Croak's mind or, for that matter, to mean anything. This is also why Music is not actually threatened by Words; he is simply deaf to Words' potential meaning. Both servants do their best to please their master. Success or failure cannot be ascribed to their unwillingness to help, but to their intrinsic incompetence.

Words and Music, as though to compensate for a difficult to identify self-referential message, exhibits a definite structure and a clear thematic development, organized in five parts: (1) exposition, (2) first interlude and first theme, of love and soul, (3) second interlude and second theme, of age and age song, (4) third interlude and third theme, of face and face song, (5) an abrupt end.

The first part begins with the orchestra tuning up and ends with Words' rehearsal. Croak is heard following the shuffle of his own slippers. The entire radioplay takes place in the dark, as we learn when Words' first plea turns into a rebuke:

> Please! (Tuning. Louder). Please! (Tuning dies away). How much longer cooped up here, in the dark, (with loathing) with you! . . . (*WM*, 287)

In this way Beckett emphasizes that there is no visual aspect to all that follows.

The animosity between Words and Music is established from the beginning. (Is it because they are cooped up in Croak's skull? Or because they do not have enough "brain" to expand on?) Music disturbs Words. Following the exposition, Croak asks Words and Music to be friends between themselves and/or his friends. He provides the play with its focus both by his arrival and by his commanding tone and speech. He apologizes for being late, and demands the first theme. The words "theme tonight" imply that there have been other themes and other such nights. (Most of Beckett's works create the sense that we are witnessing merely one arbitrary sequence in a series of continuous repetition.)

The first theme of *Words and Music* is love. Words gives the speech after the fashion of a real, live performance. Croak is not satisfied and asks Music to try the same theme. Words agonizes while hearing Music and protests wildly. There must be something in the hollow text that repels Music. Music wins this short battle. But Croak is still unhappy, and suffers from the incompetence of his "balms" in supplying him with the right message.

On the next theme, Words and Music are required to cooperate. Words tries to sing with the help of Music's suggestions, but their effort does not succeed. Croak's involvement is increased; it is as though Words and Music draw something from his life in the past. After an agonizing, slow series of verbal and musical phrases, the song of age is finally crystallized. Croak asks for the theme of Face; Words ignores him at first, but later inserts the motif, elaborating on it and on its corresponding, vague female figure.

Croak's groans become more frequent. After the song is born and sung he collapses, his club falls and he moves away dissatisfied, desperate. When Words and Music are finally able to cooperate, it is too late. The listener is left in the dark as to whether their "success" was emotionally too strong and moving for Croak to handle, or whether they simply failed by missing the issue entirely.

The medium in Beckett's radioplays is not the message. The message can never be delivered and the medium serves to focus on certain aspects of the inexpressible message. The listener is given to understand that nothing more can be said. The value in attempting to express anything at all lies mainly in a Sisyphean courage or pride; the effort continues, despite the knowledge of its futility. Silence is not just death, nor is it a testimony to the inadequacy of expression. Rather, it is the correct expression of the inability to speak or create music in any way that transcends mere sound.

Cascando

Cascando, like *Words and Music*, can be regarded as an allegory of the art of radio and, for that matter, of the struggle any artist has with his creative process; at the same time it is a manifestation of the art.[16] Having examined his artistic tools in *Words and Music*, Beckett now focuses further on what they can express. In this respect, *Cascando* marks the end of one road of exploration. The journey roughly parallels the one Beckett traveled from *Waiting for Godot* to *Breath*.

With *Cascando*, Beckett achieves maximal density and an almost absolute exhaustion of radiophonic elements, creating a perfect balance between economy of means and richness of expression. It has a mock classic beginning. "It is the month of May", yet the "dry as dust" voice and the verbal modification "for me", endow this promised resurrection a very subjective and ironic touch. The allusion to the month of May appears later for the same purpose, and is perhaps indicative of Beckett, the artist, having finally managed to write this radioplay. Beckett describes the situation of a man close to death, in need of achieving a lifelong objective, never before attained.

Beckett frequently appeals to visual images, especially in Woburn's gradual decay into mud and bilge. Yet everything happens in the dark, and even the technique of evoking those visual images is different from that of former radioplays. Here we find an attempt to hold on to every one of the senses in order to complete the story. Voice and Opener function as the inner, more reflective counterparts of each other; Beckett deliberately alternates their internal and external functions. While the dominant image is of Opener, who lifts a lid off his own skull and lets Voice speak, it is Voice who serves as the "eyes" and helps to reconstruct the event in full, both for Opener and for the listeners. The exchange of roles element creates a nightmarish atmosphere, for the listener has no way of knowing what is really happening in Opener's head. The situation closely recalls the one in *Embers*, but is still more internal, intensive, and intimate. Beckett draws the listener right into the speakers' heads. What was essentially a metaphor in the first two plays becomes in *Words and Music*, and especially in *Cascando*, a realization of the metaphor.[17]

In *All That Fall* some scenes take place metaphorically in Maddy's head. This idea is elaborated on in *Embers*, strongly implied in *Words and Music*, and quite explicit in *Cascando*: "They said, it's his, it's his voice, it's in his head" (*CAS*, 299). Opener doubts whether "it" is or is not in his head – maintaining the point of view of the listener, or any "nonself" entity. He listens to Voice in the same way that any real listener might listen to him. It is a vocal–mirror image.

The main thematic difference between the two radioplays is the need in *Cascando* to tell and complete a story. Both the function of the story and the structure of the play are indicated at the beginning.

> Story . . . if you could finish it . . . you could rest . . . you could sleep . . . not before . . . Oh, I know . . . the ones I've finished . . . thousands and one . . . all I ever did . . . in my life . . . with my life . . . saying to myself . . . finish this one . . . then rest . . . then sleep . . . no more stories . . . no more words . . . (*CAS*, 297)

The radioplay is a story about "almost"; it is almost a story about the story, about the story *ad infinitum*. Two mirrors are set opposite each other, forming a series of endless reflections. In *Cascando*, Voice and Opener's voices mirror one another vocally. But something is missing – the incomplete story between the two mirrors, the object that is being reflected. The story is never completed, and so the only thing left to do is tell how it might be found, and how incessant the search is. "Thousands and one" alludes to the Arabian story of never-ending stories. There is always one more story, the right one, to be told.

There is, however, some information to be gleaned from Voice's story about a story. A man by the name of Woburn (probably Opener and referred to in the third person) gets up to go on a strange and difficult journey, searching for something, wishing to reach some place – a light, an island. The need to arrive there is urgent, particularly because time is running short. If one can speak of claustrophobia of time, it occurs in this play. The essential always slips away, just out of reach, yet there is always a Tantalic hope that " . . . this time . . . it's right . . . finish . . . no more stories . . . sleep . . . we're [third and first person become one 'we'] there . . . nearly . . . just a few more . . . don't let go . . . Woburn . . . he clings on . . . come on . . . come on . . . [Silence]" (*CAS*, 304). Both the "story" and the radioplay present an agonizing process of trial and deeply disappointing error, a conflict between the wish to give in and the inner push to continue. There is a strong sense of escalation in *Cascando*, as suggested by the name; and a decrescendo of rhythm and volume at the end, manifesting the growing urgency of finding the "right one", yet the inability to do so. Final (and radiophonic) silence puts an end to all efforts.

In *Cascando*, Beckett reduces the animosity between Words and Music. He also deprives Music of his prior independent status. Words is no longer a personified mode of expression; rather, "it is as though they had linked their arms". In this respect *Cascando* is slightly less pessimistic than *Words and Music*. A shade of optimism lies in the end of the radioplay and in the implication that there is a need for external intervention that will lift Woburn's eyes and make him see that the island and the light are near at hand. The intervention would extract Woburn from the cyclical pattern in which he walks. Beckett does not say whether such an external intervention is possible, but Woburn's own efforts seem to be endlessly locked within themselves. He gets closer to his one and finite story without ever reaching it, much like Zeno's paradox of infinite division.

Just as nothing further can be said once the *"reductio ad absurdum"* mode of theatrical expression reaches its limit in *Breath*, so too, after *Cascando*, Beckett must change direction.

Radio I

As in *Play*, *Film*, and *Act Without Words I* and *II*, the name of the medium is the name of the work itself. In *Radio I* and *Radio II* Beckett tries to cross the dividing line between the writer–producer–actor and the audience–listener. He turns from an exploration of the means of expression and inexpressibility to the potential impression and impact that the means of expression may have on the listener. The last two radioplays draw the writer–actor–listener situation into the work itself, and in a peculiar way they internalize criticism of the play and assign it a role within the play.

In the first part of *Radio I*, a She-figure comes to a He. She arrives at a place which is, one soon learns, a room with a recording machine, perhaps a studio, perhaps some sort of radio-receiver. He can be interchanged with the author, She with the listener, while the turning of the knobs focuses on the actual technical act of turning those of the radio. She expresses an interest in how He is feeling – "Are you all right?" (*RI*, 267) – and adds that He asked her to come. He reluctantly agrees that He "meets his debts"; by inviting her He just "suffered her to come." Unlike *Words and Music* or *Cascando*, in which the self is completely enclosed, one finds here a clear concept of the Other. The relationships are not exclusively between two or more phases of and *in* one person, but between the internal phases of one person (Words, Music) *and* other people. She comes to *listen*, as she says. Rather than lifting lids from one's own skull as in *Cascando*, She does it to the He-figure by pushing knobs and turning them "to the right, Madam . . . ".

Radio I can be divided into three parts. The first part presents the encounter between He and She; the second part deals with the concern of the He-figure that "they're ending" (the voice and the music), and the attempt to get help; the third part is a strange report on the "confinements". Once the existence and the nature of voice and music have been asserted in the first part, the anguish felt for their ending is more understandable in the second. In the third part they are personified as babies. The He–She relationship sheds light on the relationship between the Words and the Music. Whatever happens in the radioplay also happens between the listener and the radio-receiver, parallel also to the relationship between He and She.

Thematic textual references reinforce this self-referential structure. She says, "I have come to listen" (*RI*, 267). When she wants some heat she says: "How cold you are" (*RI*, 268) and then asks, "Is it alive?" (as opposed to "recorded?" or "dead?"). She receives the rather funny but morbid answer: "No, you must twist" and then, "All alone?" He says, "When one is alone one is all alone" (*RI*, 268). Toward the end he says that he "cannot describe" the condition to which they are subjected. These lines are deliberately ambivalent and descriptive both of the He and She figures, and of voice and music, in their radiophonic transmission. Later, one learns that He regards voice and music as his needs, but he has an equal need to be listened to by the doctor and his secretary. She is the one who tries to communicate, whereas He stresses the motif "alone" (three times) against a notion of "they" who cannot see or hear one another. She finally leaves him to his "needs" (called "balms," "comforts", or "dogs" in *Words and Music*) because of his "cold" treatment toward her. He, however, associates his needs with "house garbage".

The second part opens after a "long pause". He remains alone and is now trying to get in touch with the outer world. In the meantime he draws the curtain violently, an act suggesting further inner enclosure. The relatively direct communication of actual encounter in the first part is replaced by the indirect, more mediated attempt to call the doctor on the telephone. During the three phone calls – two to the secretary and one to the doctor himself – voice and music gradually fade away and "fail" him; they leave him alone. He reacts in much the same way that Opener reacts in *Cascando*: "Good God"; "Come on."

In the third part, He receives a phone call in which he is informed that there was a "confinement . . . breach" (*RI*, 271); it is quite likely that the allusion is to the birth of twins (*two* confinements). This can refer either to some unknown birth of real babies or to the birth of Words and Music. Perhaps the enigmatic ending line "Tomorrow . . . noon . . . " (*RI*, 271) suggests that one or both of the twins died (due to the difficult "breech" birth) and that the funeral will take place "tomorrow". There is a direct link between the mysterious birth of the twins and the slow decline of voice and music. The impression is that their birth occurs simultaneously with their death. Actually, it is the birth and death of the radioplay *Radio I* itself.

In the end, and at least from the point of view of McGillycuddy, the protagonist, He is the one to hear about the "confinement", "breech", and probably about the death of whoever was born. This shifts the disbelief in the reality of the dying words and music which the doctor expresses in the report McGillycuddy receives.

There are many listeners and listening situations in *Radio I*. In a sense, the radioplay is "about" a listening situation and it "is" listening. Voice and music do not listen to each other. He listens to voice and music until they leave him, but hardly at all to She. She listens to He and to what He listens to – voice and music. There is also a series of telephone "listenings": He and the doctor's secretary (twice); He and the doctor; He and Miss X, who calls about the confinements. At the same time the precise meaning of *what* is said is highly evasive and deliberately vague. As in other Beckett works, the elusiveness of the content draws attention to the medium. The person who listens to all the listenings in the radioplay is the radio listener. The many silences and pauses invite the listener to become part of all the others who listen. *Radio I* is a whole radioplay within a radioplay in which the second half devours the first.

Radio II

The four characters who take part in *Radio II* are A, the animator; S, the stenographer; Fox, apparently the subject; and Dick, who remains mute. A is the dominant figure; he is cruel though sometimes polite and even flirtatious toward S, who is rather obedient but can nevertheless assert herself. Dick says nothing and only uses the pizzle following A's command. Fox is described as half-human, half-animal; he is a Lucky-figure who evokes negative emotions in A and a certain degree of compassion from S.

The images are mainly those of light and darkness (if they are images at all and not literal descriptions of fact). The "mole experience" takes place in the dark. The interrogation takes place in light (perhaps it is even too glaring for S, as A suggests) (*RII*, 275).

The situation is an inquiry or experiment performed by Animator on Fox, with the assistance of the lady stenographer and Dick. A tries different techniques, most of which are violent and cruel, in order to draw out the desired information about Fox's life. Fox supplies some information about a mole – soaping and drying it, its underground life, and so on. During the session, A and S exchange words about their previous achievements and failures with the subject. A flirts a little with S, but she does not respond. The team's main task is to mark down every syllable and facial expression of the subject, who is either reluctant or unable to deliver the clear information demanded of him. Yet, they themselves are unclear about the information they want; "Of course we do not know, anymore than you, what exactly it is we are after . . . " (*RII*, 282). Since the information Fox gives is insufficient and does not make much sense to A, he finally decides to falsify it:

> S: But, sir, he never said anything of the kind.
> A: (angry) . . . Maud would say, *between two kisses*, Amend.
> S: But, sir, I –
> A: (. . .) Amend!
> S: (feebly) As you will, sir. (*RI*, 284)

The radioplay ends with a promise for a better future when "we may be free" (*RII*, 284).

Beyond the mystery and vagueness of the plot one can detect an intricate pattern which relates to the author–character–audience relationships. Two possible mutually complementary interpretations can be supplied. According to the first interpretation, Animator is the figure who endows the characters with life (anima) and wants Fox, the sly author (Beckett), to supply him with explanations of the sombre words about the mole who lives in the dark, "unexplained" underground, and especially of the words "have yourself opened", which are often repeated.

Animator tells S that after the answers (clarifications, explanations) are received, Fox would be freed and could return to his "darling solitude". But Beckett (Fox) seems to maintain here that he does not want to have himself opened. (Indeed, once a play is written, Beckett refrains from interpreting from the outside.) If Fox is an author/playwright figure, the radioplay is a bitter attack launched by Beckett on his critics, implying that they not only torture him but actually distort his words – as A does to Fox. Dick's position in this interpretation is less clear. But perhaps he is, as suggested, the dramatic–radiophonic character that the listener–critic uses in order to misinterpret (and torture) the author–playwright. Dick's position as a mute character in a radioplay is unique. His muteness would thus be an ironic comment on the absurdity of both the author's effort and the critical act. Describing Fox as a mole (or his description of a mole he had) elucidates Beckett's view of his creation as a groping in the dark. A's role as a critic is reinforced by direct textual allusions to Dante, Sterne, and to those "old spectres from the days of book reviewing" (*RII*, 280).

According to the second interpretation, Animator is the author who, as the deliberate falsification in the end suggests, tries to "fictionalize" reality and the relationships between the characters; he gives reality some sense, albeit contrived. The stenographer in the framework story and Maud in the inner story of the "mole" are, like Dante's Beatrice, motivating inspirations as well as objective reporters of the text itself. Both are witnesses. Hence the critical interpretation exists on two levels. Dick is the listener (necessarily mute in a radioplay), who, with his whips, insists on further information from the author, or perhaps on more and more "stories".

While it is possible to combine these two interpretations, it is not easy to dispose of them altogether. The need for an allegorical interpretation ensues from the text itself:

> Of course we do not know, any more than you, what exactly we are after, what sign or set of words. But since you have failed so far to let it escape you it is not be harking on the same old themes that you are likely to succeed, that would astonish me. (*RII*, 282)

Beckett seems to be playing with his critics; he enacts the process of interpretation by means of a consistently self-referential text. *Radio II* is about interpretation, and at the same time it practises the act of interpretation in the work itself.

Whereas *Theatre II* deals with artistic criticism in theatrical terms and modes of expression, *Radio II* does so radiophonically. The allegory is reflected in the theme and situation of the radioplay as well as in its images, mutual attitudes between characters, and the highly evasive point of view (or of listening) presented.

Whether Becket (or the implied author) is presented as Fox or as the Animator, the equation clarifies a number of otherwise arbitrary lines. A says: "What counts is not so much the thing in itself . . . no, it's the word, the notion" (*RII*, 123). Here a character, in emphasizing the importance of the mode of expression, clearly represents the author. This is what interests an author; in Fox's words: "Ah, yes, that for sure, live I did, no denying . . . " (*RII*, 119). *Radio II* is concerned with the discrepancy between life as it is lived and the word or notion which may sum it up or explain it. Hence the radioplay, which is necessarily engaged in giving vocal utterance to a life lived, is caught in the same trap. *Radio II* employs the logic demonstrated in the sentence: "This sentence has five words" – a statement that self-referentially unites the mode of expression with what it says. Similarly, obscurity is at once the method and content of *Radio II*.

Every radioplay is realized temporally and in the present. Beckett incorporates this facet of radio drama into a thematic concern. The characters in the plays are all engaged in the attempt to cope with the fleeting moments of their lives. In *All That Fall* the main image is one of "lingering dissolution". In *Embers*, Henri is constantly busy marking time: "Every syllable is a second gained." *Words and Music* and *Cascando* refer to the one story that may redeem the character from his phobia of losing time. In *Radio II* there is a clear shifting of the "solution" to tomorrow.

Many of the characters are conscious not only of their obsession with talking but also of the kind of talking they perform on radio. They are unseen; their existence depends on words; they are words. Discourse in the radioplays is an event on radio insofar as it describes, expresses and represents the world of the characters. This world has two implied extensions beyond the performed event: one is the author, who may or may not be identified with the first-person narrator(s); the other is the listener, who may also be represented in the radioplay. The use of discourse (vicarious as it may be) necessarily implies a listener. Whereas Beckett's stage plays are always enwrapped in the self-referential notion of "being seen", the radioplays deal with the equally self-referential notion of "being heard". The talking–listening situation is the central motif. It is the vocal epitome of self-reference: the talkers in the particular radioplay represent the playwright whereas the listening figure (a changing role) represents the listener at home. Maddy Rooney complains about her difficulties with language, but more important is her wish to be heard.

In *Embers*, Beckett goes one step further and deliberately blurs the borders between reality and imagination both in Henri's and in the listener's understanding. One does not know whether Henri "really" hears or only imagines hearing his wife, his daughter, the piano teacher, etc. By means of the "inside" voices in *Words and Music* and in *Cascando*, Beckett implies that one always needs a listener, even if the character himself has to be divided into "talking" and "listening" phases. Unable to go deeper into the self itself, Beckett turns, in *Radio I* and *II*, to the situation of listening to "another".

Listening in the radioplays reflects listening to them. Beckett may certainly enjoy the irony ensuing from a situation in which nobody is listening to a radioplay on the air. Typically, and quite in line with the paradoxical nature of self-referential utterances, even this possibility is dealt with.

One can discern three main phases in Beckett's exploration of radiophonic expression. The first phase includes *All That Fall*, where the author makes extensive use of radio's facilities and its specific techniques: mixing, elaborate sound effects, the blending of voices, music and sound effects, a big cast, and so on. *Embers* marks a shift from the first phase to the second. Technically, *Embers* is still relatively "rich" (in terms of an elaborate use – though much less than *All That Fall* – of techniques, of fast cuts, voices, effects, etc.), but the "scene" no longer takes place outdoors. There are fewer characters and the participants are, possibly, extensions of Henri's imagination and memory. Stripping away "technique", in *Words and Music* and *Cascando*, Beckett goes further in exploring the radiophonic mode of expression. Language also becomes more economical. In *All That Fall*, Beckett presents a "rounded" and rather self-conscious three-dimensional figure; the medium through which she comes across is still a means for her portrayal. In *Cascando*, Beckett explores the very process of artistic creation on radio through voices and music (though without sound effects); hence the medium becomes the subject matter, reflecting the means of that creation. The third phase consists of *Radio I* and *Radio II*, where the roles of author and audience and the relationships between them become the single theme or "plot" of the plays. The fusion of content and technique is completed.

5 "Spirit Made Light" – Film and TV Plays

Courageous, wise and humorous, Beckett made attempts in many different media and genres to overcome the paradox of expressing the inexpressible. In his prose and poetry as well as in his plays for theatre, radio and television, he was looking for the "expressive possibilities" of the vehicle. Beckett always had an "acute sense of the problems and possibilities of the form in question . . . the work not only is predicated on the form but invariably becomes a critique of its form".[1]

The artistic manifestations of Beckett's fictitious heroes of self-consciousness change form in compliance with the medium into which they are born, but they always claim an uncompromising sense of spiritual freedom. Whether their bodies are metaphorically stuck on the stage, projected on the screen, heard on the radio or reduced to the absolute requirements of the particular medium, their souls always assert themselves.

The performative media of radio and theatre can serve as an interesting model for Beckett's TV plays. There exists a certain similarity between the development of various plays in the different media which Beckett explored. Beckett first creates a powerful play with respect to the particular medium for which the work is written; he then experiments with different components of the medium in order, finally, to imply that the message is "more important" than the medium, although the former cannot exist without the latter.

In the radio plays the *Cogito* is implicitly replaced by "I emit noises, therefore I am." In *All That Fall* Maddy Rooney says: "Do not imagine, because I am silent, that I am not present and alive" (*ATF*, 185). *Embers* already turns the medium inside-out. Henry listens to voices inside his "theatre in the skull" and features as producer and actor of his story as well as in the story-within-the-story. Attention is called to the medium itself, whereby the listener is enticed to hear the same voices and noises as Henry. He is told by his possibly dead wife Ada that he will be "quite alone" (262) with his voice, as he already is, at the time of broadcasting. *Words and Music* is an allegory of art, almost a formalization of it, as a process of exploring the artist's radiophonic means. *Words and Music* present the "expressive possibilities" of Croak, and although they do not get along very well, words and music are finally induced to cooperate with each other in order to create a song.

Having examined his tools in *Words and Music*, in *Cascando* Beckett focuses on the tools' capacity for expression. *Cascando* is a story about "almost": almost a story about a story, ad infinitum. The titles of Beckett's work are often chosen in accordance with the medium for which they were intended. Such is the case in *Radio I* and *Radio II*. The two plays switch from the internalized point of view (or listening) to a more external and critical approach. In *Radio I*, the act of listening is closely examined. The character in *Radio I* has certain "needs," he probably needs "words" and "music". This radio play concentrates on a variation: "I listen, therefore (perhaps . . .) you are." In *Radio II* Beckett exploits this medium even further by introducing a mute character called Dick. It is certainly humorous, if not revolutionary, to use a character who is unable to speak in a radio play. Here, the emphasis is on radiophonic criticism and on the discrepancy between life as it is lived and "the word, the notion" (CDW, 280) which may explain life. One character expresses himself through the sound effect of his "pizzle".

In the theatre plays, the *Cogito* is replaced by "I am present on stage, therefore I am." Didi and Gogo reassert their stage-existence after short exits. Winnie, in *Happy Days* needs "eyes on her eyes" in order "to be". Mouth in *Not I* gives birth to the actual words which constitute her unique stage presence. *Theatre II*, is "about" theatre criticism. The protagonist of *Catastrophe*, in this play-within-the-play, is inhumanly manipulated, until he raises his head and faces the "real" as well as the fictive audience with an independent, free gaze. At the same time some of the plays focus on certain theatrical means of expression such as lighting in *Play*, dialogue as well as stage properties in *Happy Days* and directing in *Catastrophe*. This meta-theatrical approach does not exhaust the interpretative possibilities of any particular play. Rather, it shows that for Beckett the medium is not merely a formal device but a highly developed and technically flawless inquiry into the expressibility of the most detailed components of the "vehicle".

In Beckett's plays, due to the dialogical nature of theatre, no character can be truly alone on stage. The notion of "other" selves will therefore be considered, together with the more principal question of *presence*; the latter being a physical necessity in theatre. But in what sense can one encounter this notion of presence which is such a fundamental component of theatre in Beckett's *Film* or in the television plays?

Experimenting with "vice-existers" in his plays and placing many of his personae on the abysmal verge of offstage (just a moment before they are absorbed by the quiet and darkness of non-being), Beckett nonetheless works with his characters' actual, though minimal presence. The characters must "be there", especially since Beckett's actors substitute the I of the character with their own I.

> The stage welcomes every illusion except that of presence . . . and inversely, the cinema accommodates every form of reality save one – the physical presence of the actor.[2]

Beckett's *Film* and his TV scripts were all written in English and produced, partly under his own supervision if not direction, between 1963 and 1983. Although belonging to a "cool", analytical medium which demands high technological requirements, Beckett's *Film* and his following five TV scripts must be counted among his most explicitly spiritual works. They not only deal with ghosts as psychological projections, but often hint that "other" beings are really "there", at least from the point of view of the medium. In this medium (with due respect to the difference between TV and film) the *Cogito* is expressed in modes of "I am seen (or "shot"!), therefore I am." In all scripts except *Quad*, the portrayed self encounters an "other": a shadow or a doppelgänger, even an envisaged quintessence of his own "feeling-thinking-willing" self depicting previous stages of his life. This other self, appearing in the "non-presence" of film or video, is the epitome of a "not yet" or "not anymore" chance given to the self. The ontological status of the entire piece, meticulously presented by Beckett, is that of a conscious, self-referential illusion, trapped by film or recorded on videotape.

There exists a perfect agreement between what is shown in the pieces on the one hand, and the expected relationship between the piece and its potential viewers/listeners, on the other. Insofar as the fictitious (but theatrically present) relationship between Winnie and Willie in *Happy Days* reflects a desired Author–Audience interaction via the dramatis personae, the video as a medium becomes a tacit partner of the TV scripts. The way in which the camera treats the self is reminiscent of how the self deals with some of its shadows and doppelgängers.

The incantation of ghosts along with the presentation of offstage space is best suited to the medium of television. Whereas the body of the TV script can be associated with the video cassette, the soul is represented by the film itself: spirit, made light. And finally, in these works Beckett presents "offstage" via "off-life" figures, beings whose depiction cannot be convincingly made in any other medium. Creating imaginary or spiritual personae on screen, figures composed of light and darkness, appears to be the closest an artist may come to expressing the inexpressible which nonetheless exists; perhaps objectively, sometimes in the viewers and always in the artist himself.

Film

Film, subtitled "esse est percipi", presents a Berkeleyan version of the Cartesian problem. While in his theatre plays Beckett establishes his characters' presence onstage through textual manifestations and no less explicit stage instructions, the "I am shot by Camera, therefore I am" can be reconciled with the fact that the camera is unable to accommodate itself to the presence of the actor. Beckett seems to fully acknowledge this phenomenon in *Film* which focuses on E(ye)'s pursuit of O. *Film* is obviously not "about something; it is that something itself".[3] In self-reflexive cinema, reflexivity rather than "presence" represents the core of the medium as well as the content of this piece. It shows that "the image of things is likewise the image of their duration"[4] and not an illusion of their presence. In fact, cinema and TV are the ideal media to cope with the kind of "vice-existence" which fascinated Beckett so much: non-presence being the essence of the medium as previously mentioned. Furthermore, a film, as a piece of celluloid with images on it, actually replays the imprints of light after the object itself has vanished.

Visual images of the self are the subject/object of *Film*. Whereas in *Play* the question "Am I seen?" creates a tautological and humorous metaphor in theatrical terms, in *Film* O constantly flees perception; he is the only one who believes himself capable of escaping unnoticed. The only non-visual element in *Film*, the "sssh!" sound, emphasizes the deliberately chosen silence of the filmed images. Fear of being perceived represents, of course, a contradiction in a medium in which "sheer existence" means being seen. *Film*, therefore, hypostasizes a cinematographic principle on the one hand, while demolishing it, on the other. The process of attempting to flee from self-awareness in *Film* is indicative of the relationship between *Film* and its potential viewers. "Wearing their eye-patches over the same eye, O and E seem to be looking at each other's mirror images" while the viewer sees the entire film either from the perspective of O or E who cannot be shown together.[5] Beckett specifies: "All extraneous perception suppressed, animal, human, divine, self-perception maintains in being" (CDW, 323). In none of his other works was Beckett ever so explicit in interpreting the "inescapability of self-perception". Only *self*-consciousness is (paradoxically) allowed to be seen in its medium oriented attempts to escape the life-giving force. From a religious or metaphysical perspective, *Film* too speaks about Man's denial of God.

Beckett "grants" O only one eye whereas E has several Os although he focuses only on one. One eye seems sufficient from a physical point of view in order to recognize the two-dimensional surface of the screen. With two eyes (to include that of E at the end of *Film*), one can already perceive the third dimension which, in films, is an illusion. It is the third eye that is supposedly necessary for spiritual insight and visions.

Film is not just commenting on its medium, or casting "a film over what it seems to reveal".[6] The medium itself is presented as a sort of doppelgänger-protagonist, haunting O who feels threatened by self-perception. Henning analyzes *Film* as a dialogue between Beckett and Berkeley, who claims that "Through its knowledge of itself, the mind has, ipso facto, intuitive knowledge of divinity . . . whether or not we feel able to believe that God is the ultimate source and support of the mind's existence, the fact remains that the mind can have a conscious awareness of its consciousness . . . " Henning maintains that "Reflection . . . is an arduous, active process that does not at all come about naturally or by itself without effort." According to Henning, self-consciousness (or what is referred to as "spirit" by Berkeley), becomes both subject and object of the act of knowing. Blocking his vision, O would like to escape the gaze of E, the gaze of self-perception and hence of self-consciousness. Yet he cannot. The degree of self-awareness only increases, "E and O", Henning concludes, "remain apart even in the movement of self-perceivedness . . . Hence there can never be full unity of the self nor any perfect self-identify."[7]

Eh Joe

Beckett's second film is written for television and "it is almost impossible to find . . . another play which is as totally conceived in terms of the small television screen and its intimate audience psychology as *Eh Joe*".[8] At the same time, Beckett defies TV by stretching his viewers' patience to the limit: for how long can one watch an endless close-up and a "low, distinct, remote" voice, which is simultaneously slow and emotionally intrusive? Joe has "avoided the self by frantic activity or dominance over others or by meaningless routine".[9] Indeed, this play too deals with the inability to escape self-consciousness. However, unlike *Film* which treats the more abstract, perhaps more spiritual angst of the exposed self, *Eh Joe* depicts the deliberately emotional realm, often on the verge of the banal and sentimental, except for the last camera movement which freezes Joe's face in an immense close-up. In *Film* the camera both leads and misleads the viewers in their pursuit of O. Moreover, the camera causes their division into perceiving and being perceived. In *Eh Joe*, because of the nine gradual close-up movements, the TV viewer is drawn into Joe's head. The notion of being "pulled into" the medium, is also an important phenomenon in Beckett's other media.

In *Eh Joe* there occurs a typical TV split into sight and sound which forces the audience to synthesize the whole from its two separate perceptual channels. The combination between the visual yet silent Joe and the oral–aural yet invisible female voice suggests a tentative identity between Joe and his external viewers. Drawn closer and closer, the viewers themselves are made to resemble the protagonist who faces them in the intimacy of their homes. At the same time we are stunned to find ourselves on the screen. Moreover, the banality of Joe's story, told by the voice that sounds at first like a superficial soap-opera (the most popular TV genre), is superbly counterbalanced by Joe's unsentimental face. The face can be seen as a triumph of the objective and spiritual element over the emotional realm since the viewers must "fill in" the emotional indeterminacies of the piece. As in *Play*, the mode and means of representation serve as correctives for sentimentality. Rosette Lamont describes the voice as Joe's *anima*; emitted by his silent lips: "Both Joe and the viewers receive enlightenment from voice's tale of two women, herself and the other. In mythic terms . . . Demeter and Kore are the two poles of the External Feminine, the mystery of their fusion celebrates a renewal independent of male sexuality. Thus, the magical unity of the older and younger female serves as a guide to the male psyche."[10] A further "spiritually" minded interpretation is Zilliacus' approach to *Eh Joe* as a "drama based on theological, Catholic givens".[11] But Zilliacus situates the play in a more psychological context, associating the voice with a woman from Joe's past and a projection of his fears. Zilliacus quotes the actor Jack MacGowran: "the television camera photographs the mind . . . ".[12] Yet one wonders whether MacGowran was right in believing that Joe finally subdues the voice. Beckett's instructions read: "[Image fades, voice as before]." Only after the image is almost extinguished, after the final "Eh Joe? . . . " Beckett writes: "[Voice and image out. End]" (CDW, 367). If the longevity of the medium is at stake here, visual Joe has lost his fight against his vocal conscience. The piece can easily be read as a private seance. Whether the voice is a projection, or a supernatural but objectively real being, Beckett does not specify.

Eh Joe represents an intimately televised invitation to share a private self-imposed Day of Justice, at least half an hour of televised reckoning. Beckett remains loyal to the medium of television whilst exploiting the elements of sight and sound and playing them off against each other.[13] Finally the viewer/listener is not certain whether he or she should give priority to either ear or eye. Does the point from which we see *Eh Joe* obliterate the sphere of hearing, or vice versa? Such deliberate ambiguity regarding the "correct" reception of the piece – both its message and modes of delivery – is also found in *Footfalls*; the audience must decide whether the invisible yet vocal V devours the corporeal May or vice versa, or whether the outcome is a dramatic stalemate.

Ironically ambiguous or not, Joe definitely embarks on an enforced retrospective, assessing the meaning of his life via his religious background as well as via the equally dominant Dantesque allusions. It finally dawns on Joe that the true love he could have had passed him by. His punishment is commensurate with his sins. Since Joe employed language as a manipulative vehicle in his relationships with women, he, in turn, is now made to suffer through language by listening to the invisible voice which whispers in his ear. As his love for "the narrow one" was in fact self-love, Joe himself is now condemned to re-experience the trauma which he previously inflicted upon his girlfriend. Joe's is a homeopathic punishment, a *purgatorio* of the self. Because of the collision between the content of Voice's text and Joe's motionless face, the spiritual aspect of life wins over the emotional one. Joe indeed joins the dead, rather than managing to throttle them in his head. The voice, physically "less present" and traditionally more spiritual, outlives the visual image.

Ghost Trio

Ghost Trio, clearly dealing with ghosts, reveals the inability to go beyond the medium and to penetrate the imaginary off-screen space which, unlike theatrical offstage, cannot be located behind the cinema screen or behind the TV set. In his third television play, Beckett narrows down the photographed space and abolishes the concrete props, such as street and staircase used in *Film*. Here, perhaps as compensation, the auditory space of the piece opens up, and for the first time Beckett adds music to a woman's voice. Moreover, the ghosts are not external, they are within.[14]

In *Ghost Trio* Beckett again changes the camera's "viewpoints". In comparison to *Eh Joe*, V, the invisible female off-voice, is less intrusive and less present. "She" is, however, more concrete than the ghostly figure of F. V, the "vocal eyes of the play" can be seen in the light of the "Virgil of the viewers", taking the latter on a guided tour of a private inferno (in "the familiar chamber"). This embedded vocal guide does not direct her words toward the inside of the work (i.e. to the TV set and the figure F), but toward the external live spectator. The female voice differs from the one in *Eh Joe*, since she cannot be an *anima* in the Jungian sense, although she might be a kind of "animator", as in *Radio II*: through her voice, quasi-unrelated sequences gain meaning.

At first sight, V seems to represent a female instructor. While for many viewers, V's text may serve as an explanation of the piece, for those who are familiar with Beckett, V's "presence" satirizes our customary approach to watching television as she really points out the obvious (i.e. the different objects inside the room, including F's movements). V's words, despite her "stating the obvious", are a medium oriented (Copernican!) device that teaches a lesson by observing observation itself.

A revolutionary approach to the medium is represented by Beckett's use of light and colour. The omnipresence of the light and the invisibility of its origin are suggestive of a spiritual, non-physical "source". The stage directions describe the light as: "Faint, omnipresent. No visible source. As if all luminous. Faintly luminous. No shadow. [Pause.] No shadow" (CDW, 408). Anyone who has tried to cope with the technical implication of "no shadow"[15] [Pause] "no shadow!" understands the particular light Beckett was looking for. "No shadow" practically means "no objects" since normally the combination of light and objects causes shadows unless the objects and, in this case F, are transparent, metaphorically spiritual, or somehow supernatural.[16]

Concerning "the colour grey, shades of grey", the spectators have the possibility of projecting their own colours onto the screen, as the world of *Ghost Trio* exists in some colourless beyond, in a perfect hypostasis of black and white.

Whereas many elements of the piece are structured in threes,[17] the visually dominant principle is a rectangle: the window against the wall, the door against the wall . . . All these rectangles are subsumed in the framing rectangle of the television screen, possibly being viewed in the rectangle of "the familiar room" of the viewer: "world within world ever expanding – or receding".[18] This formal external–inclusion principle is indicative of the spiritual self-reflexive motif by allowing the spectator a glimpse of eternity, watching himself watching himself ad infinitum.

Jonathan Kalb compares Beckett to Caravaggio; their psychological depth "becomes accessible through the lure of their illusorily simple psychological surfaces, and the use of geometry as a storytelling tool. Caravaggio prefers windows looking inward on particular souls enveloped in sublime abysses . . . "[19] Caravaggio was a daring modernist in his time, particularly in his treatment of human despair and in his doubt about divine grace; the modernity of Beckett consists in offering a secular yet somewhat consoling spirituality.

Music has usually been considered the most divine or spiritual of all the arts, perhaps because it is not marred by the characters' intervention, or, as Linda Ben-Zvi suggests, because "the mirror alone, like the music, reflects the self".[20] Beckett seems to have chosen Beethoven's trio for its outstandingly eery musical qualities. Most importantly, in the television play, the insertion of Beethoven's Largo invokes another level of existence. In *Ghost Trio* music represents those inaccessible realms of the psyche which constitute the borderline between the emotional and the spiritual.

. . . but the clouds . . .

In . . . *but the clouds* . . . two major medium oriented changes occur: the first is the camera's immobility. Scene, structure and character changes are carried out by fade-ins and fade-outs. The second change is the circular set of the decor which measures "5 m. diameter" (CDW, 418) and is surrounded by "deep shadows" (CDW, 418). In the process of gradual internalization, Beckett relinquishes the "familiar chamber" and opts for a less realistic but more expressive interplay between black and white, light and darkness, life and death, as a leitmotif.

The alternating movement between appearances and disappearances establishes a pattern which replaces the visually more static images of the two former TV plays. As if directing a rehearsal of his imagination, M, like Henry in *Embers*, summons up vocal pictures from his past. Self-direction is brilliantly portrayed in . . . *but the clouds* . . . by way of the four "directions" of the circle: "1. West, roads. 2. North, sanctum. 3. East, closet. 4. Standing position" (CDW, 418). In other words, M designs a plan for his personal stage. Moreover, it seems likely that Beckett integrated elements from *Film*. For instance, the unmoving camera can be compared to E, whereas the faintly lit circular platform represents an unfleeing O. M is visible and we can listen to his words provided that the male off-voice is his own. But unlike Joe and F, M has two *doppelgängers* referring to his two selves who alternately appear and vanish on the circle, one of them wearing street clothes while the other is dressed in a long nightdress with a sleeping cap. Rosemary Pountney observes that "in . . . *but the clouds* . . . , Beckett is concerned not with fragments of the self, but with the whole person. The protagonist, M, sees himself whole (as at the end of *Film*), held in the light circle of the imagination."[21]

Most importantly, M's self is inseparable from the woman's face which he invokes, time and again. Hensel supposes that the woman, "'reduced as far as possible to eyes and mouth' (CDW, 417) may never have appeared and emphasizes the highly self-conscious elements of the piece."[22] He describes . . . *but the clouds* . . . as a double evocation of a face and a poem (Cf. *Words and Music*) and concludes with "expectations and disappointment". Calder refers to the play's "comment on age, memory and nostalgia with economy, and with one strictly controlled camera angle and field of vision . . . The man is concentrated: a Merlin conjuring up a ghost in his memory, Yeats's 'Brilliant eye' of the poem, perhaps . . . "[23] A muse, beloved or Jungian *anima*, the woman utters the words of Yeats's poem *The Tower* inaudibly whereas M says them out loud. He knows the words and wishes that the woman would utter them, whence his desire for the performative, magical force of the spoken word, a desire which is powerfully illustrated by M's plea to the woman: "Speak to me" (CDW, 421). The woman's face and the words of Yeats are very emotional and counterbalanced by the cold, controlled precision of the evocation process and the reactions toward the success and failures of the process. "Look at me" is the visual equivalent. Moreover, Beckett's . . . *but the clouds* . . . looks at Yeats's looking eye (while gently touching the very end of Yeats' poem – the "deepening shades . . . "), observing Yeats's irony with his own: it is not clear which of the figures is indeed "alive". The ambiguity refers to both the speaker and the woman. Does Yeats imply that the physically old can still be spiritually young? Would Beckett agree with that? Or does Beckett comment on Yeats' line "But I have found an answer in those eyes / That are impatient to be gone?"

In the piece there is a play-within-a-play in which M is a creator who rehearses an act of creation. Like the famous line from the Old Testament: "In the beginning was the word", M creates words which correspond to deeds: "I came in . . . " At the same time however, M really seems to re-create via his memory. As in the Bible, M afterward sees what he has accomplished, but unlike the Bible, he does not say "and it was good". Instead, M utters: "No– . . . No, that is not right" (CDW, 419). The creative process resembles the reflective process. It is impossible to think about an object and think about thinking itself at one and the same time.

The entire event is a controlled meditation. The play is a self-reflexive act of creation that attempts to evoke the creative muse. It is "both its own excuse for being and, therefore, justification for the creative act of performance".[24] It is a mode of the secular spirituality that is achieved here, using ancient ritual techniques without irony. For instance, the movement pattern in the play resembles the cyclic orbit around the sun (which explains why the camera does not need to move). The shrouded, ghostly atmosphere evoked by the robe, the skull and the *chiaroscuro* effect are also caused by appearances and disappearances of the face and the figure. The border between the lighted area and the surrounding dark shadows, and the smooth dissolves between the three images of the piece, suggest an affinity between the world of here and now, and the hereafter; . . . *but the clouds* . . . is a study made by the soul to initiate itself into the world of the dead "till you join us" (CDW, 364).

In . . . *but the clouds* . . . there are finally two different "sound tracks"; one is the objective though agonized report; the other, Yeats' words. In . . . *but the clouds* . . . the two streams of language have "joined arms . . . two arms conflowed and flowed united on" (CDW, 446).

Quad

Quad, subtitled "A piece for four players, light and percussions" (CDW, 451), marks a deviation, parallel in Beckett's works in the other media. *Act Without Words I* and *II* are dedicated to pure movement. In *Footfalls*, May's pacing around is ghost-like. Moreover, the obsessive creatures in the dramatic prose pieces such as *The Lost Ones, Imagination Dead Imagine*, etc. also move like apparitions.

In *Quad*, Beckett uses a non-verbal combination of colour, sound and movement for the first and last time. *Quad* is his "most formal work, geometric and symmetrical",[25] in which especially "the psychological depth . . . becomes accessible through . . . the use of geometry as a story-telling tool".[26] The "feverish monotony" of the movement has been described by many critics as internal, "like Dante's damned . . . committed to an endless unyielding punishment and continuous movement of excruciating sameness".[27]

In his stage directions, Beckett requires the camera to be: "Raised frontal. Fixed. Both players and percussionists in frame" (CDW, 453). One may ask why *Quad* was written for TV rather than for live theatre. The answer is that its compressed, mechanical, and soul-less nature can be portrayed more effectively on TV than onstage; for television is essentially a cold medium. On the small screen the players' compulsive pacing around is far more impressive. In the theatre their movements would still appear too vivid, despite the inherent automatism. Enoch Brater refers to "the neutrality of dehydrated image"[28] which is indeed a look from the outside, yet with the appropriate colours and sound even this "dried out" human image is a moving social metaphor.

Quad differs from the other plays not only in terms of the individual elements of movement, colour and sound of each player, but also in terms of the orchestration of colour and sound which varies throughout the piece – "all possible light combinations given" (CDW, 452). In *Quad*, Beckett seems more interested in how people (or are they moveable dolls?), can be manipulated, rather than in their internal worlds. Being exposed to meaningless sounds and colours results in a social *perpetuum mobile*. Representing social as opposed to individual elements of human nature, the four players avoid the centre. In Beckett's other "plays for selves" and their respective doubles and shadows, the Beckettian "I" is condemned to look for its centre.

The "group" in *Quad*, composed of players wearing the three elementary colours (as well as white which contains all colours), begins to move, reaches a peak, and then fades away. The musicians occupy a higher space on a raised podium, somewhat reminiscent of the Japanese Bunraku puppet theatre. The four "movers" of *Quad* do not ask whether "anyone [is] looking at me too", as in *Waiting for Godot* and *Play* (CDW, 83; 317); they are completely absorbed by their obsessional locomotion. Indeed, *Quad* must be evaluated according to works by Pina Bausch on the one hand, emphasizing the mechanical, compulsive elements of modern life, Chaplin's "Bio-mechanics" in *Modern Times*, and the Eurythmical works of Rudolf Steiner's movement-language, on the other.[29]

Nacht und Träume

Fletcher doubts "whether this script makes for a successful or effective use of the medium" and quotes Martin Esslin for support. *Nacht und Träme* is "a bit too sentimental an image".[30] Pountney, on the other hand, states: "The figures have no discernible purpose, apart from negotiating their courses and avoiding both the centre and each other, and could thus be seen as embodying the life force – coming and going because they have no option."[31] She comments: "The climax of the dream has the right hand (R) clasped between both Beckett's hands, on the table, with Beckett's bowed head resting on them. The left hand (L) rests gently on Beckett's head."[32]

From the perspective of the medium, *Nacht und Träume* adds a super-imposed frame which Beckett did not previously use in his other television plays; it returns to the familiar room of F in *Ghost Trio* and it does not use dialogue. However, the script includes different levels of dialogue: (1) between dreamer and dreamt self (A and B); (2) between evening light and Schubert's Lied; and (3) between R and L, the hands. The hands signify the relationships between the other "couples" too. A, the dreamer, (like E in *Film*), and Beckett, as an implied author, are highly suggestive of "encounters" of the self with its doubles, demons, ghosts and spirits.

Nacht und Träume reverses cinematographic time, not only levels of reality. As a flashback mediation, a person can look back on the events of the day (or week or year) from a moment in the present to any required point in the past. Beckett exploited this mental device in *Not I*, when Mouth reflects on her life until "now this . . . this" (CDW, 382). In *Nacht und Träume*, the dreamer and his dream move back and forward, as if annihilating television time which, for practical purposes at least, is linear rather than cyclical.

While "offstage" in *Nacht und Träume* is the evening light, coming from a high window in the back wall, the two dream levels serve as metaphoric "offstages in the meticulously darkened frame of the picture".

Nacht und Träume is not only "about" the medium. The script, in particular, because of the hands and the chalice, suggests that the author perceive something that remains undetected by the viewer's eye. As an implied figure, the script writer *can* see the "offstage" of his televised space. Whether or not he is lured by a nonexistent spiritual being, the viewers shall never know; but *Nacht und Träume* certainly suggests that something is "there".

A question about the "reality" of fictitious characters is raised in the dedication ["Zueignung"] of Goethe's *Faust*,[33] in which the status of the "Schwankende Gestalten" – "wavering phantoms" – is of major concern. "Among those we call great artists", Goethe inquired into the "expressive possibilities of the vehicle", which is clearly indicated in the Prologue. He was concerned with humanity (and deity . . .), shown by the end of the Prologue in Heaven.

Goethe's wavering phantoms can also be related to the various ghosts in Beckett's plays. But can they be seen in view of a nostalgic incantation of resurrected figments, loved ones and shadows belonging to the past? Are these apparitions Goethe's source of inspiration, or do they correlate with the poet's spiritual beings who approach him with their "trüben Blick" "troubled" or "darkened gaze" (rather than Yeats's "brilliant eye" . . . ?). Goethe's "I," as an implied author, expressed in the *Zueignung*, wonders whether to hold on to the "Gestalten". He also indicates in stanza three that the "ghosts" cannot be dissociated from his "song": "E'en by their very cheers mine heart is wrung," namely that the ghosts, perhaps, serve as audience!

Beckett once explained the woman's voice in *Eh Joe*: "she really whispers in him. He hears her. Only if she lives can he have the wish to kill her. She is dead, but in him she lives. That is the passion: to kill the voices, which he cannot kill."[34] Whereas Joe's "passion" is to "kill the voices, which he cannot kill", during the last two decades of his life Beckett seemed interested in animating "all the dead voices" and visual images, especially in the already so illusory media of film and television.

In an attempt to avoid appearing old-fashioned, strange or sentimentally spiritual, both Goethe and Beckett needed an artistic medium to soften the hard transition between the worlds of the self and the modes of its expressibility. For both Goethe and Beckett's surrogate selves, namely the speaker in the *Zueignung* and the protagonists of *Film* and the TV scripts, the "Schwankende Gestalten" constitute a part of reality, at the moment when these ghosts appear. Moreover, the following quotation from Goethe's *Zueignung* can also be applied to Beckett's TV plays: "was ich besitze, seh' ich wie im Weiten,/ Und was verschwand, wird mir zu Wirklichkeiten." (All that I have, now far away seems banished/ All real grown, that long ago had vanished.) Beckett was well versed in German literature, and although a direct influence cannot be proven, some of Goethe's lines may properly serve as a motto for at least one of Beckett's television scripts: The woman in *Eh Joe* certainly "drängt sich zu" (throngs upon) and fills Joe's bosom with "Erschütterung" (distress). Similarly . . . *but the clouds* . . . is a wonderful example of "manche liebe Schatten steigen auf . . . " (shades of well-beloved faces rise) and *Nacht und Träume* "Sie hören nicht die folgenden Gesänge/ Die Seelen, denen ich die ersten sang . . . " (of my songs they may not hear the latter/Those souls for whom mine earlier songs were sung). *Quad* can be seen as a metaphor of "Der Schmerz wird neu, es wiederholt die Klage/Des Lebens Labyrinthisch irren Lauf . . . " (the pain renewed, and grief again retraces/ life's labyrinthine course).

6 Godot – Resolution or Revolution?

Waiting for Godot, no doubt, is the most popular modern theatre play in the world. It has received a legion of authorized performances, and endless unauthorized ones all over the globe, quite soon after its by now legendary Parisian premiere in 1953. *Waiting for Godot* has been given many different and interesting directorial "meanings", thus, incidentally, covering every major interpretative cultural, literary and theatrical trend, from Marxism to Structuralism, Psychoanalysis, Semiotics, Feminism – to name but a few – and their myriad variations and cross relations. In this chapter, I wish to present a case study for the universal enlisted use of Beckett's works, and to illuminate *Waiting for Godot*'s reception in Israel. The claim is that Godot was not only born and raised in the Middle East – but that he is an Israeli Culture Hero.

Less than three years after the 1953 Parisian premiere, *Waiting for Godot* opened in Tel Aviv and subsequently toured many other parts of Israel. Michael (Miko) Almaz translated the new play, formed a group of previously unknown but talented actors, and directed them. In the 35 years that followed the play has since been produced at least 15 times by professionals and amateurs, throughout the country. The groups involved include the National Theatre Habima, an all-female cast at the Tel Aviv University theatre department, the Negev Players, inmates of an Israeli prison (following the San Quentin example), the kibbutz-movement theatre company, and even Beckett's own version in the Schiller Theatre guest-show. *Waiting for Godot* was filmed and shown on Israeli television and two different shorter versions were broadcast on radio. *Waiting for Godot* is one of the most popular and most produced plays in Israel's theatrical history. It has appeared in at least five translations and has been printed by two different publishers, with thousands of copies of each edition being sold. It is taught in literature and drama departments of universities and teachers' training programmes and it is part of the official curriculum issued by the Ministry of Education to the entire country's high-school system. Lines from the play, especially the title itself, are used, abused and para-phrased by politicians, journalists and taxi-drivers, shopkeepers and local wits, most of whom have not read or seen the play. The above would appear to hold equally true for many other countries as well.

As a modern classical figure, the elusive theatrical mystery of *Godot* "himself", hovers, as a black aura, over all the Israeli stages on which the play is performed, just as he haunts theatre stages in Paris, London, Berlin or San Francisco. Godot, by dramatic character and theatrical definition, is offstage. Not only does he exist there – he is the personifi-cation *of* offstage, rather than just being off this stage or another. Whereas in the written text he can be conceived of as a "gap", an inde-terminancy; in a performed play he is the three dimensional, immediate and specific entity, technically as well as conceptually and emotionally, which can be called offstage. As a literary "black hole" and even more so through the implicit need to interpret "him" in the acted-out play, an ever growing number of interpretations are aimed at "filling him in".

Offstage Godot has tantalized Israeli directors, actors, designers and lighting people, critics and audiences alike. After years of (missed) encounters some Israelis are ready to swear that Godot was born and bred in their own neighbourhood. Others will admit that yes, he is indeed a stranger and not from a familiar place at all; albeit an amiable stranger. Godot has been engaged in a long, often painful and always one-sided dialogue with his Israeli constituency. As a once new immi-grant to a country of immigrants, Godot's familiarity has rapidly developed, and from one production to the next he has grown to be an ominous doppelgänger, a mute spokesman, and an active and acti-vating contradiction in terms: a dark mirror held up to many Israeli values, ideas and modes of behaviour. As a theatrical "sponge", func-tional *because* of its hollows and cavities, Godot has always been a passive partner; ready to first absorb and then project Israeli mental, social, political, and ideological diseases and problems.

He can be seen as a negative focus in the small, intensive, highly involved socio-dramatic Israeli scene. In fact, as some Israeli theatre and culture critics imply, Godot is "quite Jewish". They do not only note that Estragon's name "used to be" Levi. Shalev, for example, "Stealing the Gospel",[1] reads *Waiting for Godot* as a post-Holocaust play while admit-ting he is universal, a citizen of the world, who attracts personal hopes and fears throughout, the collective portrait of Godot, as painted by Israeli critics, presents him as uniquely Israeli, undergoing a process of naturalization in Israel (as perhaps in many other places).

The following sections deal with Godot as a touchstone for some Israeli whims, yearnings, and ideas. As a most difficult character to identify, Godot has drawn to himself major identity-related issues in modern-day Israel. Having finally overcome his many reviewers, Godot reveals himself at last as a critic of Israeli society.

Although most of Beckett's production teams in Israel were comprised of dedicated people with all the integrity and skill they could muster, I shall focus my observations on three main productions, since it is not the sheer artistry but the dialogue between "Godot" and society that is the focus. The great number of articles written about these shows provide a comprehensive reflection of the symbiosis between "art" and "social values", "theatre" and "criticism". At the same time, the individual value and influence of any *Waiting for Godot* production on the Israeli citizen cannot, and perhaps should not, be measured.

Godot is not an Israeli Pioneer

Still influenced by the social-realistic trends of Russian theatre and by local qualms (and mythologies-in-the-making) regarding pioneering, the critics of the first Hebrew production of *Waiting for Godot* in 1955 did not welcome the play:

> The non-realistic appearance of . . . Pozzo and Lucky makes the explanation of the play still more difficult . . . He [Beckett] repeats himself for no good reason at all in the second act which stretches out endlessly . . . [2]

Needless to say, while not all the French, British or American reviewers were enthusiastic at the time, the Israelis had even more reasons to be reluctant, if not explicitly hostile. Although modern Hebrew prose and poetry were quite au courant with contemporary styles and fashions, Hebrew drama and theatre, and a trailing genre (and medium), had not prepared a proper framework for *Waiting for Godot*. In addition, the dominant (collective) notion in literature was only then making the transition from the *WE* of a pioneering, fighting group experience to the insecurities of the lonely *I*.[3]

The clash between the individual character of *Waiting for Godot*'s "social" out-casts and the highly public and social nature of theatre seems to have hit Israeli critics at the core of their own "collective" and cultural insecurities. Weaned on shared social responsibilities, on togetherness, friendship and a fair amount of secularism, Israelis found (whatever they understood of) the plot to be totally unacceptable.

> This typically decadent play was chosen, for some strange reason, by the young *Zira* [theatre] players as material for their experimentation . . . they deserve material more of a story-line, something more constructive . . . [4]

In the spirit of "positive thinking" and further future prospects, one critic failed to understand why Lucky and Pozzo must reappear as invalids, and a second one wondered, innocently:

> Why doesn't he [Beckett] give us a positive example? Why did he write the play at all? . . . This nihilism is coquettish, ignoring the [element of] renewal of life . . . It is altogether sterile. (179)

Generally speaking, the critics attacked the play and its author rather than the artistry of the production. In the closely-knit relationships between actors, directors, audiences and critics, many of whom knew each other quite intimately in the small town of Tel Aviv, critics found it more convenient to spare their friends and slaughter the stranger, an Irishman in exile. *Ma'ariv*, claiming to be the largest daily newspaper in the country at the time, published the headline "Miserable play, excellent acting!" Only years later, after *Waiting for Godot* and its playwright had become better known and much more popular, did the critic say that what he had really meant was "a play *about* miserable people". The rejection was grounded on the somewhat self-righteous assumption that "we are not the intellectual decadents of Montmartre" (179) and, indeed, Israel of those days was looking to the future with a combination of naïvete and idealism, combined nevertheless, with more than a touch of provincialism. Even among reviewers who had tried to maintain a professional approach, one could find ideologically oriented overtones and backhanded compliments.

> What does Almaz want? Is it only a technically perfect theatre? . . . We don't want such a theatre here. (179)

Disapproval of a different kind was expressed on a traditional Jewish–Hebrew basis: "we can still enjoy a play, even if it is not a paraphrase of a distorted Ecclesiastes" (179). Naturally, the Hebrew title for *Waiting for Godot* – *Waiting for Mr God* – (Mar-El) in Almaz's translation, entailed some raised eyebrows. The name for Pozzo – Pas-El – sounds more like a mock Biblical allusion, but lines like "Hope deferred . . . " and the dialogue about the Dead Sea found an unreceptive Hebrew-speaking audience, who felt there was something inappropriate in Beckett's trying to teach them something about themselves through two such non-Israeli characters as Vladimir and Estragon.

The dominant atmosphere in the Israel of 1955 was one of a high degree of conformity, shared by the socialist elite and partly suffered by all the others. Ideological conformism was perhaps a necessary evil imposed by the post-Holocaust days, the aftermath of the 1948 war for independence, the very real need to absorb huge waves of immigrants and refugees, and the attempt to "make the desert bloom" and build new settlements. *Waiting for Godot* was first introduced to a group of people who came from over a hundred different countries and spoke over seventy different languages. They recognized the importance (functional, at least) of these values while, at the same time, feeling that the realization of the long yearned for Jewish State also marked the beginning of the end of that very dream, and the approach of a much more individualistic period within a harsh political reality.

Critics were still trying in those grey days to harness theatre to "positive" ideologies and deeds, wishing for a clear, simple image of hope and courage to emanate from art in general and to make theatre as a public meeting place, in particular. It is little wonder that Bertolt Brecht was much more popular at this time. The intense thirst for culture, assisted by a readiness to accept American, British and French plays, was quenched by a strangely assorted repertoire and the introduction of original, new Hebrew plays. "Meaning" was a key word; more in the nature of wishful thinking than as a description of any particular play performed in those days. Beckett's sense of meaninglessness was hard to digest, not so much against a background of sheer rejection, but because it touched on a deeply rooted sense of insecurity. Under the headline *"We are Waiting Too"* – a rather ambivalent phrase that also implies the age-old Jewish Waiting for the Messiah, one critic says:

> He . . . allows himself to use a confused and embarrassing style, with a great deal of senseless, meaningless and purposeless 'depth.' (179)

"Lack of purpose" was certainly the most abusive term. Vladimir and Estragon did not, for instance, reinforce a simple notion such as active engagement to build a new kibbutz. However they did import a whiff of European elegance, subtlety, morbid humour and other cultural phenomena which some of the Israelis, as ex-Europeans, knew and appreciated. Moreover, Godot represented a nostalgia, in the Israeli context, for a "God who hides his face", as the kabbalistic mysticism has it, during the annihilation of European Jews.

Among the few critics who favoured the 1955 *Waiting for Godot* production, two can be singled out as having a more sensitive approach. Haim Gamzo felt that:

> a young and educated audience . . . that dislikes regular routine shows, should encourage this experiment, since this time we see on stage living people who speak a lively language. (182)

He too thought that the second act of the play was superfluous, but he nonetheless enjoyed the mixture of tragedy ("Trauer") and comedy and was sensitive to a number of religious elements, including the Hebrew name for Godot, Mar-El (Mr God), which he liked, without giving a reason why. Perhaps, one may assume, he thought the name brought Godot closer to the Hebrew audience. Haim Gamzo, Ezra Zussman and other critics compared Beckett to Kafka, not only because the Habima Theatre had presented Max Brod's version of *The Castle* and its elusive master; but because an analogy serves to extricate a critic from the embarrassment of ignorance. In comparing an unknown piece with a relatively known one, he is in command of at least one out of the two. Whereas Gamzo "did not find a Kafkaesque style" in *Waiting for Godot*, another critic maintained that:

> Beckett's symbolism does not compare with Kafka's rigour. However, there is something touching and poetic in his work, testifying that he is a poet but perhaps not a playwright. (179)

Zussman, a perceptive man of letters, goes further than the expected comparisons of Beckett to Joyce (the famous "Beckett was his secretary" argument turns up time and again). He includes Kafka, Proust and even Steinbeck (in his *Of Mice and Men*) and brings in the National Hebrew Poet Laureate Bialik, ironically admitting that the two have not read each other. Zussman finds a fascinating similarity to Bialik's poem *When the Days Grow Long*, where elements of mechanical repetition, boredom, waiting for God/the Messiah in the midst of a drab existence are expressed (among others) in taking off a shoe. Realizing the cultural gap between Beckett and Bialik and undermining his own (educational!) argument, he adds:

> A play that has won great success in London and Paris, is still as much of a risk and a bewilderment here; and may stand the chance of failure. (181)

Of the 52 (!) complimentary tickets sent to critics to review *Waiting for Godot* at the Zira Theatre in 1955, a surprisingly large number did indeed show up. An unsurprising number of them proceeded to reject the play.[5] However, compared with other critical evaluations of contemporary plays, *Waiting for Godot* was relatively respectfully handled. Not being much of a pioneering socialist, Godot was sent back to his offstage, but his tentative and temporary expulsion was executed with a fair amount of doubt, grace and embarrassment.

Zussman, almost praying for *Waiting for Godot* to mean something, analyses the scene by the tree in the second act:

> It is a sign of a miracle; the miracle may happen even to these 'dry blocks of human trees' . . . this is why this couple of vain-walkers hug the old green tree in the manner that praying people do. (181)

A less sophisticated but quite characteristic note was provided by another critic, who admitted to having understood only a little of the play but:

the characters say and do little things which are, for me, touching and meaningful. (180)

According to interviews, the audience response to *Waiting for Godot* was much warmer than that of the critics.

Godot is an Occupied Area

The second production of *Waiting for Godot* took place in 1961 with an amateur group that included two professional actors. The show received little critical attention, but the few critics who did react seem to have been better informed than in 1955. Judged as an amateur production, directed by Moshe Amiel and retranslated by Edna Shavit (*Lucky* in the previous production), two critics remarked, with luke-warm sympathy, on the interpretation:

> I wonder whether the director's perception . . . was sufficient to challenge the special requirements [of the play] . . . and it may be too much to ask of an amateur production . . . The acting was surprisingly good . . . (183)

Slightly more positive, under the heading *A Conversation between Mutes*, the second review stated:

> For some moments these two *Less Miserables* were shockingly powerful and convincing . . . Nonetheless, I fail to understand why we were denied the ease and elegance of Beckett's fast, fluent and witty dialogues. (183)

As in 1955, once again a woman was chosen to play Lucky. This time it was one of Israel's finest actresses, Ruth Geller, who at the time was relatively unknown.

Five years later, in 1966, and one year before the 1967 war, Edna Shavit again used her own translation and directed *Waiting for Godot* at the Tel Aviv University theatre. Due to the semi-educational character of the production, critical attention was deliberately avoided, but audience and professional response was enthusiastic and rapidly passed on by word of mouth. Years later this production was still being mentioned as excellent in comparison with more recent ones. Shavit tried twice more to run *Waiting for Godot*. In 1974, a year after the shock of the October War, her revived production toured army camps, in order, perhaps, to "endow the soldier's suffering with meaning"(!) (203); reactions, again, were highly positive. Her third version, in 1980, was decimated by the critics as "heavy", "boring", "sentimental", "too loud", "self-indulgent", "A tired Godot"; this time the translation was also attacked as not being sensitive enough to the original transitions between poetry and farce.

In 1968, after the "smashing victory" of the Six Day War, Israel was now ready to receive a fully, universally acclaimed modern, classical masterpiece. Habima, the national theatre, publicizing it as a major event, commissioned a number of top artists, chosen for their combination of audacity and renoun: Yossi Yizraeli, the energetic, young and original director; Moshe Shamir, a famous author (and a right-wing politician at the time) lent his translation to the production; and Yigal Tumarkin, painter and sculptor of no little fame, was the stage-designer. Tumarkin prepared an elaborate, ornate and circus-like large stage, filled it with bigger than life colourful puppets stuck inside closets hanging on abstract trees, added piles of old clothes, and a number of photos, including those of Marilyn Monroe (who, unlike Didi and Gogo, *did* commit suicide) and Samuel Beckett (who might have, had he seen the show). Beckett's stage instructions were largely ignored and a number of cuts were made and changes inserted into the dialogue. Any religious indications were omitted altogether. Catchy music, played by a circus band, was easily recalled and hummed by the audience during the intermission. As far as Yizraeli was concerned, he was, as quoted in a preview interview, interested in

> fun, games and a pleasant theatrical activity, and I only hope it is going to be a show with delightful entertainment qualities; as I did my best to provide the audience with fun. (200)

In preparing the theatrical tour de force of 1968, there were almost as many previews, interviews, and background reportages as there were critical evaluations after the premiere. A preview can easily serve as a convenient bridge between the public relations department of a theatre and the as yet non-committed but news-hungry entertainment-section editors. A preview will thus use a semi-descriptive style, giving the expected production every possible advance credit, supply the philosophical, historical and political context and collaborate with the socio-financial interests of the new show. Long articles were dedicated to such themes as *Time in Waiting for Godot and in Henry IV*, to *How do we wait for Godot this time*, *Avant garde Becoming a Classic* and *Hope Deferred*.

Avoiding the "unfair" and real critical preconceptions of *Waiting for Godot* in 1968, previews drew public attention to previous *Waiting for Godot* productions. They discussed Beckett and his various idiosyncracies and presented encompassing "waiting" notions, including personal gossip on actors, while generally and elegantly ignoring hard-core questions pertaining to the "legitimate" interpretation of the play and its "valid" modes of presentation.

Some previewers actually took part in an almost unprecedented public relations party in which the very waiting for *Waiting for Godot* proved, retrospectively, to be as equally important as the play itself. This time, with no longer 52 newspapers ready to cover the cultural event, as in the explicitly political and intensely involved days of 1955, fewer but more widely distributed papers were competing with one another to deliver the most interesting and exclusive story on *Waiting for Godot*. The prevalent atmosphere was that of the post-war euphoria: first we take the West Bank, then we take Godot.

Godot had been made into a long sought-for, vigorously fought-for, finally "liberated" spiritual–artistic offstage territory, on the other side of the border. In the actual interpretation of the play, what could have been understood as existential malaise was turned by the press into a victorious national pride. It should be noted, however, that the show itself had nothing whatsoever "national" about it. Rather, it was by omitting certain elements that the "national celebration" write-ups sneaked in.

Gamzo ends his positive review with the words "In Yizraeli's direction there is risk, but daring too. The daring was worthwhile" (194). Ohad, still writing a preview, but after having seen a rehearsal as one of the pre-premiere run-in shows, uses a particularly charged term:

> Habima gave Yossi Yizraeli a free hand, Yossi Yizraeli, in return, gave Habima the most beautiful show ever presented there since the destruction of the temple. (192)

Ohad used the Hebrew word "house" (Ba'yit) which means the twice destroyed though only once rebuilt Jerusalem temple. In the 1968 context this ironical quasi-messianic review also meant that the Habima theatre was using *Waiting for Godot* as a gala-show to reopen its reconstructed and expensive auditorium. No wonder that under such conditions, Godot, as a successful sales promoter on the one hand, and artistic conquest on the other, lost, as Kaniuk wrote, all of its *Angst*. Only the circus was left (195).

Hedda Boshes praised this circus as "a ray of colour thrust onto the otherwise mediocre, drab and gray Israeli stage" (196). Dov Bar Nir went one-step further in his somewhat hazy compliment:

> This production makes it possible to turn Beckett into commercial theatre. No more 'classical' boredom, but a living effervescent show presented in the National Theatre for the broad public. (198)

A slight obstacle presented itself during the pre-production victory procession. When the Kibbutz Theatre group also wanted to mount *Waiting for Godot* at about the same time, they were denied the rights (which were held first by the Cameri theatre, then by Habima) in order, one assumes, to prevent them from competing with the exclusivity of the Habima production. Two years later, the Kibbutz Theatre managed to finally stage their version, after the 70 Habima performances – not a large number in Israeli terms – were over. Their show was not considered successful, either by critics or by audiences.

After *Waiting for Godot* was officially opened at Habima there were a number of critics who did not participate in the "we conquered Beckett" hit-campaign. While praising the show, Uri Kesary nostalgically reminisced about Almaz's 1955 production:

> All circles ostracized Beckett, Habima included, in 1955 . . . yet it was a real inner need that Almaz felt for Beckett. (189)

Kesary also raised the question of the need to abide by Beckett's stage instructions, and wondered how Beckett would have reacted to seeing his own picture as part of the Tumarkin–Yizraeli stage design. Avraham Oz is much more explicit in his reservations:

> If I were a doorman in charge of the gates of classical theatre, I would not have let Yizraeli's show enter. (195)

His reasons, while giving full credit to the director's professional and technical abilities, are directed against what he had believed to be directorial distortions, misconceptions, and a one-sided interpretation. As an example, he presents the quadruple fall of Vladimir, Estragon, Pozzo, and Lucky.

> it was a mechanical skit, bereft of depth and feeling. Perhaps the audience enjoyed the gag, but it was deprived of its (cathartic) right to pity. (195)

Kaniuk expressed his reservations about the overly elaborate (and "horribly beautiful") stage, and claimed that the Yizraeli show had lost all the "wastelandness and horror". The sharp humour of the play was propelled on a platform of anxiety . . . which was absent. Kaniuk also felt that the music, although quite lovely, was somewhat superfluous. The actors, he concluded, never even once "touched the heart of the audience" (195).

Whereas the 1955 pioneer production was conceptually more Lucky-oriented, the 1968 presentation was certainly under the influence of Pozzo; both dominant and cruel, self-centred and flashy, pitiful and pathetic *and* blind.

Godot of 1968, due to critical response and certainly not because of any deliberate insensitivity on behalf of any of the participants, seems now, some 34 years later, to have been a demonstration of "everything you (out there in the world) can do, *we* can do better". Reflecting, in a social–artistic way, the post-engagement contortions of Israel's imaginary grandeur after the victorious war, Godot too was enlisted to march in the laureate procession, and only too few of the critics whispered

"memento mori" in his ears. As a consummated cultural conquest, that
production was later renegotiated with the Palestinians in Ilan Ronen's
Waiting for Godot in 1984.

Godot is the Palestinian *Intifada*

Godot hovered above Israeli stages again and again. The aforemen-
tioned Shavit productions (1974, 1980) were separated by Beckett's own
direction in the Schiller Theatre guest show in 1977, which was, most
probably and not surprisingly so, as critics noted, the best *Waiting for
Godot* Israel has seen. In 1980 Robert Skloot directed *Waiting for Godot*
with an all-female student cast at the Tel Aviv University theatre; an
interesting exercise which, again – as a student show – was paid little
attention by the critics. In the meantime, Israelis were given a chance to
see more of Beckett's plays, which refined their tastes and sharpened
their critical faculties.

Toward the end of 1984 an experienced and painstaking Ilan Ronen
took up *Waiting for Godot* once again and prepared two parallel versions
with the same group of actors, two of whom, Yussuf Abu Warda and
Makram Khouri were completely bi-lingual in Hebrew and Arabic.
With Arab–Jewish relationships deteriorating, somewhere between the
Lebanon War (1982–5) and the beginning of the Palestinian *Intifada*
(1987), words such as "Was I sleeping, while the others suffered? Am I
sleeping now? . . . The air is full of our cries. (He listens.) But habit is a
great deadener . . . At me too someone is looking, of me too someone is
saying, he is sleeping, he knows nothing, let him sleep on. (Pause.) I
can't go on!" (*WFG*, 83) gained a unique, highly contextualized political
meaning.

This third major production of *Waiting for Godot* was initiated by the
Haifa theatre, an already politically minded establishment, with at that
time clear left-wing, liberal, pro-Palestinian tendencies. The performance, at one and the same time a highly explosive comment on Israeli
society, an enormous success with Arab and Jewish audiences and an
extremely well-received show by most critics, was not overly orthodox
in purely Beckettian terms. Phrases with poetic and religious overtones
were reduced or eliminated. The set, a half-destroyed half-erected, scaf-
folded concrete building, told the audience that Didi and Gogo are,
without having yet said a word, Palestinian day workers from the Gaza
Strip or the West Bank, who come to Israel to earn a hard living. The
production was relying on the Israeli audiences' previous knowledge of
the "original" *Waiting for Godot*, and hence its readiness for considerable
changes, adaptations and new interpretations. Relinquishing, in
advance, some of Beckett's "universal" appeal, the Haifa theatre used

Waiting for Godot for blatantly social and political issues.

As expected, right-wing politicians and ideologists were stirred, deeply moved and outraged. Some of them strongly defended Beckett's artistic rights to be "properly" interpreted rather than distorted by left-wing directors. As self-appointed theatre critics, *they* attacked what critic Amir Oryan called "the only vital role theatre can still fulfil in this complex century – to shake Israeli conscience and emotion and present a relevant, here and now comment on reality" (213).

Rabbi Druckman, supporter of the West Bank Jewish settlers, expressed his view that "the role of art is to perfume the air", but the Haifa *Waiting for Godot* went for artistic commitment and social daring, the smell of which was not particularly appealing, to him, at least. Pozzo was presented, through costume and gesture, choice of words (Anton Shammas's powerful new translation into Hebrew and Arabic) as well as diction, as an easily recognizable Israeli master. Lucky's speech, in classical "high" Arabic was considered by many to be particularly moving, in Doron Tavori's rendition of him as a supersensitive debilitated slave. Many other superlatives were poured on this production, and for the first time a number of Arab-reviewer's reports were specially translated into Hebrew. They too were highly favourable (214).

More than any previous *Waiting for Godot* productions, this one soon became a springboard for after-performance discussions, some of them rather heated, between audience and stage. Whereas in 1968 previews were the main bearer of the production's message, in 1984 reports on audience reaction were by far the more interesting. Audience response, quantitatively greater than in any other *Waiting for Godot* production and more intensive than in most other theatre shows in Israel, became an intrinsic part of this production.

As reported by Sarit Fuchs in *Godot and the Palestinian Problem*, Arab teacher Miriam Mar'ee "did not expect her pupils to understand that much of the play. Yes, there are Jews who will consider the show as political agitation, but the time has come . . . that the Jews should understand our feelings through that caricature" (213).

"I have nowhere else to go", says Arab-Israeli actor Khouri, when asked by a Jewish-Israeli teacher what he means by saying, onstage "Let's go" and does not move. Jewish-Israeli actor Doron Tavori (Lucky) bursts out:

> An existential, poetic play? I'm ashamed to admit I don't know what this means . . . In my opinion oppressor and oppressed are conceivable only against the background of a specific reality. Do you want to hide this show from Arabs and play it to Jews only? (213)

Some critics defended the "real Beckett" in an attempt to remain faithful to him, to *Waiting for Godot*, to the theatre and to the audience. By 1984

Beckett's *Waiting for Godot* had become actual, relevant, political. Godot becomes the voice of conscience and reveals the Israeli public to themselves in an unpleasant light. It is no more a "simple" Pozzo-oriented 1968–kind-of *Waiting for Godot*, but a complex image of Lucky the Palestinian, whereby Pozzo the Israeli is *us*, as in "all mankind . . . ".[6] Vladimir and Estragon are funny, clever and philosophical Palestinian workers and Godot is, most likely, a vague warning echo of a future revolution, although Arab and Jew may disagree as to which revolution it is; which of the thieves was saved, which was damned.

Filled with emptiness, any Beckett play, and certainly the most famous of all, *Waiting for Godot*, calls for active involvement. In the last 35 years *Godot*, the epitome of *offstage*, has managed to entice the Israeli theatrical scene into absorbing and reflecting many of its self-images. As a non-socialist he was put on hold. As an occupied territory, he was a circus-master. In 1984, Godot, radiating ominous signs from offstage, was a warning that whoever does not recognize the self-consciousness of the Other, will not be granted his own self-consciousness. In this respect there exists a frightening similarity between the personal and the political levels.

7 I's and Eyes: A Hermeneutical Circle

In an imaginary dialogue between Beckett and his audience, the playwright may ask: "How could you have responded if you were not there? (Pause.) How could you possibly have said Amen if, as you claim, you were not there?" (FF, 403). The audience may choose Clov's words in responding: "What? (*Pause.*) Is it *me* you are referring to?" (*EG*) Beckett's dramatic considerations for the audience in his plays are often ironic but nevertheless concrete and implicitly quite demanding. His characters, perhaps following their author, are "morbidly sensitive to the opinions of others". Observed from the perspective of chaos theories, the line "if it's the connection, the least jog can do it", is quite perceptive. (*TII*) Like the wings of the legendary Chinese butterfly whose flutter raises storms over America, Beckett's dramatic "absence in presentia" suggests that he does indeed "admit the chaos". The delicate balance between the (implied) playwright, the actor and his or her role in the play, the audience and the (professional?) critical stand are the very foundations of the theatrical situation, discussed in this chapter and closing a hermeneutical circle.

Behind the overt efforts to portray the infinite through an ever-growing process of condensation of expressive means, there remains the irrefutable fact that Samuel Beckett was a publishing author. His works are widely read and produced. Even a full recognition of the paradox ensuing from the discrepancy between the (allegedly) negative message of Beckett's works and the very act of trying to communicate that message, does not extricate Beckett from the ultimate need to choose between silence and writing–producing. No matter how much his plays are filled with "silences" (and only silence can hope to "affirm" ultimate negation), or bleak notions on the fate of Man, Beckett finally opts for the absurdity of communicating his ideas rather than the slightly lesser inconsequence of keeping silent. Having committed himself to at least a minimal communication by the very fact of writing, Beckett can never truly retreat to full-fledged solipsism, although often he seems to be preaching such a philosophy. The agony, so often felt in his works, of attempting to express the inexpressible, should therefore be regarded as the innermost conviction of an artist who tries to convey to others what he believes to be his human and artistic essence. The fact that Beckett does so with meticulous artistic precision, a hilarious sense of humor, and great skill, helps to explain both his world acclaim and the highly personal quality of his works.

Beckett as author is never totally eliminated from his works.[1] Indeed, in the plays where the playwright rather than the implied author is the central subject behind the characters, Beckett draws particular attention to himself. The playwright is the maker of all the semantic content, to which the plays are respectively linked.[2] In fact, only the literary work itself can be *objectively* self-referential. The essence of theatre involves a tripartite relationship between playwright, actor, and audience. The notion of audience, from Beckett's point of view, is an implied figure: it is to be detected and discovered. Similarly, the playwright can be discovered by examining the text from the audience's point of view. Beckett actors are not only intermediaries of texts, but through their own self-referentiality they are intermediaries of self-consciousness: from that of the playwright to that of the audience. The playwright can be detected in his plays by examining the "I" of the role, which, in Beckett's plays (indeed, in most theatrical situations), is a triple I. It is the "I" of Beckett, the "I" of the actor (as both person and role), and finally and hopefully, the "I" of the audience.

The hermeneutical circle begins with the playwright's initiative, moves on to the self-reference of the actor and ends with – at the very least – an invitation extended to the audience to "refer to themselves" as the protagonists of the "real play". Samuel Beckett's works, despite their solipsistic semblance, are a model of honest, courageous communication.

The Playwright's "I"

The generic uniqueness of the "author's voice" has been dealt with by Herta Schmid, who distinguishes between three sorts of drama: "personal drama", in which the auctorial subject withdraws behind the dramatic world and action; "conversational drama", in which the role of characters and the situational frame is subordinate to the characters' verbal activities, and the auctorial subject appears more distinctly through the inconsistences in the subject matter; and "situational drama", in which the framework of the situation points distinctly to the auctorial subject.[3] Fieguth observes that, "In the course of Herta Schmid's discussion, it becomes more and more apparent that the auctorial subject cannot be separated from a presupposed recipient's acts of perception."[4] Beckett's plays fall under all three categories. They are "personal", because the auctorial subject in the plays withdraws somewhat behind the consistency of the three unities of time, place and action. They are "conversational" (*Gesprächsdrama*), for Beckett's heroes are almost always engaged in verbal activity that not only subordinates the situational framework, but often compensates for it. And the plays are "situational" due to the overall importance of the dramatic effect of characters being confined to wheelchairs, ash-bins, mounds, etc. The auctorial subject can be traced in the three sorts of drama as well as in yet another important element, namely the stage instructions.

Whereas in a novel the dialogue text and the author's text constitute one verbal structure, in drama (in general), and particularly in Beckett's plays and radioplays, these two "texts" are quite distinct. If one accepts that the stage directions are the author's text in a direct way, one sees that Beckett's intervention in his plays is both frequent and intensive. Beckett's auctorial text is very detailed and specific in regard to where, when and how actors should perform their roles. There are many instructions concerning tone, emotion, pitch, speed, body posture, location on stage, etc., all of which indicate that Beckett is very careful in designing contextual and subtextual elements of the bare text.

Furthermore, Beckett sometimes creates a bridge of ironic understanding between himself and a reader (rather than a spectator) of his play, in the form of jokes played at the characters' expense. Notes such as "he puts on his glasses and looks at the two likes", or "he tries to look intelligent", are typical self-reflexive semi-jokes which testify to the degree of their writer's self-consciousness as well as his attempt to expose the theatrical artifice by deliberately appealing to a reader. No audience can possibly get the gist of such stage directions; they remain a purely textual joke between playwright and reader.

Beckett's stage directions are usually limited, in the more active plays, to a description of movement, handling a stage property, or a brief qualification of feeling or tone the actor should follow. Yet, quite often, the stage directions acquire, if read independently, a poetics of their own. Such is the fairly long description of Krapp's fumbles at the beginning of *Krapps' Last Tape*, a description that resembles the one of the pebbles in *Watt*, the "hat-scene" in *Waiting for Godot*, or the meticulously planned "dialogue" between auctorial text and monologue text in *Happy Days*. When read, the stage directions serve as a corrective to the text. When performed, the auctorial text loses its poetic, corrective–correlative quality and turns into practical instructions:

Vladimir: Now: . . . (joyous). There you are again . . .
(indifferent) There we are again . . .
(gloomy) There I am again. (*WFG*, 54)

Yet the stage directions, when performed, are to be carried out carefully: they are the explicit and intentional intervention of the playwright in his play. In Beckett's plays the characters – the carriers of the dialogue-text – often seem to rebel against the meaning of the auctorial text although "They do not know about it."[5] Such an assumption, as Feiguth observes, "presupposes a perceiving subject that establishes a level on which this conflict can take place". In Beckett's plays the "perceiving subject" is the audience, whose involvement and self-reflexion are thus invited. Such is Hamm's response in *Endgame*, and the more extreme case of the protagonists of *Play*. In *Play*, they even talk back to their auctorial text when it is read out or actualized as moving off the spotlight. A *Piece of Monologue* is in the form of "stage instructions" read aloud by the actor; the *auctorial text* and the *dialogue text* switch roles throughout.

The most impressive and prevalent notion of an implied playwright is found behind the obsessive "self-expressors" in the plays. Almost all of Beckett's dramatic heroes perform in their dramatic life what Beckett said about Van Velde: "Unable to act, obliged to act, he makes an expressive act, even if only of itself, of its impossibility, of its obligation."[6] Beckett's *dramatis personae* extensions of their author are fully aware, in a non-metaphorical manner, of their mode of existence. On radio, characters such as Maddy Rooney, Henri, Croak and Words (together!), Opener and Voice, He and She, and even Animator, Dick and Fox, are all trying to express themselves vocally and to give vent to their author's need to live-by-talking or, at least to "make an expressive act". On stage, the characters resort to the particular stage techniques of doing the same: they are fully aware of their stagy-ness, which indicates that their playwright is just as much aware of his role as playwright. The Beckettian world (Beckett said, "the Proustian world") is "expressed metaphorically by the artisan because it is apprehended metaphorically by the artist: it is the indirect and comparative expression of indirect and comparative perception."[7]

Many of Beckett's heroes are practising artists, storytellers, writers, actors: they are people, albeit fictitious, who try to express their playwright by expressing themselves. Lucky, when finally speaking up, expresses the typical self-referential agony of speaking about speech. Hamm (and to a lesser extent his father) is an actor, a storyteller. He often breaks off his story in order to remark on the conditions in which the story is told; in the attempt he tells another story about the initial story and why it can or cannot be told. Winnie – actress and storyteller – is just as much aware and self-conscious of her situation as Hamm.

Krapp is a failing author – "17 copies sold . . . " – who, like Beckett, dares to fail: "To be an artist is to fail." All three characters in *Play* feel the inescapable need to talk and tell about their closely entangled mutual lives. The emphasis in *Come and Go* is placed on laconic, highly indeterminate phrases, which involve the characters in brief encounters with self-expression. In *Breath*, self-expression is compared with a whole life squeezed into thirty-five seconds of inhaling and exhaling. Mouth, in *Not I*, is not only motivated but also blocked by her enormously obsessive and excruciating need to "give vent". The characters of *That Time* and *Footfalls* are similarly motivated. In *Theatre II*, the implied playwright is C who is simply "there"; the talking about him is done by others. C represents Beckett himself on stage. In the two *Acts Without Words*, Beckett tries to "talk" without words. "The presentness of something already contains in itself a direct relationship with the hearer. To witness something depicted and conceived as happening in the present one has to be present in person, whereas to learn about something entirely past, neither the physical immediacy of communication nor therefore a public is necessary at all."[8] George Lukàcz's distinction between drama and novel relate to self-reference too, although theatrical self-reference is filtered through the performance of actors, and their unique "presentness" and immediacy. In theatre, self-reference can only be performed in the first person singular and in the present tense. Consequently, that self-reference which the playwright inserted in his play can work if and only if the actors also perform it, in the sense of both "acting" and "doing". It is logically necessary to assume that self-reference has to be performed. Hintikka has shown it in regard to Descartes' *Cogito* which is a performative act;[9] Beckett's self-referential characters follow, basically, the same rule. The actors who play them have to be self-reflexive, whereby the "self" they reflect upon is not only the fictitious character's self but their own real one.

In theatre, the mediation between an actual self-reflexive playwright and his implied or actual audience's self-reflexion, can be achieved by an actual, performing self-reflexive actor. The distinction between the reflection and confirmation of the self through its encounters with self-less objects describes the pattern of behavior assigned to many of Beckett's protagonists, reflecting the playwright's own wish to have his self-consciousness confirmed by that of "another", namely the actor, and through him, the audience. Through the positing of the self-reference of the medium, Beckett proposes that there exists a parallelism between on-stage relationships (e.g., Winnie and Willie in *Happy Days*), and the stage-audience and playwright relations. The play and the actors mediate between the self-consciousness of the playwright and the "other" self-consciousness of and in his audience. Beckett leaves the option for the audience to respond as self-asserting human beings or as self-less objects in the same way this option is left open for Willie.

Beckett's stage, moreover, has a subtle built-in actor–audience situation. The pattern designed in *Happy Days* is characteristic to his other plays too. Beckett the author can be associated with the actor-figure who acts out something to be seen and heard by an audience-figure, both on stage and in the auditorium. Reduced to its bare essentials, theatre could suffer the loss of costume, lights, make-up, and many other relatively minor elements. It would, however, necessarily maintain the basic formula that constitutes the theatrical situation: "A (actor) impersonates B (role), while C (audience) is looking", Beckett's theatre lays a special emphasis on the mutual relationships between these A–B–C factors of the play. The author being constantly aware of the paradoxicality of the situation makes this very paradoxicality the subject matter. The paradox, from the actor's point of view, is that of having to demonstrate and to impersonate. From the audience's point of view the paradox lies in the clash between identification (sympathy, empathy, "addiction") versus reflexion (in the cognitive, more alienated sense of the word), and illusion versus inlusion.[10]

The two sets of paradoxes, which initially belong to the actor and the audience, are made into lines uttered by actor-roles and audience-roles. The double irony of the Beckettian theatrical situation lies not only in the texts, but also in the actors' challenge against their theatrical roles. Most important is the active enlisting of the audience: a passive, dull audience – which refuses Beckett's and his actors' invitation to accept the author's expressed views about the world, people, their situation and their communicability – is made to be the object of the irony. If, however, the audience responds "properly" and sees the relationships on stage as reflecting its own relationships to the stage, then, and only then, does Beckett succeed in using the theatrical situation to express something that is happening beyond it, namely the partnership between any two, or more, human beings:

> The understanding of a text is not an end in itself and for itself; it *mediates* the relation to itself of a subject who, in the short circuit of *immediate* reflection would not find the meaning of his own life.[11]

In a theatrical performance "understanding", as mediated through an actor, calls for the "short circuit of immediate reflection." There exists not only a parallelism between the relationships Winnie–Willie and Beckett–audience. The intra-textual references to self-reflexive author and self-reflexive audience reflect the extra-textual references between real author and audience. Beckett can be regarded as the initiator of a self-reflexive circle. He writes his own self-reflexion into the play; the play becomes self-referring in relation to its writer, to itself, and to its audience; finally, the audience is invited to become self-reflexive. Only if this cycle is completed is the playwright's intention fully realized, and the spectators become actual co-creators of the play, and able to interpret their own lives through Beckett's text as spoken and acted by an author.[12] Even if the audience does not become self-reflexive, its very presence is a necessary condition for the playwright's "true" consciousness, for a person (or an audience, or Willie) should be "recognized as a person even though he himself does not attain the truth of being recognized as an independent self-consciousness".[13]

Actors and Roles

All Beckett's characters are engaged in the awareness of the creative process, especially in words, so much so that talking for them becomes a metaphor for living, a substitute for living, and a mode of living in the Cartesian sense of "I utter, ergo I am." They are aware of their verbal existence and they crave silence so as to stop it all. But, and dialectically so, as long as they *talk* about wanting silence (death) they keep on living.

> While every other form of art translates from real life into an objective structure which is different from life, the actor is supposed to do the opposite . . . As a real person the actor is no more the stage character created by art than coloring is a portrait . . . [14]

Only the actor standing there has any existence at all. Taking for granted that theatre is an independent art and not a realization of the dramatist's textual intention given to an actor to "play", "interpret", "present", "represent", etc., the actor's performance is, in terms of the art, the endpoint itself.

Hardly any other dramatist does so much in order to mutilate, minimize, ridicule, and finally, eliminate altogether the function of a living person (actor) on stage. Beckett has always been very interested in the production of his works. His attitude to directors, actors, etc. has been described in a number of biographical essays as well as in production logs. His involvement is yet another indication concerning the connection between the implied and the actual playwright, and more than circumstantial evidence for the importance of self-reflexion.

Beckett's active participation in the performance of his plays, from the days of *Waiting for Godot* (1953) to the engagement with the Schiller Theatre in Berlin, suggests that he does not deal with any "right" interpretation of his plays but, rather, with the artistic extensions of an authentically imposed self. Alan Schneider has indicated that Beckett has a strange way of making himself "present in absentia":

> I've always rehearsed as though he (Beckett) were in the shadows some-

where watching and listening, ready to answer all our doubts, quell our fears and share our surprises and small talk. Sometimes, without sounding mystical or psychotic, I've felt that he was indeed there.[15]

Such a feeling that Beckett is "indeed there" issues, in part at least, from the self-referring notions in the text – notions that gain vivacity when performed, and which can be explained by literary terms rather than by parapsychology.

Beckett not only treats his actors with warmth, care and understanding (he "allows you any amount of freedom you want, provided he feels it does not conflict with the text"),[16] but the written role itself shows great concern for whichever actor is willing to identify with it. It is practically impossible to assume that Beckett would not think of the actual man or woman who plays a Winnie or a Hamm. Madeleine Renault, Martin Held, Billie Whitelaw, and a long list of actors who have worked with Beckett, testify to this effect.[17]

A Beckett actor is not just a mediator of a text but a person whose text is delivered as self-referring – the self not being the self of the *role*, but the self of the acting *person*. The actor is given self-referential texts and the only way he can possibly relate to them is by internalizing them. A self-referential sentence refers not only to the role (e.g., Vladimir, Krapp, etc.), but *to the actor in it*. Given self-referential sentences such as "where were we yesterday – here" (namely on stage at this or that specific theatre in town), and patterns like "They cry – ergo they are," it is obvious that the very fact of putting an act on stage is *performatory*; it creates a situation rather than describes one.

Waiting for Godot is full of such self-reflexive lines, which serve to strip off, as well as reconfirm, theatricality. Some of the lines are more explicit than others yet taken together they all fall into the category of self-referential patterns, which Beckett is so meticulously careful to pass on to the audience through his self-referential actors. "Charming spot . . . inspiring prospect," "Godot . . . who has your future in his hands . . . at least your immediate future," "professional worries." Such lines refer to actors who make it clear that they talk about their jobs as actors while performing them. They talk about Godot whose arrival may put an end to tonight's show, for outside they may not necessarily wait for him. They talk about their clownish routines as being "worse than the pantomime – the circus – the music hall – the circus", but such a routine is, nevertheless, highly theatrical. They know that theatre is not what one does but how one does it: "but it's the way of doing it . . . " When Vladimir has to relieve himself he asks Estragon, who sends him to the toilet of the house ("end of corridor, on the left"), to keep his seat. (Here he behaves as a member of the audience!) In fact, the whole of Act II can be regarded as the following day's performance of Act I, in which the characters on stage try to amuse one another while waiting for somebody who (even the audience knows by now) will never come. Hacking away at possible illusions they say: "Recognize? What is to recognize? All my life I've crawled in the mud and you talk to me about scenery!" (*WFG*, 40).

Time passed in the theatre is not necessarily fictitious time. The characters in *Waiting for Godot* de-fictionalize it constantly. The time spent is real, un-fictionalized time; its very passing is intensified and there is a clash between linear and cyclical time through the constant recurrence of events and by the mere waiting. The characters do what bored audiences do in a play: instead of being enveloped by whatever goes on the stage, they stop watching, ask for the time, check what has happened so far and what still lies ahead of them. It is the place, the uniquely "framed" theatrical space and situation, which has to be focused on in order to enhance theatricality. Combining time and space, Vladimir and Estragon say: "The beginning of what? – This evening. – It's been an occupation," and toward the end: "I assume it's very near the end of this repertory, for I begin to weary of this motif" (*WFG*, 79). As actors, they are busy, predominantly with their immediate surrounding. In Beckett's plays, the physicality of the stage surrounding is of great importance, since difficult "conditions" (for both actors and characters) function as metaphorical and non-metaphorical at the same time.

In *Endgame*, the time–space enclosure is reinforced yet saved from sentimentalism and sheer boredom by a keen, self-addressed sense of irony. Here Beckett hardly leaves one theatrical element untouched. Clov draws curtains, like stage props, on the windows. He says, "Nice dimensions, nice proportions" (*EG*, 93), meaning the stage itself and the scenery as scenery. Hamm begins his lines with, "Me to play." Soon after, and it is only the beginning of the play, he says, "Have you not had enough? Clov – Yes! (pause) of what? Hamm – Of this . . . thing" – again meaning the very "thing" they are doing.

As in *Waiting for Godot*, they cannot leave each other. The "centrifugal" "Let's Go – we can't" is here replaced with the "centripetal" (and equally confining) "I'll leave you – you can't." As long as Hamm and Clov play the Endgame, they are inseparable. They are not playing in a play or being actors in a play, they are *the* play itself. They don't mean anything beyond what they say and do. Hamm can relax: they are not going "to mean anything". In an indirect reference to his audience, Hamm complains, "Ah the creatures, the creatures, everything has to be explained to them." He refuses to explain or to provide a meaning, but supplies, like so many other Beckett actors–storytellers–characters, a story to exemplify his being there. So does Nagg, who tells the story about the tailor who progressively made the trousers worse and worse – like God made the world, like Hamm himself decaying, like his own *telling* of the story. Being blind like Pozzo, and being symbolically so much like the audience, Hamm is obsessed with the idea of being seen. Asking whether the dog is gazing at him, he reminds one of Winnie, "Oh I know it does not follow . . . that because one sees the other, the other sees the one," or of Vladimir, "At me too someone is looking." All the characters in *Play* derive their *raison d'être* to utter such lines from an audience that sees them: "Am I as much as being seen?" (*PL*, 317).

Hamm talks about "bringing in other characters" into his own play within a play but does not know where he would find them. Could he see, he would have picked them from the first row. He knows, in a sharp and double ironic line, that what keeps Clov with him is nothing but "the dialogue". He is feeling rather drained – as any actor who ever played Hamm's role may testify – because of the "prolonged creative effort" performed in front of the audience. Those people in his story, whom he could have helped, are again none other than actual or potential members of the audience. He is talking about "an aside", "arming up", "soliloquy", "an underplot" and finally, with a great sense of panache, about "This is what I call making an exit." Having behaved throughout the play as an actor who refuses to take off his mask, Hamm reminds one of Marcel Marceau's famous numbers where the clown *cannot* take off his mask. Hamm, with human dignity and decency, as well as with tremendous courage, thanks his supporting co-actor and immediate on-stage audience: "I'm obliged to you, Clov." Clov, being just as much of an actor as he is an audience to Hamm, does not delay his reply: "(turning sharply) Ah, pardon, it's I am obliged to you," as though knowing that he who thanks is more of a star in a show than he who is thanked. Hamm, still maintaining the upper hand, says "It's we are obliged to each other." Not seeing (blind as he is) that Clov is still there, he is ready to begin again, all alone, "Me to play." Clov, the audience, has had enough. Hamm the actor has not.

A close reading of the first few pages of *Happy Days* reveals its high degree of theatrical, indeed "actorial", self-reflexiveness:

> Maximum simplicity and symmetry. Blazing light. Very pompier trompe-l'oeil backcloth . . . she is discovered sleeping . . . capacious black bag . . . bell rings piercingly. (*HD*, 139)

The very symmetrical arrangement of the scene already suggests deliberate and self-conscious theatricality. It is an *en-face* view suggesting direct appeal to the audience, hiding nothing and making no pretense at "reality". The light is a theatre spotlight, and the backcloth is supposed to look deceiving, and to expose rather than hide its own theatricality. The ringing of the bell can easily be perceived as the theatre bell and as a sign for both actress and audience to take their places. It reminds one of other Pavlovian-type reflexes that occur in other Beckett plays, and suggests that Winnie is fully subservient to the imposed ringing.

Happy Days has two beginnings. The first ("another heavenly day") is a ritualistic, actor-like pattern of behaviour: the actress prepares herself, as though she is still in her dressing room and about to go on stage. As she is there already, she performs the little ritual of praising the day and the Lord rather quietly: "Lips move again in audible addendum." The play really begins, however, with the self-reflexive words: "Begin, Winnie (pause) Begin your day, Winnie." Throughout the play Winnie keeps spurring herself on. She tries to establish, alternatively, a communication with stage props and with Willie, in the attempt to confirm herself in her unique situation of being literally, as well as metaphorically, stuck on stage. She first establishes contact with her bag, her toothbrush and toothpaste, after which she is ready to acknowledge and look for the other character on stage ("Hoo-oo!"). Winnie even compares Willie to her toothpaste: "Poor Willie (examines tube, smile off) – running out." She then turns to examine herself and her tooth. She continues with a comment on drama: "What are those wonderful lines?" in which Beckett makes the text itself self-reflective, as he does with the cliché words Winnie utters all along. Then, another focusing on a theatrical element: "Holy light – (polishes) – bob out of dark – (polishes) – blaze of hellish light."

All these meticulously enumerated theatrical elements – set, props, actors, light, etc. – contribute to the high awareness of theatricality in the play. The rapport with a listener, an audience, is certainly the most pressing element goading Winnie to go on:

> Ah, if only I could bear to be alone. I mean to prattle away with not a soul to hear, something of this is being heard, I am not merely talking to myself, that is in the wilderness a thing I could never bear to do – for any length of time. (Pause) That is what enables me to go on, to go on talking like that. (*HD*, 146)

Winnie is an actress in quest of her role. Many of her monologues are reflections on what one can possibly do and say in her situation: "These things tide one over. That is what I mean. That is all I mean." She tries to pull Willie to her side in her struggle over "her day", her play: "I think you would back me up there" she says, and later realizes that Willie, as her audience, has "done more than your bit already" so "just lie back and relax" – as the audience does.

Winnie's song can be seen as one of her plays-within-the-play (others are Mildred, and the Shower and Cooker stories). "One cannot sing just to please someone, however much one loves them. No, song must come from the heart." This line echoes the entire situation of an actress, her need to have "true" motivation and use "gutsy" stuff to back up her lines with "real" emotion. When Willie finally attempts the long yearned-for actual approach, Winnie says: "I'll cheer you on," but then, "Don't look at me like that." Willie, if one accepts his presence on stage as representing the audience, dares to try and break through the frail illusion and seclusion of an actress on stage. He does what the audience *should* do if *Happy Days* were not a play, namely to go and dig Winnie out of her mound, or kill her. The theatrical gap is here laid open before a live audience – at a point where the stage-character "freezes". At this point (which is toward the end of the play), the so far well-devised self-reflexive pattern threatens to fall apart. But Beckett leaves the final act of tearing away the actress-mask, and the assumed self-sufficient theatricality, to hang in mid-air. The very end is left open: Willie does reach out for Winnie, but we never know whether he succeeds in making actual contact.

Play presents a situation of people fighting silence and darkness, "They being one." The play is divided into two halves. The first half is a banal love story, made interesting through a smart technique of lighting and intercuts of speech. The second half is a reflection on the first. It uses the first half as *reflected material*; the initial banality of the triangular love story is replaced with painful quests regarding the very situation of the previous inquisition by light. Beckett uses the love story as consciousness, and the second half as self-consciousness, which needs something to be conscious of. All three characters are bothered by the impersonal light, which is in the form of a theatre spotlight. Once this is understood to be what it is, namely a self-reflexive theatrical metaphor, one can charge the light with further meaning such as "light of conscience", "the eye of another", a "divide light", or even a light representing the audience whose eyes follow the moving spotlight and behave in the same inquisitive manner – not really knowing what to expect from the three figures in urns.

Inasmuch as the light causes the actors to react, it also conditions the response of the audience. It creates the pattern of looking at the figures as in a three-fold ping-pong game. It is an interrogating light not because of what it is, but because of what the figures *say* of it. The light, which is addressed to the audience as well, is the real protagonist of *Play*. The situation in *Play* is a dramatization of the need to respond to another consciousness. The need is there, but there is no certainty that the other, the light, has a consciousness at all. Perhaps it is "Mere eyes. No mind." By using the theatrical situation, Beckett puts in doubt whether there is any consciousness of "another". In *Play*, he uses a triangular love story because in such an emotional muddle people are supposedly in an intense position regarding what they really feel, and how they truly respond to each other. They often attempt an internalization of the other's state of mind. Hence the mentality of the objective, personality-lacking nature of the light, which does not enable them to get away easily with deceiving one another or even themselves.

The three characters in *Play* are well aware of the strange unreality of their situation ("urns, hellish-half light", etc.) They are even aware of its theatricality, or better, "hellish half-theatricality". "I know now all that was just . . . play." Here M probably refers to the first half which now, in the second half of *Play*, seems to him remote. He wishes that this second part, the fully conscious one, will also have been just play. He doesn't know what Beckett knows: the games one plays with consciousness are as theatrical as the ones he, M, played with women, and a person is no less prone to self-deception than to the deception of others.

Not I begins before the curtain rises and ends after its fall. Mouth talks before and after the visual convention of opening and closing is triggered. The play thus gives the clear impression that, in a way similar to other Beckett plays, this play too attempts to transcend beyond its own medium-limits. Although once again being highly aware of its own theatricality, *Not I* – like *Waiting for Godot*, like *Play* – has no real beginning and no real end. It tries to extend beyond the stage, as though whatever is presented is just a short curve in a huge spiral. The audience is made to feel that it witnesses an arbitrary sequence in a never-ending prattling of a seemingly unrelated, though in fact extremely well devised, string of words and phrases.

In *Not I*, the distinction between theatricality and reality is harder to tell apart. The visual image of a mouth lit "upstage audience right" and fiercely talking, as if on fire, is perhaps one of the most striking uses made of a dramatization of a speech act. Except for the Auditor, nothing else acts on stage but the speaking organ – the mouth. More than any other Beckett character, Mouth does what it says and says what it does, thus effacing the otherwise relatively clearer border between theatrical illusion and realistic reference that exists in the other plays. The first intelligible word of *Not I* is "out", which suggests actual and verbal birth, both "into this world" (*NI*, 14) and onto the stage. The mouth itself, and the girl who may be its owner, are both a "tiny little thing". Both Mouth and the girl "stare into space", both share a "stop . . . then on . . . a few more . . . " – a pattern similar of progression in life as well as in speech. Both refuse to accept self-identity: the girl or woman (a number of ages in her life are referred to), due to some traumatic experience, is fiercely opposed to using the first person singular. Mouth cannot say "I" because it has no "personality" and does not know whether it has a body and whether this body is "standing . . . or sitting". The brain is still working, nevertheless. The "ray of light", at one end and the same time, is the theatre projector and that inner light which flashes (metaphorically?) through Mouth's brain. Both the Mouth and the character it talks about (herself!) are "so disconnected". "The buzzing" is simultaneously what the character says it hears as well as being the very noise of the words it produces, being both object and subject. Mouth talks away its stream of words and about them: "and now this stream . . . this steady stream . . . " It is talking about a character who was always speechless and now pours everything forth, while not admitting it is "her voice at all", and having "no idea what she was saying!" – yet knowing she is deluding herself in so doing.

At this point in the play Mouth indulges in a meticulous description of speech: "gradually she felt her lips moving . . . the tongue . . . jaws . . . cheeks . . . etc." She analyzes the action of speech six times, closely watching her own speech act. Like the audience (and in a way she is her own audience because of her refusal to say "I"), she "cannot catch the half . . . not the quarter . . . " of what she says. And now she can't stop, and can't stop saying she can't stop. Now she can only talk; therefore there is no use in her "straining to hear" and "piece it together". "She" is "dragging up the past" – fragmented bits and pieces of scenes, such as walking aimlessly in the field, the supermarket, and her appearance in Croker's Acres in the court.

In *Not I*, Beckett equates language with life. Both are described as a response to or result of some guilt; they are, therefore, a punishment. Not being sure even of this, because there is no pain involved, she is trying to make something of it. The overall effect of the speech is, by content, an inner dialogue in which, once externalized, the limits between speaker–subject and spoken-about-object are diffused.

Mouth's speech sounds like an abortion of words to match the baby abortion hinted at in her speech. Her "sudden urge to . . . tell" is an act of giving birth to bubbling baby words. The speech is an extended, verbalized vagitus, as in *Breath*. She "must have cried as baby – perhaps not – not essential to life – just the birth cry to get her going." What it finally and really is, neither Mouth nor the audience ever get a chance to find out: "what she was trying . . . what to try . . . no matter." Yet both take part in one of the most amazing theatre experiences – that of the "trying" itself.

When actors play characters in a performance they (both actors and characters) become "vice-existers", in more than one sense. The question arises in regard to *how* and in *what* sense do actors-in-their-roles represent the playwright's attitude, his thoughts, his feelings and his situation. If it is true that the playwright manifests his existence in a play, he must do so by having actors represent him, actors who in their turn actually represent characters who represent the playwright.

The presentness and immediacy of the theatrical work changes the distance and the mode of interaction between the writer and the recipient of the work. In the theatre, the audience is actually present; there-fore the *direct* though *fictitious* appeal of the author to his reader is replaced with an *indirect* though *actual* appeal of an actor to an audience. In a novel, authors can differ from each other by the literary distance they create between themselves, their characters, and the readers. There are different sorts of distance, such that ensue from a moral or intellec-tual level, or distance in time or space. In theatre yet another sort of distance is introduced, namely that which ensues from the medium of a performing art.

The existence of actors on stage implies that the playwright is both more *remote* from his audience, because he is replaced or represented by the actor, and *closer* to his audience because of the live interaction that takes place between his "representatives" and the recipients of his works. The greater distanciation (no direct appeals from an author) in drama as a *genre* is fully compensated for by contracting the distance through the medium of theatre.[18]

In drama, it is not the text but the speech act of an actor that mediates between playwright and audience. The notion of the implied play-wright in Beckett's plays is closely linked with that of the audience. The many references made to an audience necessarily point back to both their speakers–actors and to the writer – the original source. Beckett's active intervention in the production of his plays may be understood not only as attempts to impose the author's interpretatoin, but as attempts to endow the actor with the same self-referential quality that he and his dramatic characters have.

The *self*-referential quality of the plays and their numerous elements mentioned, are reducible to the different phases of the implied play-wright's high degree of self-consciousness. Dialectically, it finds its most *un*-narcissistic vent in the very act of presentation. In offering this self-reflexive circle, Beckett relies on the existing conventions of theatrical lighting, design, make-up, and style of acting. If revolutionized or dras-tically changed, these conventions cannot serve their main function of self-reflexion. The apparent conventionality of Beckett's theatre serves as a deliberately well-known background to which the audience may relate while actually being referred to by themselves. Had Beckett radi-cally revolutionized his theatrical modes of presentation, he would have side-tracked the main issue of focusing on the self-reference of the creative process, of himself, his play and the recipients.

By using the medium of theatre, Beckett is engaged in the courageous attempt of actively communicating that which is hardest to communi-cate. Beckett's drama is, therefore, not *about* communication, but an actual act *of* communication, and an attempt to attain it by creating a real dialogue between the characters on stage, and an author and his poten-tial audience. An audience can treat other people (including an author) as an object, too. Beckett has done his share in asserting true self-consciousness of the "other". It is for the audience to complete the "circle" of *mutual* consciousness.

Notions of Audience

Inasmuch as a playwright reaches out toward his audience through his play, so are the members of the audience required to reach back to the author through the very same medium. It is worth repeating, in the context of audience as opposed to the context of the playwright, that the "presentness" and immediacy of the theatrical work changes the distance and mode of interaction between the writer and the recipient of the work. In the theatre, the audience is actually present. Therefore the direct though fictitious appeal of the author to his reader is replaced with an indirect though actual appeal of an actor to an audience. In the theatre, distance is introduced, as ensuing from the medium of a performing art. The speech act, when performed on stage, involves a two-way communication between actor and audience, instead of an implied and one-way communication between author and reader, even though this mode of communication is often a metaphor.[19] The very existence of actors on stage implies that the playwright is both more *remote* from his audience, because he is replaced or represented by the actor, and *closer* to his audience because of the live interaction that takes place between his "representatives" and the recipients of his works:

> The reference is resolved by the power of showing a reality common to the interlocutors. Or if we cannot show the thing being talked about, at least we can situate it in relation to a unique spatio-temporal network to which the partners in discourse also belong.[20]

Drama does not and cannot abolish the ostensive reference of the spoken text. "The dramatic situation is not an objective reality external to the language; it is an immaterial meaning generated by the language itself."[21] In Beckett's plays, where from the point of view of the actors' very existence on stage the "situation" is of ultimate importance, the audience is not only not exempt from involvement, but actually built into the actor's being "thrown there".

Beckett's awareness of his audience is manifest in a number of dramatic and theatrical techniques, other than the obvious fact that theatre is intended to be presented in front of an actual, live audience. With varying degrees of intensity we find at least one of the following approaches to the audience in the plays: direct appeal (verbal and non-verbal); indirect appeal (again, both verbal and non-verbal); and a deliberate depiction of an actor-audience relationship on stage in a given play as part of the theatrical situation itself. As a result, possible approaches to the play are already built into it, supplying the audience with critical guidelines for their evaluation of the play. At the same time, however, this built-in self-criticism of the play partially deprives the audience of a valid and original evaluation of it *outside* the theatrical encounter. This, certainly, is completely different in a silent reading of a text.

These different dramatic modes of referring to the audience partially overlap, yet taken either separately or together they indicate that the actual audience *of* the play (in contrast to the notion of the audience *in* the play) is invited to regard itself as being made up of those people *about* whom and *for* whom the play is written and presented.

The direct verbal appeal is a direct second-person address to the audience, in which the actor addresses his lines to (or about) the audience straight to its face. Such appeals are scarcer in Beckett's plays than might be expected from a writer whose characters are often obsessed with a yearning for communication. Beckett does not usually address his audience directly. In *Waiting for Godot*, Vladimir refers to "that bog" and "muck heap"; Hamm in *Endgame* says the same. Again in *Waiting for Godot*, the audience is referred to as "not a soul in sight", or as corpses and skeletons. But in the subsequent plays, Beckett makes no more direct verbal addresses until as late as *Footfalls*, in which the voice says "whom the reader will remember" (*FF*, 403). The scarcity of this approach ought not, perhaps, to be lamented, because the surprise effect is soon dissipated.

In his earlier plays, Beckett refers to people in the third person and calls "them" by names such as Men, Humanity, My Likes, Creatures, Souls, Skeletons, Corpses, Mankind, Everybody, Somebody, Someone, Anyone, Gentlemen, Wayfarers, Some Kind of Person, etc. All these labels, which can be treated as indices of a general notion of "They", serve as a simultaneous reference to both the actual audience and to all of humanity outside the theatre.

Extensive use of this reference can be found in *Waiting for Godot*, and also, with diminishing frequency, in the later plays. "They", a grammatically indirect appeal to an audience, acts as camouflage for a "You", suggesting that Beckett himself, his actors and audience, share in the same fate of passing time in a highly self-conscious, self-referential manner. The self-referential quality of the actors' speech acts enhances that of the audience. Beckett's protagonists are given many lines in which they develop a notion of "They" and integrate it into themselves. Pozzo says, "I cannot go along without the society of my likes" (*WFG*, 24). Vladimir says explicitly, "At this place, at this moment of time, all mankind is us, whether we like it or not" (*WFG*, 73). And also, "At me too someone is looking" (*WFG*, 80). Hamm wants to know whether even the toy dog is looking at him, "Is he gazing at me" (*EG*, 112). Perhaps more than most other Beckett characters, Winnie is obsessed with "They" who are none other than the audience sitting in front of her – "Someone is looking at me still, caring for me still" (*HD*, 160). The most poignant remark of this sort is "What? Is it me you are referring to?" (*EG*, 130).

The integration of the third person (singular or plural) into one's own first person is best shown in *Not I*. Mouth's deliberate avoidance of the first person is the most intense expression in Beckett's drama of the attempt to hold the "I" and the "They" in a tense relationship of attraction and rejection, tacitly inviting the audience to substitute their "I" for hers.

In the early plays most of the stage activity is both centred and meticulously frontal. Hamm wishes to be seated right in the middle. Winnie finds it very hard to look anywhere but forward, and so do the two women and the man in *Play*, the three women in *Come and Go*, the mouth in *Not I* and the head in *That Time*. The frontal approach is the most natural pose toward a theatre audience, and yet in Beckett's plays it is different from a natural theatrical device. As well as enhancing the artificiality of the theatrical situation, the frontal (either centred or slightly off-centre) location of the action on stage serves to reinforce the need for the audience's response, tacit though it may be. Acts such as Krapp throwing the banana peel into the auditorium, or retreating to his dark backstage source of liquor, should be interpreted as part of the confrontation-avoidance pattern of facing an audience.

Beckett's characters, like their author, both avoid and face themselves. Insofar as they avoid or face themselves or each other (in language and in non-verbal action), so too do they avoid or face the audience. However, by virtue of being on stage they are inevitably conditioned to at least some sort of minimal "facing". Whereas in older theatrical traditions a protagonist is interrogated for certain deeds – actions or failures to act – in Beckett's plays a protagonist's very presence on the stage indicates a situation of interrogation from the outside as well as from the inside.

The theatrical situation of being on stage compels the characters to do something, to justify their being there at all, as many of them are made to realize, perhaps even as their own audiences. In *Waiting for Godot* and in *Theatre II* one of the key lines is "Let's go." But the characters cannot go away; they are bound to stay on stage, in front of an audience.[22] Hamm is constantly aware of his need to play, and even goes so far as to ask: "Did anyone have pity on me?" (*EG*, 130); but he immediately undercuts his own appeal to the audience with a self-conscious, ironic remark: "Did you never hear an aside before?" The audience no longer knows whether the line is "an aside". Similarly, Winnie wants to know (as a person and as an actress too) what she is supposed to do in her weird situation: "There's so little one can do . . . One does it all . . . 'Tis only human" (*HD*, 146); "One can not sing just to please someone" (*HD*, 155). But Winnie keeps on going *because* "someone [be it Willie or the audience] is looking at me still . . . eyes on my eyes" (*HD*, 160).

The same need to utter, act or simply to be in front of the audience is made very clear in *Play*, in which the three characters feel required by the light to explain, tell, or do. This attitude is reducible to: "Am I as much as being seen?" (*PL*, 61). The external pressure a character feels subjected to in the presentation of his or her life, is epitomized in *Not I*, both in the story within the play, about the woman in court, "speak up woman . . . mouth half open . . . " (*NI*, 381); and in the play as a whole, which is a perfect unity between the content of the speech and its mode of presentation – "start pouring it out . . . mad stuff . . . no one could follow" (*NI*, 382).

The notion of audience is achieved through the balance between the spoken text and the conditions under which the lines are delivered (in terms of posture and movement, as well as pitch, speed, and so on). The audience in Beckett's plays is not simply described in the text as an external motivator for the characters' behaviour, the text also assumes the presence of the actual audience that has to suffer and sit through the listening and watching of the often agonizing plays. The answer to the question as to whether the members of the audience regard *themselves* as the addresses is left free for them to decide. Beckett's offer to them to respond is, however, a standing invitation as long as the play is on.

Beckett's individual approach to the question of audience is meant to establish dramatic situations in which the relationship between stage and audience is reflected in the plays themselves. An audience–actor relationship can best be defined within the dialectical axis of alienation–identification. Any rhetoric of stage implies both a conscious, well-formed expression of spontaneous feeling and a primal, experiential empathy – on behalf of both actors and audience. Uri Rapp terms this intrinsically theatrical double attitude – similar to the "willing suspension of disbelief" – "inlusion". "Inlusion" is a meta-level of experience-participation in which a person experiences both himself, and the plot in which he partakes in *as* theatrical.[23]

Characters in Beckett's plays often treat each other in precisely this way. Estragon, Vladimir, Pozzo, and Lucky relate to each other as the audience relates to them, namely with an ambivalent "inlusive" attitude that combines empathy and detachment, alienation and identification. Whenever Vladimir and Estragon are alone on stage they go through innumerable routines of quarrelling and reconciliation, together with routines of pitying each other and being emotionally absolutely blank to each other. Of the two principal characters, Estragon usually main-

tains the role of actor, and Vladimir the role of omniscient or understanding audience. With Pozzo and Lucky, Pozzo is the spectator and
Lucky the performer. The greater mutuality between Vladimir and
Estragon is reduced, in Pozzo and Lucky's case, to a rather one-way attitude. When the two couples meet, they treat one another as an audience
treats actors. As soon as they get to know each other a little better, the
attitude of estrangement is replaced by one in which there is a flexible
shifting between empathy–antipathy, affection–disgust, or simply
indifference. Vladimir and Estragon examine Lucky. "They resume
their inspection", and comment on him, "He's not bad looking . . .
Perhaps he's a half wit . . . a cretin" (*WFG*, 25). He looks as strange to
them as they may look to the audience.

In Lucky's speech, in itself a mock locutionary, illocutionary, perlocu-
tionary speech act, all the other three characters watch him, each
following Lucky in his own typical individual mannerism, imitating the
same pattern in which the audience can be said to experience the whole
play, and particularly this specific scene. This is made explicit when
Didi and Gogo say they could play at Pozzo and Lucky. Earlier in the
play, Lucky asks for audience reaction to his speech: "How did you find
me? (Vladimir and Estragon look at him blankly). Good? Fair?
Middling? Poor? Positively bad?" (*WFG*, 36).

The play that reflects actor–audience relationships on stage in the
most stunningly precise way is *Happy Days*. Winnie's attitude to Willie
reflects not only the attitude of the playwright to his audience, but the
attitude of any one person to any other. The spatial setting of Willie
already indicates that he is not a "regular" co-actor. He disturbs the
symmetry of the stage by lying to the side and back of Winnie. Willie is
both Winnie's husband and her audience-on-stage. He not only "give[s]
her the impression she exists", as Estragon might say, but is also a
precondition of her entire act. Willie is thus the representative on stage
of the audience in the auditorium. However, Winnie appeals to him and
talks to him only by talking to the front, to the real audience. Beckett
succeeds here in creating the illusion that it is Willie who witnesses
Winnie's "dialogue" with the audience, rather than the audience
witnessing her talking to Willie:

> Can you see me from there, I wonder? Oh, I know it does not follow when
> two are together – (faltering) – in this way – (normal) – that because one
> sees the other, the other sees the one. (*HD*, 149)

Happy Days is replete with utterances that refer both to Willie and to the
audience:

> "Don't go off on me again . . . I may need you . . . no hurry, just don't curl
> up on me again,"

And even more explicitly:

> Ah yes, if only I could bear to be alone, I mean prattle away with not a
> soul to hear . . . something of this is being heard, I am not merely talking
> to myself. (*HD*, 145)

Winnie uses this approach in foreshadowing Willie-the-audience's
potential response:

> Oh I can well imagine what is passing through your mind; it is not enough
> to listen to the woman, now I must talk to her as well. (*HD*, 149)

One of the most striking self-reflexive lines in the play, to which the real
audience is not expected to reply, is: "Ah yes, so little to say, so little to
do, and the fear so great, certain days, of finding oneself" (*HD*, 152).
Here Winnie expresses her fear of being left without any audience at all.
Act II also begins with this craving to be seen:

> Someone is looking at me still. (Pause) Caring for me still. (Pause) That is
> what I find so wonderful. (Pause) Eyes on my eyes. (*HD*, 160)

From here onward Winnie is engaged in exercises in order to check
herself against herself (e.g. by sticking out her tongue or examining the
contents of her bag). But all such attempts cannot possibly be practised
by Winnie-the-actress without the presence of an audience. Having
internalized Willie's possible self-reflexiveness, Winnie tries a mock-
Cartesian equation: "I say I used to think that I would learn to talk alone
. . . But no . . . Ergo you are there" (*HD*, 38). Lines such as this refer to
the characters, to the actors who play them, and to the relationships
between the implied author and his dialogue.

The song that Winnie finally sings at the end can be regarded as a
metonymy for the whole play; it compares the state of a "stuck" actress
to that of a "stuck" author. In the same way as Winnie needs "true motivation" to sing on stage, the playwright too needs something – more
than "love" for an audience – in order to write and present a play,
instead of a play about a play. Winnie does sing her song at the very
end, and even Beckett did write a play.

Winnie is looked at by a Mr Shower,[24] and evokes an impression of
taking part in a play-within-a-play, creating a double reflexion and a
double situation of actress and audience:

> This man Shower or Cooker – no matter – and the woman – hand in hand
> – in the other handbags – standing there gaping at me – " . . . What's she
> doing?" he says – "What's the idea!" he says, "stuck up to her diddies in
> the bleeding ground" – coarse fellow – "what does it mean?" He says –
> "what's it meant to mean?" (*HD*, 164)

The man and the woman are reflections of Willie and Winnie. They too, man and woman, hold bags, and they too, are looking. They may be regarded as representations of Beckett who "looks" at Winnie or as yet another "audience" doing the same. This is a doubly reflexive scene of incredible sophistication and many layers of mutual mirroring. Hence, no doubt, the deliberately confusing use of personal pronouns.

Looking is a reassurance of presence and existence, as well as a nearly explicit call for help. Gadamer says: "Only if the other is not merely the other of the first self-consciousness, 'his other', but is rather free precisely in opposition to a self, can it provide confirmation of the first self-consciousness,"[25] and this is precisely the case here with the intricate relationship between Beckett – through Winnie–Willie – and the audience. Through his mouthpiece on stage, Beckett comes full circle back to openly admitting another "self" – that of Willie that of Winnie and that of his own audience. It is an urgent *need* to respond to the "other's" consciousness, even though he doesn't know whether the other *has* self-consciousness at all! *Happy Days* uses theatre in order to explore the expressive possibilities of the author, through the vehicle of theatre, in order to reach out, both *on* stage and *from* the stage, to the audience.

In *Not I*, the function of the Auditor, the audience-on-stage figure, is reduced to four gestures of "helpless compassion"; the "sideways raising of arms . . . lessens with each recurrence till scarcely perceptible at third" (*NI*, 375). Unlike in *Krapp's Last Tape*, where live Krapp is his own audience and the recorded Krapp the "actor", in *Not I*, Beckett reduces the activity of his audience-on-stage to a bare minimum. The tall speechless figure is there to show how little an audience can help. And yet the Auditor's four movements are conceptually necessary as well as theatrically effective. This figure is a condensed, perhaps more abstract Willie-figure, who plays audience to a Winnie-figure (Mouth), who, in turn is being sucked yet another degree into her mound. This figure is desperately needed as a witness – an actual and present human being who ought to be there when another human being is suffering,[26] to express even that little bit of helpless compassion. Just as Mouth is the minimal visual theatrical expression of a talking human being, so the figure of the Auditor is the minimal, though still perceptibly externalized, manifestation of audience response.

Whereas in *Waiting for Godot* the roles of actor and audience change and shift (except for Lucky who acts "actor" all along), in *Endgame*, Hamm consciously refuses to peel off his "actor" role. Not only Clov, his main audience, but his parents also, who die on him (of darkness!) are a nervous, unwilling audience sick of playing the audience role. Winnie is still willing to simulate the role of audience: "Perhaps he is crying out for help all this time and I do not hear him!" (*HD*, 163). But

Willie's reaching hand and the possibility of mutual help between people in general and the stage characters who represent them, are abandoned in *Not I*. In the plays after *Not I* Beckett tries a new variation of the notion of audience. In *Come and Go* and in *Play*, the three characters serve as audience to each other. The effect of this device compels the real audience in the auditorium to accept the mutual relationship between W1 W2 and H, and between Flo, Vi and Ru; and, at the same time, to function almost simultaneously in the actor–audience complex.

In *Footfalls* and in *That Time*, Beckett seems to be going back to audience notions already suggested in *Krapp's Last Tape*, but develops them further. In *That Time*, the face of the protagonist serves as audience for his own three voices (in different stages of his life) which talk to him. The self becomes its own audience, and the two functions of actor and audience are to be found in one and the same person. One can detect here, and much more so in *Rockaby*, how the character relinquishes the "other" – an Auditor, a witness, an audience – and becomes the other of itself.

Interestingly, only four of Beckett's characters are alone in the strict sense of having no other person to relate to: Krapp, the listener in *That Time*, the man in *A Piece of Monologue*, and the woman rocking on her chair in *Rockaby*. In all the other plays the actor is never completely abandoned, and always has someone else on or off stage to help him. When, as in these four plays, an actor is alone, there occurs a split in himself, and his older (or younger or "other") self emerges to assist in a "dialogue", in this way preserving the relationship of actor to audience.

In *Footfalls*, the audience is deprived of any certainty as to which character to identify with as its "reliable" representative on stage. V and May present two equally reliable and valid points of view. They dwell, so to speak, in each others' inner spaces and it is unclear whether both of them are dead or alive, or whether only May is alive or dead, or vice versa. It is also unclear what degree of objective, realistic truth is ascribable to the long speeches of either of them. The two women are an internalized audience of each other. They consider each other in their minds and allow the audience to take part in the process. The end of the play suggest that they are finally united, and that vocalized V has swallowed visual May, which is perhaps why the narrow strip of the tiny stage is now empty. Surely this extreme relativity of point of view reflects the actual audience as well. Here Beckett tries to undermine the (already narrow) foothold of his audience: "How could you have responded if you were not there?" (*FF*, 403).

Whereas a Beckett novel-character indulges in self-reflectiveness, the Beckett actor does so "live". His soliloquy must therefore be understood not just as a dramatic convention, but as an actual self-referential speech act. Doing the job of interpreting his own deeds and explaining (as best as Beckett allows him) his very existence on stage, a Beckett actor is likely to deprive the audience of their traditional task of interpreting the play, while implicitly demanding they "interpret" *themselves*. Insofar as one regularly pays attention to the actor-in-the-role, in Beckett's plays one focuses on the actor as actor, and on his attempts, well substantiated by the lines given, to be fully conscious of the situation, both existentially and theatrically; by being conscious of one's consciousness, one becomes highly self-conscious.

The Critical Voice

The critical voice in Beckett's plays is a rather tricky issue. Beckett himself said that had he known who Godot is, he would have said so himself in his play. Such a statement is probably true for his other plays as well, which are no less baffling as far as their "meaning" is concerned. Beckett's dramatic texts invite the audience to fill in the interpretative gaps, but offer hardly any real support or preference to one interpretation over any other. Albeit indicating the self-reflexive quality of the text, one has not yet exhausted the possibilities of what it may possibly mean after all, for the self-reflexive quality *per se* is not necessarily a "meaning". The link between the playwright and audience is shown here through the prism of the self-referential voice of Beckett – as represented by critical remarks and "critical roles" performed on stage, and focus on hermeneutics rather than on the methodology.[27]

Being a keen critic himself, Beckett seems aware of the problems his works present to fellow critics. His awareness can be traced in the texts themselves, and it adds yet another perspective to the understanding of his attitude to the audience. In dealing with the critical voice in Beckett's plays, I emphasize Beckett's own reflected attitude to potential criticism, rather than focus on the initial openness of the text.

The only direct reference Beckett made to a critic is the "Curate – Cretin – Crritic!" line in *Waiting for Godot*. However, I propose that *Theatre II* is wholly dedicated to dramatic criticism. Between the snide remark in the first play and a full treatment of the subject in the later *Theatre II*, one finds many indirect references to the interpretability of the plays in the plays themselves. Recurrent references to meaninglessness in *Waiting for Godot*, *Happy Days*, *Endgame* and in *Play*, and most impressively in *Not I*, are remarks addressed primarily to the play itself, as well as to life outside it. This idea is reinforced by Beckett's attitude to the stage and to the theatrical situation in general.

The recurring answer to questions pertaining to meaning in *Waiting for Godot* all end with different variations on "I don't know," with deliberate evasions and digressions into other topics, and, finally, with yet another emphasis on inescapability. Beckett, in an interview, not only said that he would have written who Godot is, had he known, but in fact says in the play that he does not know. In *Endgame*, the critical function is ascribed to Hamm, who criticizes Beckett's play, its content and its mode of presentation: "the whole thing is comical." And comical it is – in *any* context, theatrical or otherwise. Admitting of such he deprives and reassures the audience that his own mixture of feelings is fruitful. In *Play*, the consciousness of having no interpretation is heightened by the characters' constant looking for one. The audience not only has to supply its own interpretation, but has actually to make out the play and sort out the collage of lines thrust at it. Using audio-visual techniques, the audience must combine the three versions and knit them into a sensible whole unit in the first half. In the second half, the audience, together with the characters, tries to find meaning in what it has previously experienced. In both parts the audience is not much better off than the characters in knowing what *Play* is all about.

Beckett is better at asking the questions than at giving the answers. Every possible unequivocal solution to questions such as "Are the figures alive," "Who or what is the spotlight?" etc., is negated. Inasmuch as not one of the three figures is given a favorable point of view over the other two, such is the case with a particular interpretation of *Play*. The play contains its unanswerable questions, and acts them out instead of answering them. The only logically sufficient meaning of *Play* lies in its actual presentation, and the same goes for the performance of the other plays: because they are not about something, except that self-referential something itself, the plays need "only" be staged!

In *Not I*, as mentioned before, the critical voice is found in the doubt role of Mouth as being "I" and "not I" together. She describes the goings-on while doing them. Here again she deprives the audience of their otherwise natural right to extricate themselves from the situation by analyzing it. Mouth, Winnie and all the rest are highly self-conscious about the situation, and more often than not quite brilliant in describing it.

In Beckett's dramatic practice, as well as in the tentative theory that can be drawn from it, one finds a deliberate alienation between audience and character. But such alienation, in Brechtian terms, only tricks one into further involvement, commitment and identification. All that is left is an ever-lasting process of quest and search, in which the actors serve as spotlights, goads and Godots, etc., to their audience. But now, in *Theatre II*, it is the critical aspect of the theatrical situation that is performed.

In *Theatre II* there are three men, A, B and C, on a stage which is (relatively) full of objects, symmetrically arranged with an open double window, two small tables, two chairs, two reading lamps, a door, as well as props such as a briefcase, papers, a watch. "C standing motionless before left half of window with his back to stage." A and B enter, and throughout the play perform a series of actions and conversations while treating C in the third person, although he is obviously there and alive – as we learn later on. They are there in order to "sum up", perhaps adding something to what C himself did not know already. The two men rummage through C's personal papers in an attempt to "make out" who and what he is, what his life is like and to "have him". Their tentative results: "A black future, an unpardonable past." They behave like two notaries in charge, perhaps, of executing his will. C himself is probably just about to jump out of the window. The two men try to find a justification for C to keep on living. They try to find some sense in his papers.

During their work A and B express boredom and quite a definite wish to pack up and go. Their job is tedious, and they don't seem to be very successful in finding what they are after. They are sidetracked by their own little stories, and by the two songbirds (one dead). Soon after, at the end, they suggest that C is dead, too – as indicated by A, who "takes out his handkerchief and raises it timidly to C's face". The situation, the relationships between the characters, the stage metaphors and, of course, the content of the discourse, all point to the fact that the play is primarily an allegory on the relationship between the author and his critics. C is the author – or rather his on-stage agent – whereas A and B are critics in their half-interested task of "making out" the implied author. The first notion Beckett made of the "critic" in *Waiting for Godot* receives here a full treatment, not altogether cold but quite condescending. If C embodies Beckett himself (or any person in need of other people to "make out" his life), then his presence on stage, back to the window, is a double message to both his critics on stage as well as to the ones in the auditorium. "You can't reach me but please try hard!" Shouldn't "they" simply talk *to* him instead of *about* him?

Having settled on stage, A wonders "why he needs our services . . . a man like him . . . and why we give them, free men like us", in this way establishing the incongruity of the situation, at least from C's viewpoint. The constant consulting of a watch (and many more references to the time of day, the date, etc., later in the play) suggests the habitual preoccupation with the urgency of time with which Beckett's plays are always imbued. Here, specifically, the urgency is achieved by linking the passage of time with the need to "sum up" C before he jumps out of the window. In a line often repeated in *Theatre II*, and unmistakably reminiscent of *Waiting for Godot*, A suggests "shall we go" (or "let's go") and a typically Estragon–Vladimir short repartee ensues:

B: Rearing

A: We attend
B: Let him jump.
A: When?
B: Now. (*TII*, 238)

A and B coolly discuss the height and the chances of C to "land on his arse, the way he lived, his possible way down from the sixth floor, the spine snaps, and the tripes explode". The detached and funny description only enhances the discrepancy between what A and B do (their function as C's "Saviours"), and what they feel about C (their complete carelessness and gross rummaging in his personal effects). For them their job is just an occupation which does not carry with it the importance of life and death as it does for C. They treat his "work, family, third fatherland, cunt, finances, art and nature, heart and conscience, health, housing conditions, God and man, and so many disasters" (*TII*, 85) with indifference. They say they have been to the "best sources" – no doubt another ironic remark Beckett puts in their mouth, perhaps in regard to the rummaging of real critics.[28]

The main activity of the play is the reading of notes written, as is gradually made clear, about C. The notes refer to C's biography, which is all in fragments and is supposed to shed some light on C's present situation and on his life in general. There are ten fragments, some of which are mentioned more than once, since A and B keep referring back to them as being possible clues:

(1) The memory book – about the elephant;
(2) on love and miscarriages (formal juridical style, of a separation?);
(3) on remembering only the calamities of the national epos;
(4) on family – never shedding tears;
(5) on his life when tipsy; horror worked into humorous skits;
(6) on the watch;
(7) on playing with dog excrement near the post office;
(8) on the heiress aunt;
(9) on the milkmaid's bottom;
(10) on confidences – "morbidly sensitive to opinions of others" – and, finally, the story about running away from home.

Having gone through these fragments, A and B comment on them and the play leads on to the eye-to-eye encounter between A and C. Most of the fragments include a funny touch, ridiculous names of people and places, and juxtaposing the content of the note with the profession or place of the writer. All the fragments portray a glum picture of the person; the final result of the collage can be summed up by what is found under "confidences" – "need of affection . . . inner void . . .

congenital timidity . . . morbidly sensitive to the opinions of others".

This last line appears seven more times, therefore proving to be the key line in the play. There is a gradual approximation to what seems to be the crux of the matter while going through the papers, especially in the last fragment, which is apparently an autobiographical one. The dynamics of seemingly approaching the core of the issue beings B closer to A, as though he is afraid of revealing some dangerous truth, or an intimacy that they could not find thus far. At this point A goes to look at C's face, but C, whose secret has not been revealed through papers, does not reveal his secret. B notes: "Could never make out what he thought he was doing with that smile on his face." One cannot possibly avoid thinking bout Beckett himself, smiling at his real critics, to the legion of which the author of this line has just been added.

The constant, slow accumulation of facts on C's life is a deceptive device. Even after getting closer to him, B says: "Looks to me we have him." They don't really have him at all and A answers "We're getting nowhere, get on with it." This effect has been used before. The stringing of more facts and stories, is more perplexing than clarifying, because there is no evident focus to them. The accumulation is an asymptotic approximation, never a realization. A and B do not understand that they have already arrived at some answer, namely, that C is "morbidly sensitive to the opinion of others".

In *Play*, three people tell a three-faceted story. In *Theatre II* there is just one story, the main "meaning" of which is that there remains an onto-logical gap between who and what a person is (C) and how *others* (A and B) can "make him out" through loosely related writings about him. A and B have no criteria with which to judge what is "right" and what is "wrong". Their summing-up is "a black future, an unpardonable past – so far as he can remember, inducements to linger on all equally prepos-terous and the best advice dead letter" (*TII*, 246).

The last part of the play deals with the "pathological horror of" the songbirds. A and B find one of the two love birds dead, and A indulges in a sentimental outburst of emotion: "Oh you pretty little pet, oh you bonny wee birdie!" and says about the bird something that is also char-acteristic of C, "And to think all this is organic waste! All that splendour!" B retorts with a typically funny and ambivalent Beckettian line, "They have no seed!" There is no mention of why the bird died, but the previous mention of the cat hints at the answer. Soon after finding the dead bird, A and B discover that C has perhaps died too. They let the cloth fall on the bird-cage. A "takes out his handkerchief and raises it timidly towards C's face". He, in a way, is the songbird; "there is nothing we can do," says B, a line as true about the bird as it is about C.

Beckett supplies a lighting scheme which serves to "shed light" on a person's life: the light flickers, plays strange tricks, and goes on and off arbitrarily. This is a play which represents an attitude toward the possibility of "making out" a person. In *Theatre II*, Beckett ridicules the critics who try to "make him out" through that typical rummaging in papers and through trying to fit grim but insignificant details into a whole that has no unity, but is just there.

An interesting line develops from *Waiting for Godot* to *Theatre II* in regard to the notion of the implied playwright. Assuming that Godot is a disguise for Beckett himself, one sees that he succeeds in establishing a unique relationship between the playwright and the play, the creator and the work. He is constantly "present in absentia". *Waiting for Godot* is strangely a waiting for a playwright who, in a sense, is not only the author but the *subject matter* of the play. Because Beckett does not in fact know what the play is "about" (otherwise he would have said so in the play), he is in the play and out of it at one and the same time. In *Theatre II*, C is no other than a live though silent embodiment of a playwright who is relatively more explicit than implied. A and B are theatre (or literary) critics who are looking for he who is right there, in the same way that Vladimir and Estragon are waiting for he who will come only in *Theatre II*. Beckett's plays are a minefield of references that clearly indicate that Godot and C are theatrical embodiments of their author. They, as well as the other characters, are deeply stuck in attempts to explain themselves and their situation to an audience. By the same token, the very act of writing and presenting a play can only be interpreted as Beckett's incessant wish to do the same.

Epilogue: Six She's and other *Not I* Proxies

Technically, emotionally and conceptually, Samuel Beckett's *Not I*[1] is considered a most demanding play. Having directed it six times in English, Hebrew and German over the last 25 years, I asked the actresses with whom I was privileged to share an often excruciating but always highly creative process, to write about their experiences. I am truly indebted to all these actresses, with a range of over 50 years between the oldest and the youngest, who were willing to contribute some of their professional as well as intimate experiences to this epilogue chapter. I wish here to give voice to the real "proxy selves" who filtered their personality through Beckett's *Not I* text, and through Mouth's lips, cheeks, tongue, and all those contortions without which verbal expression is not possible.

The actor cannot be a "good" proxy unless she fills-in the character's self with her own. Beckett's highly self-referential plays, particularly, force actors to posit their selves in front of a live audience, in a live theatre space, in order for the (self-) reference to take place. Consequently, only if the actors refer their Beckettian texts directly to themselves and not only to their roles, can the play really "work", at least as far as the self-referential aspects are concerned. *Not I*, moreover, is not "about" self-reference, "it is that something itself".[2]

Presented with a self-negating, self-avoiding or self-rejecting and almost fully disembodied dramatic character, actors of *Not I* must indeed "drag up the past" and make it present in and for the here and now of the unique, never-the-same tonight's performance. They are practically conditioned to learn about their roles primarily from the physically immediate, often painful and confining whereabouts on stage.[3] In such spaces they are virtually forced to harness their whereabouts *vis-à-vis* their selves. The actress must refer to a She when she vehemently avoids the first person singular. Is the circumscribed and denied "I" the "self" of the actress? Logically it is not, because the actress is not She (as in "What?.. Who?.. No!.. She! . . . ") and therefore she, the actress, can say so without lying. However, the "I" cannot be determined as the "I" of any given member of the audience either. Yet tentatively, illusorily, or artistically it is indeed the "I" of whoever posits his or her I for the fictitious characters, be it author, director, actor, or audience. In order to initiate such a hermeneutic search for real or fictitious selves in the theatre, it must therefore be the "I" of the actress who starts the cycle in a live performance.

Joy Coghill-Thorne was glad it was not "I"[4] and explains that the rehearsal process was a

> [. . .] Horrific experience. The exploration was challenging and fascinating, making one Beckett's for life. Luckily, that is all that I experienced, for we never got to the performance stage for lack of the rights. The person who owned them was Jessica Tandy who told Robin Phillips that she prayed for a heart attack every time she waited to begin. She did it very seldom . . . [. . .] It is not the experience of the text. That is indeed demanding but marvelous. It is the insistence on the PACE. I believe that is wrong.. to be used that way.. as an emotional machine . . . having the effect of a long scream of life.. oh yes I understand the effect and the impact of that effect . . . but to me that is using the theatre . . . and using an actress's soul for the sake of a theatrical effect. I think he went too far and this is a form of torture.. but then, that is a bit melodramatic. Not all actresses work the same way. Some would glory in the number of words and the challenge of fulfilling his mandate . . . but I was glad that it was not I!!!!! There.

Coghill and I had worked for over six months on the play. A highly acclaimed actress, and no novice to Beckett's drama, she had previously played Winnie in *Happy Days*, and together we did *Play* and *Eh Joe*, performed at the Guelph Festival, 1975. (I had never heard anything as moving and precise as her interpretation of the woman's voice in *Eh Joe*, before or since.) Her response to our working process on *Not I*, 26 years later, is utterly genuine as best as I too can recall. Indeed, some of the reports by the other actors also reflect feelings of being used, misused, or even abused by Beckett's extreme emotional and technical demands. I wonder, retrospectively, whether a performance, which never took place in this case, would have changed Coghill's reaction, either because of the performative exposure itself, necessarily a totally different experience to a rehearsal situation, or because of the audience's response. In her brief and not un-Beckettian letter, Coghill, nevertheless, raises an ethical–emotional (and professional) issue regarding the profound mental recesses of actors who play Beckett, a so far practically untouched area.

Hanna Hacohen, responded to my request with:

You entreat me to find meaning within myself, to let it ensue from my own make-up . . . And so, with great clarity, I remember another reading, and another. Suddenly, enlightenment, I tell you most of the [Not I] story [. . .] I am about fifty, full of life and turbulence, constantly denying myself. Why? *Not I*, she – Mouth, but Mouth IS I . . . Trying, for the sake of this working process on the play, to peel away the extraneous burdens of my life and remain as an 'inside only', an emotion, a most primary experience of being. I try to flatten the musician in me, the voice teacher at the peak of her career, into a Mouth, into muteness. Into the outburst of an absolute necessity to express a voice . . . [. . .] My clashes with Mouth intensified the more I was required to peel her off, revealing more and more profound layers. When I did not want to identify with the nothingness of her world (in my view), I cried. My inner unpreparedness to accept her terrible misery, made me scream [. . .] My inner rebellion and Mouth's scream became unified, in your view, into the right thing [. . .] Beckett managed to make me truly accept her into my world, make her my mirror, a magnifying mirror. [. . .] When the day arrived, when I was sitting on the seat on the ladder, tied, packed, concentrated, and the entire me filled with joy and fear, all of me was ready. For what? For a striptease? A theatrical performance? I felt more like a missile ready to be launched – 'out'! And – the light beam! . . . [. . .][5]

Hacohen described the experience also as "night after night, the essence of life . . . ", a perfect reflection not only of an individual feeling, but of Beckett's art as well, as an amazingly creative mixture between selves. Hacohen, who had vehemently fought against the text, created a dialogue with it, interpreting her life in the light (and darkness) of *Not I*, and vice versa.

Angelina Gazques wrote:

Wie die Fliege in meiner Luftroehre ums Ueberleben kaempfte – und ich auch.[6] Wenn das einzige, was uebrig bleibt, ein sprechender Mund ist, angeleuchtet von einem dummen Lichtstrahl, und wenn dieser Mund unaufhoerlich sprechen muss um nicht ganz zu verschwinden – dann kann eine Fliege, tanzend auf dem Lichtstrahl, zu eine existenziellen Bedrohung werden. Und dann, mit einem diese hastigen atemzuge, wird die Fliege zum Verschluss der Luftroehre . . . und *sie*? Was macht *sie* [. . .] ein Hoechstmass an Konzentration und – ich. Dem?? Ich in sein *sich* selbst in sich schaffen – den und haltenden Taetigkeit ist fuer mich zum zentralen Abendteuer in der Arbeit an *Nicht Ich* geworden. [. . .] "Auf die Spitze der eigenen Individualitaet zu stellen".

Like the fly in my throat, fighting for survival, so did I. If the only thing left is a speaking mouth, lit by a dumb beam of light, and if this mouth must speak incessantly in order not to disappear completely, then a fly, dancing on the light beam, become an existential threat. And then, with one of those hasty breaths, the fly becomes a stopage of the air pipe . . . and *she*? What does *she* do? [. . .] At the peak of concentration – and I. The I creating itself in its own self – this activity has become for me the central "holding" adventure in working on Not I – to "be placed at the peak of one's own individuality". (Rudolf Steiner)[7]

In one of the shows, a real fly, attracted by the light beam, focused on her mouth, flew straight into Gazques's open throat and choked her, for an apparently short moment, but much too long for her. Her re-telling of this anecdote not just as a retrospective smile of comic relief, but as a metaphor to what she had felt ever since, is an epitome of her relationship with 'Not I'. Gazques, trained in Dornach's anthroposophical drama school, has a superb command of her speech organs, together with a stunning talent for memorizing texts. She is the only actor with whom I directed *Not I* in two languages, German (her native tongue) and English. The intrinsic *Gestus* of the two languages, even though performed by the same person, delivered two quite different *personae* of the same Beckettian character. Rather than philosophical or psychological, the working process was short, intensive, and almost exclusively performance-oriented. Gazques channeled her professional talents to the task without indulging in biographical matters, with which, incidentally, she had then been heavily burdened. Nevertheless, she strongly focused on a unique mode of self-creation through the Beckettian character. The last phrase in her letter sums up her experience of the process in Rudolf Steiner's words, reflecting her own conclusion: At the peak of one's individuality.

Mirjam Hege has played major roles in all of the Goetheanum's main productions for many years, in some of which she has delivered up to 15-minute long complicated monologues by Steiner, Goethe, and others. In addition to a very impressive, variegated deep voice, she also has a unique sensitivity to musical elements such as pace, rhythm, and emotional colorings (as she rightly states). Our work on *Not I*, however, had been hard going, filled with mutual misunderstandings (like hers of Beckett, mine of her . . .) yet utterly rewarding.

Dies sei meine Chance, mir selbst zu beweisen, dass ich diesen Text sprachlich und emotional bewältigen könne. Ich hatte nie auch nur annaehernd ähnliches gemacht bis dahin. Sehr bald allerdings merkte ich, dass ich ständig an meine Grenzen kam, den Text zu denken, zu üeberschauen. Ich war gewöehnt, Texte zu durchfühlen, Zeit zu haben für seelische Umstellungen, Farbe im Stimmtimbre zuzulassen . . . [. . .] Jetzt plötzlich dieses vorwärtsdräengen, Mund immer in Bewegung [. . .] zwischen

Leben, zwischen Tod ein Funke, ein Aprilmorgenlichtsfunke fluktuirend
zwischen Nichts und Sein.[8]

This is my chance to prove to myself that I can master this text emotionally and speech-wise. I have never done anything even remotely similar
to this. But very soon I noticed that I often reach my limits to think the
text, to have an overview. I was used to feel my way through the text, to
have time for mental modifications, to admit colour in the voice [. . .] and
now suddenly this thrust forwards, mouth always in movement [. . .]
Between life and Death, a spark, an early April morning light between
nothingness and being.

Of all the actresses I have worked with, Hege came closest – at least
in intention – to certain spiritual qualities prevalent in Beckett's text. In
the same evening of four Beckett plays, Hege performed V in *Footfalls*,
and her voice (playing "Voice"!) created a virtually visual entity on
stage.[9] But in performing *Not I*, Hege, like Coghill, for one, seemed to
have quarreled with Beckett over the discrepancy between a highly
taxing technique on the one hand, and her own wish for an uncompromising personal expressiveness.

Ruth Geller emphasizes the immense personal and professional difficulties in working on the *Not I* text, situation and character. With refined
irony she explores the Hebrew term for "learning by heart" as a personal
"through the mouth". But it was not her mouth alone that suffered; hers,
Mouth's and Beckett's "tongue, cheeks, lips . . . " but Geller's breath, and
her very sanity, were called in question.[10]

[. . .] Das Hebräisch Wort für "auswendig" is "beal-peh", "durch den
Mund", also "mündlich". Mir blieb nichts anderes übrig, als die wörter
hinteraunander in den Mund zu legen. [. . .] der Text müsse wie "automa-
tisch", quasi von sich aus, aus dem Mund herausquellen. Genau so sind
die Bühnenanweisungen, die Samuel Beckett vorschrieb [. . .] Der
Schauspieler muss auf seine presentative und visuelle Persoenlichkeit
verzichten, was er ungern tut. [. . .] Heute überlege ich, wie weit man sich
vom gesprochenem Text entfernen kann, und im welchem Masse man
sich als representierndes Subject ausschalten kann, um dem Text diese
Selbsstanendigkeit zu ermöglichen. [. . .] Vorwärts reden, – rückwaerts
denken, erinnern! Kein Wunder, dass ich Zeit brauchte, um mich zu
"spalten". Ich litt physisch und mental. Ich spürte anfangs beim
Einstudieren einen Druck im Kopf, so dass ich unterbrechen musste.
[. . .] Ich hatte Momente in denen mir schwartz vor den Augen wurde,
Angst die Besinnung zu verlieren. Sogenannte Begleitser-scheinungen.
Ich war damit „besessen", vergass meinen Atem zu regeln.
    Ich begann an meiner Normalität zu zweifeln. Keiner der Mittel mit
denen man gewöhnlich an einer Rolle hinantritt waren hier zu
gebrauchen. Ich konnte den Text immer wieder lesen, konnte immer
wieder in gleichem Masse begeistert und erschüttert sein. Aber wie

schalte ich meine Gefühle und Gedanken, meine Kritik, meine Phantasie, meine Einfühlungsgabe aus? [. . .] An einer Stelle endeckt *Not I*, dass sie ihre Gesichtsmuskeln bewegt, ihren Mund, Lippen, Zunge. Sie ertappt sich beim reden. Das Bewusstwerden ihrer hervorgebrachten Laute, hörbar auch fuer sie, ist der Beweiss das sie noch "ist". [. . .] *Not I* [und] *Happy Days* sind meine aufregendsten und beglückendsten Theaterarbeiten.

The Hebrew word for "by heart" is "beal-peh", "by mouth". I had no other option but putting the words in my mouth [. . .] The Text must come out by itself, so to speak, gush out of the mouth, as Beckett indicates. [. . .] The actor must give up her presentative and visual Personality, which one does not like [. . .] Today I wonder how far you can estrange yourself from the spoken text, how detach yourself as a "representing Subject", so as to endow the text its independence [. . .] Speak forwards, think backwards, remember! No wonder I needed time to split myself. I suffered physically and mentally. In the beginning I felt a pressure in my head, and often had to stop rehearsing [. . .] I had moments of actual blackout, and fear to lose my senses [??] I was obsessed, forgot to regulate my breathing. I began to doubt my sanity. The means with which I normally entered a new role were useless. I could read the text again and again, and be fascinated and deeply shaken by it. But how should I engage my feelings and thoughts, my critique, my imagination, my sympathy and empathy? [. . .] At a certain point "Not I" discovers that she moves her facial muscles, mouth, lips, cheeks, tongue. She catches herself talking. Her consciousness of the uttered words, heard by her too, is the proof that she still "is" [. . .]

Hovering between her life experience and the character's, Geller describes the fascinating brinkmanship of the character as hers: "Aber wie schalte ich meine Gefühle und Gedanken, meine Kritik, meine Phantasie, meine Einfühlungsgabe aus?" "But how do I switch off my own feelings and thoughts, my phantasy, my sympathies?" The answer is indirectly given in Geller's words in her next line: "Sie ertappt sich beim reden. Das Bewusstwerden ihrer hervorgebrachten Laute, hörbar auch fuer sie, ist der Beweiss das sie noch 'ist'". Though she never performed the piece, she considers it to be one of her two favorite works; the other one is also Beckett's.

Shirly Steier wrote: "I loved her. Pitied her, feared her for being mad at me . . . "[11]

[. . .] The words themselves make you dizzy [. . .] I get the feeling that it is I that motivates 'it all', and yet it all happens by itself, and I am actually quite passive . . . a very unusual feeling on stage . . . my body stormed with the words, making a physical connection to things I could not have been attached to intellectually. [. . .] A gap between conflicting strong emotions and actual insanity. [. . .] I loved her. Pitied her, was afraid that she'd be mad at me for not 'delivering' her sufficiently well . . . That she chose to speak through my mouth, but might regret it if I let her down, if I didn't 'glide' into her enough, didn't give her the final compassion to really 'be'! [. . .] Then I thought to myself . . . she chose to speak through my mouth, but this is exactly the way she expresses herself, she even says: What? Who? No! She! About her own self [. . .] Which of us two is wrong? [. . .]

I begin [. . .] It all becomes clear: The shame, the pain, the smallness, its strength, it is I, it is indeed I! The familiar words start flowing followed by the pictures: Croakers Acres – I know the place. If I saw it, I'd recognize it. [. . .] All the words that tell about the brain and the mouth, the lips, the cheeks, and the buzzing, all the time the buzzing [. . .] If I had tried to connect to old age and death rationally, I would have run away and lied to us all. I communicated with my deepest and closest fears, just like the poor old woman with her life and her death. In the end I lose control, then regain it and am conscious again of my whereabouts.

Steier's letter relates to my 2001 production of *Not I*. Steier, 26, is a graduate acting student at Tel Aviv University's Theatre Department, commensurate, perhaps, with the following description: "Beckett requires a 'holy' actor no less than Artaud and Grotowski . . . Thus, acting effectively involves a kind of quest for an indescribable grail inside the author's stage directions and the music of his words, a process, long and torturous to some, of learning to trust the text . . . "[12] Steier might be surprised to learn that she is being compared with "holy" actors. It is she who writes: "I loved her. Pitied her, I was afraid that she would be mad at me for not 'delivering' her sufficiently well . . . That she chose to speak through my mouth, but might regret it if I let her down, if I don't 'glide' into her enough, if I don't give her the final sacrifice/absolution to really 'be'!" While many actors, often semi-consciously, feel that they sacrifice something very essential within themselves for the sake of other selves (such as playwrights and directors who choose not to play, or characters who need actors in order to be acted-out), Steier spells it out almost explicitly. "Beckett tends to focus on performance as a mode of self-consciousness, in relation to his characters' attempts to stage their own presence (or absence) and in terms of the author's continual interrogation of the act of representation . . . The plays also draw attention to their own status as performers."[13]

Beckett's Mouth uses words and mouth-movement to express an awareness of her theatricality, i.e. that she is "there" in a deliberately artificial, artistic situation. Her lines, acknowledging this theatrical situation, are delivered from the straights of particularly agonized Beckettian space, from which both actor and character call in doubt the authenticity of "a self", be it the character's, the implied author's self, or frequently, as we have seen, even the actor's. Character and actor are thereby paradoxically negating and confirming "selfhood" at one and the same time. Whereas the character may reject her self "so called", the actor playing the role must ascribe at least a minimal quality of selfhood to particular lines.

It is in the performative act of self-creation in Beckett's texts, when it is indeed self-referentially performed, that the true self-reference of an actor really expresses individually the self of the author and thus extends an invitation to the audience to posit their selves too. In *Not I* the threshold situation is expressed in the correlation between text and situation of the character in space; between I and Not I. In order to be truly self-referential, the actors must, in fact, be completely themselves.

Notes

Preface

1 Melvin J. Friedman, ed., *Samuel Beckett Now* (Chicago and London: University of Chicago Press, 1970), 3.
2 Ruby Cohn, *Samuel Beckett* (New York: McGraw Hill, 1975), 13.
3 Ruby Cohn, *The Comic Gamut* (New Jersey: Rutgers University Press, 1962), 296.
4 Wolfgang Iser, *The Implied Reader* (Baltimore and London: Johns Hopkins University Press), 262.
5 Hanna C. Copeland, *Art and the Artist in the Works of Samuel Beckett* (The Hague: Mouton, 1975), 20.
6 Hans Georg Gadamer, *Hegel's Dialectic* (New Haven: Yale University Press), 62.
7 The original is: "Something to give us the impression we exist", in Samuel Beckett, *Waiting for Godot* (London: Faber & Faber, 1971), 69.

Introduction: Self-Organization in the Middle of Chaos

1 Heinz-Otto Peitgen and Peter H. Richter, *The Beauty of Fractals* (Berlin: Springer-Verlag, 1986), 21.
2 James Gleick, *Chaos* (London: Abacus, 1995), 5.
3 Steven Connor, ed., *Waiting for Godot and Endgame* (New York: Macmillan, 1992), 2.
4 See Lois Oppenheim, *Directing Beckett* (Ann Arbor: The University of Michigan Press, 1994), 1–19.
5 Oppenheim, *Directing Beckett*, 3.
6 Samuel Beckett, *Proust + Three Dialogues* (London: John Calder, 1965), 103. See also Peitgen and Richter, *The Beauty of Fractals*, 22.
7 See Jaako Hintikka, "Cogito, ergo sum: Inference or Performance?" in: Alexander Sesonke and Noel Fleming, *Meta-Meditations, Studies in Descartes* (Belmont, CA: Wadsworth, 1965) 50–76. See also Rudolf Steiner, *Die Philosophie der Freiheit* (Dresden: Verlag Emil Weises Buchhandlung, 1936), ch. 3
8 J. L. Austin, *Philosophical Papers* (London: Oxford University Press, 1970), ch. 10.
9 Following the paging in Samuel Beckett, *The Complete Dramatic Works*

(London and Boston: Faber & Faber, 1986).

10 Gleick, *Chaos*, 140.

11 Peitgen and Richter, *The Beauty of Fractals*, 6.

12 Ibid., 8.

13 Oppenheim, *Directing Beckett*, 175.

14 Peitgen and Richter, *The Beauty of Fractals*, 9.

15 Kitty Ferguson, *The Fire in the Equations* (New York: Bantam, 1994), 207.

16 See Ruby Cohn, "Ghosting Through Beckett" in Marius Buning and Lois Oppenheim, eds, *Beckett in the 1990s* (Amsterdam–Atlanta: Rodopi, 1993), 1–12; and Katherine Worth, "Beckett's Ghosts" in Steven E. Wilmer, ed., *Beckett in Dublin* (Dublin: The Lilliput Press, 1992), 62–74.

17 Roger Penrose, *Shadows of the Mind* (London: Vintage, 1994), 419.

18 Gleick, *Chaos*, 6.

19 *Machshavot* 44 (1976): 80–8.

20 For example, *HaAri* (Rabbi Yiztchak Luria), Safed, sixteenth century.

21 Hans Georg Gadamer, *Hegel's Dialectic* (New Haven: Yale University Press, 1976), 64.

22 Connor, *Waiting for Godot and Endgame*, 131ff.

23 Menahem Mendel of Kutzk, early nineteenth century.

24 Gleick, *Chaos*, 311. I shall not attempt a comparison between Libchaber's helium-in-a-small-box (Gleick, 193) experiment and Beckett's *Imagination Dead Imagine*, but some of the similarities are quite striking.

25 Ferguson, *The Fire in the Equations*, 215. Furthermore, an interesting element in Beckett's writing is that Godot will always come "tomorrow": Like Stoppard's Rosencrantz and Guildenstern whose coin always flips "heads", a random sequence is generated. Something has gone wrong in such a universe because even randomness cannot be relied upon, and chaos itself cannot be patterned, coded, or expected. The only way is really to wait. Ibid., 206.

26 Wheeler, *Machshavot* 44 (1976): 85.

Chapter 1: Philosophical Notions

1 Samuel Beckett, *Proust and Three Dialogues with George Duthuit* (London: John Calder, 1965), 120.

2 Samuel Beckett, *Dante . . . Bruno. Vico . . Joyce* (In *Our Exagmination* etc.) (London: Faber & Faber, 1972), 14.

3 Beckett, *Proust*, 66.

4 Martin Esslin, ed., *Samuel Beckett* (New Jersey: Prentice-Hall, 1965), 6ff.

5 Jürgen Habermas, *Knowledge and Human Interests* (Boston: Beacon Press, 1972), 162.

6 Paul Ricoeur, *Metaphor and the Main Problem of Hermeneutics*, trans. David Pellauer (Northfield, MN: St. Olaf's College), 95.

7 R. D. Laing, *The Divided Self* (Harmondsworth: Penguin, 1974), 106.

8 Hans Georg Gadamer, *Hegel's Dialectic* (New Haven and London: Johns Hopkins University Press, 1976), 61–2.

9 See Robert Alter, *Partial Magic* (Berkeley: University of California Press, 1978), x.

10   See Ruby Cohn, "Philosophical Fragments in the Works of Samuel Beckett", in *Samuel Beckett*, ed. Martin Esslin, 172. In the same collection of articles see also Hugh Kenner, "The Cartesian Centaur". See also Jaako Hintikka, "Cogito, Ergo Sum, Inference or Performance", in *Meta-Meditations*, ed. Alexander Sesonke and Noel Fleming (Belmont, CA: Wadsworth Publishing Co., 1965), 58.

11   Cohn ("Philosophical Fragments", 172) is right again in saying: "The Unnamable reminds one not of the Cartesian Geulincx but of Descartes himself, for monologue is a virtual discourse on *Lack of Method*, on the impossibility of method, given the human mind – 'let us not be over-nice' working in words".

12   Cohn, "Philosophical Fragments", 174–5.

13   Hintikka, "Cogito", 62–3.

14   Betting, apologizing, naming, etc. – "in all these cases it would be absurd to regard the thing that I say as a report on the action which is undoubtedly done . . . We should say, rather, that in saying what I do, I actually perform the action". In J. L. Austin, *Philosophical Papers* (New York: Oxford University Press, 1961), 220 ff. In regard to the links between speech-acts and the literary function, etc., see Richard Ohmann, "Speech Acts and the Definition of Literature", *Philosophy and Language* 4 (1971), 1–19; "What's a Speech-Act?" in J. R. Searle, ed., *Philosophy of Language* (London: Oxford University Press, 1971), 39 ff.; and Ora Segal, "The Theory of Speech Acts and its Applicability to Literature" (in Hebrew) *Hasifrut* 18–19 (December, 1974), 113–19.

15   Hintikka, "Cogito", 75.

16   See Niklaus Gessner, *Die Unzulanglichkeit der Sprache* (Zurich: Juris, 1957).

17   Jean-Paul Sartre, *La Liberte Cartesienne* (Paris: Trois Colines, 1946).

18   Beckett uses quite a similar expression: "The laugh laughing at the laughter". Samuel Beckett, *Watt* (New York: Grove Press, 1959), 48.

19   Jean-Paul Sartre, *Being and Nothingness* (New York: Washington Square Press, 1966), 57 ff.

20   Sartre, *Being and Nothingness*, 59.

21   Paul Ricoeur, *Freud* (New Haven and London: Yale University Press, 1977), 43. See also, with direct reference to Beckett, though using a different approach, David H. Hesla, *The Shape of Chaos* (Minneapolis: University of Minnesota Press, 1973), 187 ff. "When Consciousness posits some transcendent object in the world, it is accompanied by the pre-reflective cogito, but when it posits itself, it becomes the reflective cogito. When consciousness reflects upon itself, its structures itself as reflecting and reflected . . . The self is nothing other than itself, but it is itself as the reflecting-reflected dyad". Hesla goes further and supplies a useful examination of consciousness on the one hand, and "that of which consciousness is conscious. The complications – grammatical intellectual, and existential – arise from the fact that one of the beings of which consciousness may be conscious is itself".

22   If one accepts Ricoeur's words, and self-reflexiveness is not "immediate", one understands why Beckett is fully committed to the present tense and to *presence* in the theatre.

23   Hesla, *The Shape of Chaos.*

24   Ibid.

25   An extensive discussion on the topic took place in *Mind*, between Jörgensen, Kattsoff, Ushenko, Encarnacion and others. See *Mind*, nos. 247 (July 1953) and 253 (January 1955); see also R. L. Martin, ed., *The Paradox of a Liar* (New Haven: Yale University Press, 1970): "The theory of types have, if tenable, shown how paradoxes can be avoided but they have not shown how they could arise", says Jörgensen, whose argument against the paradox of reflexiveness is based on claiming that "Knowing is a temporal process", and therefore, "we could not speak about an act of knowing that does not yet exist in the sense that it would be nothing at all". Whether we trest paradoxes, as Russell suggests, as "experiments of logic", or as Jörgensen suggests, as "traps of logic", the point remains that Beckett's self-reflexive sentences are definitely paradoxical in nature, but they are neither sheer "traps" nor just "experiment". They are, as previously argued, an act, a performance. They do not *describe*, they *do*. See also S. Shoemaker, "Self-Reference and Self-Awareness", *Journal of Philosophy* 15 (1968), 555–67.

26   Beckett, *Proust*, 125.

27   Samuel Beckett, *The Unnamable* (New York: Grove Press, 1965), 291.

28   Ricoeur, *Freud*, 37 ff.

29   Ricoeur, *Freud*, 28. "The only thing that can come to the aid of equivocal expressions and truly ground a logic of double meaning is the problematic of reflection".

30   Roland Barthes, *Mythologies* (Frogmore, St. Albans: Paladin, 1973), 152.

31   Barthes, *Mythologies.*

32   Raymond Federman, "Beckettian Paradox: Who is Telling the Truth?" in *Samuel Beckett Now*, ed. Melvin J. Friedman (Chicago and London; University of Chicago Press, 1975), 103–17.

33   Following notions developed by Henri Peyre, *Literature and Sincerity* (New Haven and London: Yale University Press, 1967).

34   "What the solipsist means is correct only it cannot be said; it shows itself. What the solipsist means is that the world is my world. This inexpressible truth shows itself in the fact that 'the limits of language' (of that language which I alone understand) means the limits of the world". P. M. S. Hancker, *Insight and Illusion* (London, Oxford, New York: Oxford University Press, 1972), 188 ff.

35   As in Richard Kuhns, *Structure of Experience* (New York: Harper & Row, 1970), rather than Booth's too general remark for his purpose: "The showing power of language is realized and explored in performance; the saying power of language is realized and explored in argument and in experiment" (p. 240).

36   Susan Langer, *Philosophical Sketches* (New York: Mentor Books, 1964), 79 ff.

37   Samuel Beckett to Alan Schneider.

38   Wayne Booth, *Rhetoric of Irony* (Chicago and London: Oxford University Press, 1975), 259.

39   Iser, *Reader*, 43.

40   Ibid., 41.

41   Booth, *Irony*, 525.

42　Iser, *Reader*, 272. See also George H. Szanto, "Samuel Beckett, Dramatic Possibilities", *Massachusetts Review* (Autumn 1974). "There is nothing in Beckett's work except form. Therefore any interpretation is available to one seeking out meaning of the context" (pp. 735–63). Obviously critics such as Booth, Szanto and others rely not only on a general assumption. They enlist, quite justifiably, Beckett's own words: "To find a form that accommodates the mess. That is the task of the artist now."

43　Austin, *Philosophical Papers*, 44.

Chapter 2: The Message of the Medium – Theatrical Techniques

1　Samuel Beckett, *Proust and Three Dialogues with George Dathuit* (London: John Calder 1965), 84.

2　Jindrich Honzl, "Dynamics of the Sign in the Theatre", in *Semiotics of Art*, ed. Ladislav Matejka and Irving R. Titunk (Cambridge, MA: MIT Press, 1976), 76.

3　In Ruby Cohn, *Back to Beckett* (New Jersey: Princeton University Press, 1973), 129.

4　Interview with Charles Marowitz.

5　Cohn, *Beckett*, 157.

6　John Fletcher and John Spurling, *Beckett* (New York: Hill and Wang, 1972), 118.

7　Eugene Webb, *The Plays of Samuel Beckett* (Seattle: University of Washington Press, 1974).

8　Fletcher and Spurling, *Beckett*, 118.

9　John Fletcher, *Samuel Beckett's Art* (London: Chatto & Windus, 1971), 58.

10　In S. Beryl and John Fletcher, *A Student's Guide to the Plays of Samuel Beckett* (London: Faber & Faber, 1985), 258.

11　James Knowlson, *Light and Darkness in the Theatre of Samuel Beckett* (London: Turret Books, 1972), 11.

12　Tom Driver, "Interviews with Beckett", in Gravert Federman, ed., *Samuel Beckett, The Critical Heritage* (London: Routledge & Kegan Paul, 1979), 220.

13　Stanton Garner, *Bodied Spaces, Phenomenology and Performance in Contemporary Drama* (Ithaca and London: Cornel Univesity Press, 1994), 87–93.

14　Shimon Levy, *The Medium and the Message* (Tel Aviv: Hakibbutz Hameuchad, 1997), 32 ff.

15　For an interesting discussion of colour in Beckett's work, see Lawrence E. Harvey, *Samuel Beckett, Poet and Critic* (New Jersey: Princeton University Press, 1970), 339ff.

Chapter 3: The Poetics of Offstage

1　Without actually hypostatizing the notion of *offstage*, a number of scholars have written about its function:

　　(a) Issacharoff speaks of the mimetic and diegetic as two major forms of dramatic space. "In the theatre mimetic space is that which is made visible to an audience and represented on stage. Diegetic space on the other hand, is described, that is, referred to by the characters" (p. 215). Issacharoff also distinguishes between theatre space (architecture), stage space (stage and set), and dramatic space. Michael Issacharoff, "Space and Reference in Drama", *Poetics Today*, vol. 2, no. 3 (Spring 1987): 211 ff.

(b) Ubersfeld says: "Purity of the void. Everything that matters – life and death, sex and power, conquest and passion – is off-stage . . . " Anne Ubersfeld, "The space of Phedre", *Poetics Today*, vol. 2, no. 3 (Spring 1981), 209.

(c) Patrice Pavis says that the contrast between space shown in a concrete situation, and space evoked by the spoken word, is a sufficiently clear criterion for it to be signalled in the stage/off stage duality. He also maintains: "Le hors-scene comprend la realite qui se deroule et existe en dehors du champ de vision du spectateur". Going further, he distinguishes between space visible by the characters on stage yet "masque au publique (teichoscopie) . . . coulasses."

2   Shimon Levy, "Offstage Notions in Chekhov's Plays" (in Hebrew), *Prosa* (October 1987), 30ff.

3   See Katharine Worth, ed., *Beckett the Space Changer* (London: Routledge & Kegan Paul 1975), 186; "The visible bareness already makes a powerful impact, but Beckett increases it by building up the impression of an offstage area that infinitely extends the bareness and emptiness . . . "

4   In Tom Driver, "Beckett by the Madeleine", Columbia University Forum (Summer 1961).

5   Alain Robbe-Grillet, "Presence in the Theatre", in *Samuel Beckett*, ed. M. Esslin (New Jersey: Prentice-Hall, 1965), 114.

6   Jonathan Kalb, *Beckett in Performance* (New York: Cambridge University Press, 1989), 149.

7   Steven Connor, *Samuel Beckett – Repetition, Theory and Text* (Oxford: Blackwell, 1988), 192.

8   Alan Shneider, "Anyway You Like it, Alan", *Theatre Quaterly*, vol. V, no. 19 (1975), 28.

9   Interviews with Beckett actors can be found in Linda Ben-Zvi (ed.), *Women in Beckett* (Urbana and Chicago: University of Illinois Press, 1990); Jordan R.Young, *The Beckett Actor* (Beverly Hills: Moonstone Press, 1987); Nicholas Zurbrugg, Interviews with David Warrilow and Billie Whitelaw, in *The Review of Contemporary Fiction* vol. VII (1987); Billie Whitelaw, . . . *Who he?, An Autobiography* (London: Hodder and Stoughton, 1995).

10 Rudolf Steiner, *Philosophy of Freedom* (London: Rudolf Steiner Press, 1964).

11 Hintikka, *Cogito*, 58.

12 See Mary Bryden, *Samuel Beckett and the Idea of God* (London: Macmillan 1998), 1.

13 Ruby Cohn, "Ghosting Through Beckett", in *Samuel Beckett Today/Aujourd'hui*, no. 2 (1993): 1–11.

14 Clas Zilliacus, "Act Without Words I As Cartoon and Codicil", in *Samuel Beckett Today/Aujourd'hui*, no. 2 (1993): 298.

15 Herta Schmid, Strukturalistische Dramentheorie (Kronberg: Scripter 1973), 81.

16 Anna McMullen, *Theatre On Trial, Samuel Beckett's Later Drama* (London: Routledge, 1993), 113.

17 See Rubin Rabinowitz, "Repetition and Underlying Meaning in Samuel Beckett's Trilogy", in Lance St John Butler and Robin J. Davis (eds), *Rethinking Beckett* (London: Macmillan, 1990), 31–67; Steven Connor, Samuel Beckett, *Repetition*, 115–69.

18 Lois Overbeck's interview with Brenda Bynum, in Linda Ben-Zvi (ed.), *Women in Beckett* (Urbana: University of Illinois Press, 1990), 53. Also: Jonathan Kalb, Beckett in Performance (Cambridge: Cambridge University Press), 238.

19 Jack Miles, *God, A Biography* (New York: Vintage, 1996), 28–38.

20 James Knowlson, *Damned to Fame* (London: Bloomsbury, 1996), 680.

21 Beckett to Lawrence Harvey; in Shimon Levy, *The Medium and the Message* (Tel Aviv: Hakibbutz Hameuchad, 1997), 76.

22 Gottfried Buettner, *Samuel Beckett's Novels* (Philadelphia: University of Pennsylvania, 1984), 153.

23 Michael Robinson, *The Long Sonata of the Dead* (New York: Grove Press 1969), 69–70.

24 H. Porter Abbott, *Beckett Writing Beckett* (Ithaca: Cornell University Press), 158.

25 Katharine Worth, "Beckett's Ghosts", in S. E. Wilmer (ed.), *Beckett in Dublin*, (Dublin: The Liliput Press, 1992), 72.

26 Jean-Michel Rabate, "Beckett's Ghosts and Fluxions", in *Samuel Beckett Today/Aujourd'hui*, no. 5 (1996): 37.

27 Phil Baker, "Ghost Stories: Beckett and the Literature of Introjection", in *Journal of Beckett Studies*, no. 5: 1+2 (1996): 59.

Chapter 4: The Radioplays

1 To borrow Grotowski's term. See Jerzy Grotowski, *Towards a Poor Theatre* (Holstebro: Odin Theatres Forley, 1968).

2 Marshall McLuhan, *Understanding Media* (London: Sphere, 1967), 332.

3 Dylan Thomas, *Under Milkwood* (New York: New Directions, 1953), 3.

4 Marshall McLuhan and Edmund Carpenter, *Explorations in Communication* (Toronto: Beacon Press, 1960), 65, 72.

5 John Cage, *Silence* (Middleton, Conn.: Wesleyan University Press, 1968), 8.

6 Hildegard Seipel, *Untersuchungen Zum Experimentellen Theater Von Beckett und Ionesco* (Bonn: Romanishces Seminar, 1963), 242 ff.

7 Victor Zuckerkandl, *Sound and Symbol* (New Jersey: Princeton University Press, 1969), 184.

8 Donald McWhinnie, *The Art of Radio* (London: Faber & Faber, 1959), 133 ff.

9 Irving Wardle, ed., *New English Dramatists, Radioplays* (Harmondsworth: Penguin, 1968), 21 ff.

10 Zuckerkandl, *Sound and Symbol*, 184.

11 By way of example, sound effects are used realistically in H. G. Wells' *War of the Worlds*, or any other typical thriller; metaphorically in Alan Sharp's *The Long-Distance Piano Player*; and symbolically in Louis McNeice's *The Dark Tower*. One can imagine a complete radioplay composed only of sound effects, and in that respect the sound effect approximates the border between concrete music and music on the one hand, and concrete music

and words on the other. *Visages* by Luciano Berio is a good example.

12 Martin Esslin, "The Mind as a Stage", *Theatre Quarterly* 3 (1971): 5–11.

13 William York Tindall, *Samuel Beckett* (New York: Columbia University Press, 1964), 41.

14 Martin Esslin, ed., *Samuel Beckett, Volume of Twentieth-Century View* (New Jersey: Prentice-Hall, 1965), 7 ff.

15 See also Frances Gray and Janet Bray, "The Mind as a Theatre: Radio Drama Since 1971", *New Theatre Quarterly*, vol. 1, no. 3 (August 1985): 295.

16 Martin Esslin, *Mediations* (London: Eyre Methuen, 1980), 142 ff.

17 Compare with Clas Zilliacus, *Beckett and Broadcasting* (Abo: Abo Akedemi, 1976), and with Katharine Worth, "Beckett and the Radio Medium", in J. Drakakis, ed., *British Radio Drama* (Cambridge: Cambridge University Press, 1981), 191–217.

Chapter 5: "Spirit Made Light" – Film and TV Plays

1 Linda Ben-Zvi, "Samuel Beckett's Media Plays", in *Modern Drama* 28 (2 September 1985): 23 and note 6, p. 37.

2 André Bazin, *What is Cinema* (Berkeley: University of California Press, 1971), 95.

3 Samuel Beckett, "Dante . . . Bruno. Vico . . Joyce", in *Our Exagmination* etc. (London: Faber & Faber, 1972), 14.

4 Bazin, *What is Cinema*, 15.

5 Nico J. Brederoo, "Beckett's Film: An Essay", in *Samuel Beckett Today/Aujourd'hui*, ed. Marius Buning et. al. (Amsterdam–Atlanta: Rodopi, 1992), 158 ff.

6 Ruby Cohn, *Back To Beckett* (New Jersey: Princeton University Press, 1973), p. 209.

7 Sylvie D. Hanning, "Film: A Dialogue between Beckett and Berkeley", in *Journal of Beckett Studies* 7 (1982): 99.

8 Martin Esslin, *Mediations* (London: Eyre Methuen, 1980), 151.

9 Sidney Homan, *Interpretations For Performance* (Lewisburg: Bucknell University Press, 1984), 149.

10 Rosette Lamont, "Beckett's *Eh Joe*: Lending an Ear to the Anima", and Katharine Worth, "Women in Beckett's Radio and Television Plays", both articles in Linda Ben-Zvi, ed., *Women in Beckett* (Urbana and Chicago: University of Illinois Press, 1990), 233.

11 Clas Zilliacus, *Beckett and Broadcasting* (Abo: Abo Akademi, 1976), p. 188.

12 Ibid., 198.

13 Ibid., 195.

14 Ruby Cohn, *Ghosting Through Beckett*, lecture held at the International Beckett Symposium in The Hague, 1992. Also, along similar lines, Katherine Worth, *Beckett's Ghosts* (tentative name) at the Beckett Theatre Festival in Dublin, 1991.

15 As I have, in the 1981 Tel Aviv University production in Hebrew.

16 Rosemary Pountney, *Theatre of Shadows* (New York: Barnes and Noble Books, 1988), 199.

17 John Calder, "The Lively Arts: three plays by Samuel Beckett", on BBC 2,

17 April 1977 as well as in *Journal of Beckett Studies* 2 (1977): 117.
18 Ben-Zvi, "Samuel Beckett's Media Plays", 35.
19 Jonathan Kalb, *Beckett in Performance* (Cambridge: Cambridge University Press, 1989), 99.
20 Ben-Zvi, "Samuel Beckett's Media Plays", 36.
21 Pountney, *Theatre of Shadows*, 204.
22 Georg Hensel, *Beckett* (München: DTV, 1977), 172.
23 Calder, "The Lively Arts: three plays by Samuel Beckett", 120.
24 Homan, *Interpretations For Performance*, 223.
25 Stanley E. Gontarski, "*Quad* I and II: Beckett's sinister mime(s)", in *Journal of Beckett Studies* 9 (1983): 137.
26 Kalb, *Beckett in Performance*, 100.
27 Beryl S. and John Fletcher, *A Student Guide to the Plays of Samuel Beckett* (London: Faber & Faber, 1985), 260.
28 Enoch Brater, "Toward a Poetics of Television Technology: Beckett's *Nacht und Träume* and *Quad*,' in *Modern Drama*, vol. 28, no. 3 (September 1985): 48–54.
29 Rudolf Steiner, *Speech and Drama* (London: Anthroposophical Publishing Company, 1960), 24, 252–3.
30 Fletcher, *Samuel Beckett's Art*, 268.
31 Pountney,*Theatre of Shadows*, 209
32 Ibid.
33 Johann Wolfgang von Goethe, *Faust* (München: C. H. Beck Verlag, 1986), I am referring to the English translation by Albert Latham (London: Everyman), 9–10.
34 Kalb,*Beckett in Performance*, 103.

Chapter 6: Godot – Resolution or Revolution?

1 Mordechai Shalev, "Stealing the Gospel" in *Alpaiim*, vol. 1, June (1989): 59–160.
2 Shimon Levy, ed., *Thirty Years of Hebrew Beckett Criticism* (Tel Aviv: Dyonon [a limited experimental edition], 1986), 3.
3 Gershon Shaked, *New Wave in Hebrew Fiction* (Tel Aviv: Sifriat Poalim, 1971), 11–25.
4 Levy, ed., *Thirty Years of Hebrew Beckett Criticism*, 3. The page number indicators at the end of all the following exracts relate to page numbers only in this collection of Beckett materials in Hebrew, between 1956–1986.
5 From an interview I made with Edna Shavit in May 1985. Prof. Shavit, a young actor at the time, played the first Israeli Lucky and was also in charge of public relations for the first Hebrew *Waiting for Godot*.
6 See Linda Ben-Zvi, "All Mankind is Us", in Ruby Cohn (ed.), *Beckett: Waiting for Godot* (London: Macmillan, 1987), 67ff.

Chapter 7: I's and Eyes: A Hermeneutical Circle

1 Wayne Booth, *The Rhetoric of Fiction* (Chicago and London: University of Chicago Press, 1965), 155 ff.
2 Jiri Veltrusky, "Dramatic Text as a Component of Theatre", in *Semiotics of*

Art, ed., Ladislav Matejka and Erving R. Titunik (Cambridge, MA: MIT, 1976), 110.

3   Herta Schmid, *Strukturalistische Dramentheorie* (Kronberg TS: Scripter, 1973).

4   Rolf Fieguth, "A New Struckturalist Approach to the Theory of Drama and to General Genre Theory", *PTL* (Descriptive Poetics and Theory of Literature), vol. I, no. 2 (1976): 389 ff.

5   Schmid, *Strukturalistische Dramentheorie*, 81.

6   Samuel Beckett, *Proust and Three Dialogue with George Duthuit* (London: John Calder, 1965), 125; see also Lawrence Harvey, *Samuel Beckett, Poet and Critic* (New Jersey: Princeton University Press, 1970), 401–40. The author notes an interesting connection between Beckett's own criticism and the criticism about him.

7   Becket, *Proust*, 88.

8   George Lukàcz, *Approximations to Life in the Novel and the Play* (Harmondsworth: Penguin, 1973), 283.

9   Jaako Hintikka, "Cogito, Ergo Sum, Inference or Performance", in *Metameditations*, ed. Alexander Sesonke and Noel Fleming (Belmond, CA: Wadsworth Publishing Co., 1965), 58 ff.

10 Rapp maintains that both actors and audience are aware of their dual role as part of the theatrical situation: the actor represents an "unexisting" world in a "realistic" way, trying to bridge between the *intended* and the *perceived* meaning of the play, whereas the audience comes to *see* as well as be seen. Uri Rapp, *Sociology and Theatre* (in Hebrew) (Tel Aviv: Sifriat Poalim, 1973), 252 ff.

11 Paul Ricoeur, "What is a Text?" in *Symbolic Language and Philosophical Anthropology*, ed., D. M. Rassmussen (The Hague, Martinus Nijhoff, 1971), 135 ff.

12 Ricoeur, "What is a Text?"

13 Gadamer, *Hegel*, 62.

14 Georg Simmel, "On the Theory of theatrical Performance", in *Sociology of Literature and Drama*, ed. Elizabeth and Tom Burns (Harmondsworth: Penguin, 1973), 104.

15 Alan Schneider, "Anyway You Like it, Alan", *Theatre Quarterly*, vol. V, no. 19 (1975): 28.

16 Jack McGowran, Interview with Richard Tuscan, *Theatre Quarterly*, vol. III, no. 11 (1973): 16.

17 See, for example, Volker Canaris, *Samuel Beckett, Das Letzte Band, – Regiebucj* (Frankfurt: Suhrkamp, 1970); John Calder, ed., *Beckett at Sixty* (London: Calder and Boyers, 1967); Walter Asmus, "Beckett Directs Godot", *Theatre Quarterly*, vol. V, no. 19 (1975).

18 Norman N. Holland, *The Dynamics of Literary Response* (New York: North, 1975), 280.

19 Dorothy Mack, "Metaphoring as Speech Act", *Philosophy and Rhetoric 7* (1974): 245.

20 Paul Ricoeur, *The Hermeneutic Function of Distanciation*. A presentation (Northfield, MN: St. Olaf's College, 1973).

21 Jiri Veltrusky, "Basic Features of Dramatic Dialogue", in Ladislav Metajka

and Erving R. Titunik, eds, *Semiotics of Art* (Cambridge, MA: MIT, 1976), 130.

22 Allain Robbe-Grillet opens his article on Beckett's *Presence in the Theatre* with Heidegger's words: "The condition of man . . . is to be there. The theatre probably reproduces this situation more naturally than any other of the ways of representing reality. The essential thing about a character in a play is that he is 'on the scene'! There . . . " With regard to Beckett, Robbe-Grillet says: "For this is what we have never seen on stage before, or not with the same clarity, not with so few concessions and so much force. A character in a play usually does no more than *play a part*, as all those about us who are trying to shirt their own existence. But in Beckett's play, it is as if the two tramps were on stage without a part of play". Alain Robbe-Grillet, "Samuel Beckett, or Presence in the Theatre", in Martin Esslin, *Samuel Beckett, Volume of Twentieth-Century Views* (New Jersey: Prentice-Hall, 1965), 108.

23 Rapp, *Sociology*, 62.

24 In German, *"Schauen"* and *"gucken"* – pronounced "Kuken" – mean "seeing", "watching". It is likely that Beckett used the English names in their German sense.

25 Hans Georg Gadamer, *Hegel's Dialectic* (New Haven: Yale University Press, 1976), 62.

26 "Was I sleeping, while the others suffered? Am I sleeping now?" or, "To all mankind they were addressed, those cries for help still ringing in our ears!" (*WFG*).

27 Richard E. Palmer, "Post-Modernity and Hermeneutics", *Boundary* 2, vol. 5, no. 2 (Winter 1977): 363–88.

28 Deirdre Bair has published A Beckett Biography (New York and London: Harcourt, Brace, Jovanovitch, 1978). Would Beckett, who "neither helped nor hindered" Professor Bair, regard this extension work "a rummaging?" Ironically, many of Beckett's real critics, unlike their portraits in *Theatre II*, treat him with great reverence and loving care: James Knowlson's *Damned to Fame, The Life of Samuel Beckett* (London: Bloomsbury, 1996) is a superb example of writing biographies, not only Beckett's.

Epilogue: Six She's and other *Not I* Proxies

1 My first Not I was the renowned Canadian actress Joy Coghill in 1976. Then came musician and voice teacher Prof. Hanna Hacohen (1982). Angelina Gazques from Germany and Mirjam Hege of Switzerland, both from the Goetheanum Theatre Group in Dornach, Basel, were next (1995). Later still I worked in Israel with Ruth Geller (1996)` and last but not least with Shirly Steier (December 1999) in Tel Aviv.

2 Samuel Beckett, *In Our Exagmination . . .* (London, Faber & Faber, 1972), 262.

3 Similar to Nag and Nell in their trashbins, or W1, M and W2 in their burial urns in Play.

4 From an E-Mail letter, dated 15 January 2000.

5 From a letter in Hebrew, dated 25 June 2000, my translation (S.L.)

6 From a letter in German, dated 25 January 2000.

7   Relating, probably, to Rudolf Steiner, *Philosophy of Freedom* (London: Rudolf Steiner Press, 1964).

8   From a letter in German, dated 22 February 2000.

9   "Beckett hears in these performers the voice that speaks to him when he is writing. The metaphor of voice here sinks to a deeper, and more mystical level; the actors' voices are no longer repetitions of Beckett's own voice, but rather of that deeper more authentic voice that speaks through him and his writing," Steven Connor, *Samuel Beckett – Repetition, Theory and Text* (Oxford: Blackwell, 1988), 192.

10 From a letter in German, dated January 2000.

11 From a letter in Hebrew, July 2000, my translation (S.L.).

12 Jonathan Kalb, *Beckett in Performance* (New York etc.: Cambridge University Press, 1989), 149.

13 Anna McMullen, *Theatre in Trial* (New York, London: Routledge, 1993).

Bibliography

Abbott, H. Porter, *Beckett Writing Beckett* (Ithaca: Cornell University Press, 19??).

Alter, Robert, *Partial Magic* (Berkeley: University of California Press, 1978).

Austin, J. L., *Philosophical Papers* (London: Oxford University Press, 1970).

Bair, Deirdre, *Beckett, A Biography* (New York and London: Harcourt, Brace, Jovanovitch, 1978).

Barthes, Roland, *Mythologies* (Frogmore, St. Albans: Paladin, 1973).

Bazin, André, *What is Cinema* (Berkeley: University of California Press, 1971).

Beckett, Samuel, *Dante . . . Bruno. Vico . . Joyce* (In *Our Exagmination etc.*) (London: Faber & Faber, 1972).

——, *Proust and Three Dialogues with George Duthuit* (London: John Calder, 1965).

——, *The Complete Dramatic Works* (London and Boston: Faber & Faber, 1986).

——, *The Unnamable* (New York: Grove Press, 1965), 291.

Ben-Zvi, Linda, "Samuel Beckett's Media Plays", in *Modern Drama* 28 (2 September 1985).

——, "All Mankind is Us", in Ruby Cohn (ed.), *Beckett: Waiting for Godot* (London: Macmillan, 1987).

Beryl, S. and Fletcher, John, *A Student's Guide to the Plays of Samuel Beckett* (London: Faber & Faber, 1985).

Booth, Wayne, *Rhetoric of Irony* (Chicago and London: Oxford University Press, 1975).

——, *The Rhetoric of Fiction* (Chicago and London: University of Chicago Press, 1965).

Brater, Enoch, "Toward a Poetics of Television Technology: Beckett's Nacht und Träume and Quad", in *Modern Drama*, vol. 28, no. 3 (September 1985).

Brederoo, Nico J., "Beckett's Film: An Essay", in *Samuel Beckett Today/Aujourd'hui*, ed. Marius Buning et al. (Amsterdam–Atlanta: Rodopi, 1992).

Bryden, Mary, *Samuel Beckett and the Idea of God* (London: Macmillan 1998).

Buettner, Gottfried, *Samuel Beckett's Novels* (Philadelphia: University of Pennsylvania, 1984).

Cage, John, *Silence* (Middleton, CT: Wesleyan University Press, 1968).

Calder, John, "The Lively Arts": three plays by Samuel Beckett on BBC 2, 17 April 1977 as well as in *Journal of Beckett Studies* 2 (1977).

Cohn, Ruby, "Ghosting Through Beckett" in Marius Buning and Lois Oppenheim, eds, *Beckett in the 1990s* (Amsterdam–Atlanta: Rodopi, 1993).

——, *Back To Beckett* (New Jersey: Princeton University Press, 1973).

——, *Samuel Beckett* (New York: McGraw Hill, 1975).

——, *The Comic Gamut* (New Jersey: Rutgers University Press, 1962).

Connor, Steven, ed., *Waiting for Godot and Endgame* (New York: Macmillan, 1992).

——, *Samuel Beckett – Repetition, Theory and Text* (Oxford: Blackwell, 1988).

Copeland, Hanna C., *Art and the Artist in the Works of Samuel Beckett* (The Hague: Mouton, 1975).

Driver, Tom, "Beckett by the Madeleine", Columbia University Forum (Summer 1961).

——, "Interviews with Beckett", in Gravert Federman, ed., *Samuel Beckett, The Critical Heritage* (London: Routledge & Kegan Paul, 1979).

Esslin, Marshall, *Understanding Media* (London: Sphere, 1967).

——, "The Mind as a Stage", *Theatre Quarterly* 3 (1971).

——, ed., *Samuel Beckett, Volume of Twentieth-Century View* (New Jersey: Prentice-Hall, 1965).

——, *Mediations* (London: Eyre Methuen, 1980).

Federman, Raymond, "Beckettian Paradox: Who is Telling the Truth?" in *Samuel Beckett Now*, ed. Melvin J. Friedman (Chicago and London: University of Chicago Press, 1975).

Ferguson, Kitty, *The Fire in the Equations* (New York: Bantam, 1994).

Fieguth, Rolf, "A New Struckturalist Approach to the Theory of Drama and to General Genre Theory", *PTL (Descriptive Poetics and Theory of Literature)*, vol. I, no. 2 (1976).

Fletcher, John and Spurling, John, *Beckett* (New York: Hill and Wang, 1972).

Friedman, Melvin J., ed., *Samuel Beckett Now* (Chicago and London: University of Chicago Press, 1970).

Gadamer, Hans Georg, *Hegel's Dialectic* (New Haven: Yale University Press, 1976).

Garner, Stanton, *Bodied Spaces, Phenomenology and Performance in Contemporary Drama* (Ithaca and London: Cornell, 1994).

Gessner, Niklaus, *Die Unzulanglichkeit der Sprache* (Zurich: Juris, 1957).

Gleik, James, *Chaos* (London: Abacus, 1995).

Gontarski, Stanley E., "Quad I and II: Beckett's sinister mime(s)", in *Journal of Beckett Studies* 9 (1983).

Grotowski, Jerzy, *Towards a Poor Theatre* (Holstebro: Odin Theatres Forley, 1968).

Habermas, Jürgen, *Knowledge and Human Interests* (Boston: Beacon Press, 1972).

Hancker, P. M. S., *Insight and Illusion* (London, Oxford, New York: Oxford University Press, 1972).

Hanning, Sylvie D., "Film: A Dialogue between Beckett and Berkeley", in *Journal of Beckett Studies* 7 (1982)

Hensel, Georg, *Beckett* (München: DTV, 1977).

Hesla, David H., *The Shape of Chaos* (Minneapolis: University of Minnesota Press, 1973).

Hintikka, Jaako, "Cogito, ergo sum: Inference or Performance?" in Alexander Sesonke and Noel Fleming, *Meta-Meditations, Studies in Descartes* (Belmont, CA: Wadsworth, 1965).

Holland, Norman N., *The Dynamics of Literary Response* (New York: North, 1975).

Homan, Sidney, *Interpretations for Performance* (Lewisburg: Bucknell University Press, 1984)

Honzl, Jindrich, "Dynamics of the Sign in the Theatre", in *Semiotics of Art*, ed. Ladislav Matejka and Irving R. Titunik (Cambridge, MA: MIT Press, 1976).

Iser, Wolfgang, *The Implied Reader* (Baltimore and London: Johns Hopkins University Press).

Issacharoff, Michael, "Space and Reference in Drama", *Poetics Today*, vol. 2, no. 3 (Spring 1987).

Kalb, Jonathan, *Beckett in Performance* (Cambridge and New York: Cambridge University Press, 1989).

Knowlson, James, *Light and Darkness in the Theatre of Samuel Beckett* (London: Turret Books, 1972).

——, *Damned to Fame, The Life of Samuel Beckett* (London: Bloomsbury, 1996).

Kuhns, Richard, *Structure of Experience* (New York: Harper & Row, 1970).

Laing, R. D., *The Divided Self* (Harmondsworth: Penguin, 1974).

Langer, Susan, *Philosophical Sketches* (New York: Mentor Books, 1964).

Levy, Shimon, "Offstage Notions in Chekhov's Plays" (in Hebrew), *Prosa* (October 1987).

——, ed., *Thirty Years of Hebrew Beckett Criticism* (Tel Aviv: Dyonon [a limited experimental edition], 1986).

——, *The Medium and the Message* (Tel Aviv: Hakibbutz Hameuchad, 1997), 32 ff.

Lukacz, George, *Approximations to Life in the Novel and the Play* (Harmondsworth: Penguin, 1973).

Martin, R. L., ed., *The Paradox of a Liar* (New Haven: Yale University Press, 1970).

McGowran, Jack, Interview with Richard Tuscan, *Theatre Quarterly*, vol. III, no. 11 (1973).

McLuhan, Marshall and Carpenter, Edmund, *Explorations in Communication* (Toronto: Beacon Press, 1960).

McMullen, Anna, *Theatre On Trial, Samuel Beckett's Later Drama* (London: Routledge, 1993).

McWinnie, Donald, *The Art of Radio* (London: Faber & Faber, 1959).

Miles, Jack, *God, A Biography* (New York: Vintage, 1996).

Ohman, Richard, "Speech Acts and the Definition of Literature", *Philosophy and Language*, 4 (1971).

Oppenheim, Lois, *Directing Beckett* (Ann Arbor: The University of Michigan Press, 1994).

Palmer, Richard E., "Post-Modernity and Hermeneutics", *Boundary 2*, vol. 5, no. 2 (Winter 1977).

Peitgen, Heinz-Otto Peitgen and Richter, Peter H., *The Beauty of Fractals* (Berlin: Springer-Verlag, 1986).

Penrose, Roger, *Shadows of the Mind* (London: Vintage, 1994).

Peyre, Henri, *Literature and Sincerity* (New Haven and London: Yale University Press, 1967).

Pountney, Rosemary, *Theatre of Shadows* (New York: Barnes and Noble Books, 1988).

Rabinowitz, Rubin, "Repetition and Underlying Meaning in Samuel Beckett's Trilogy", in Lance St John Butler and Robin J. Davis (eds), *Rethinking Beckett* (London: Mamillan, 1990).

Rapp, Uri, *Sociology and Theatre* (Tel Aviv: Sifriat Poalim, 1973).

Ricoeur, Paul, "What is a Text?" in *Symbolic Language and Philosophical Anthropology*, ed., D. M. Rassmussen (The Hague: Martinus Nijhoff, 1971).

——, *Freud* (New Haven and London: Yale University Press, 1977).

Robbe-Grillet, Alain, "Presence in the Theatre", in *Samuel Beckett*, ed. M. Esslin (New Jersey: Prentice-Hall, 1965).

Robinson, Michael, *The Long Sonata of the Dead* (New York: Grove Press, 1969).

Sartre, Jean-Paul, *Being and Nothingness* (New York: Washington Square Press, 1966).

——, *La Liberte Cartesienne* (Paris: Trois Colines, 1946).

Schmid, Herta, *Strukturalistische Dramentheorie* (Kronberg: Scripter 1973).

Schneider, Alan, "Anyway You Like it, Alan", *Theatre Quarterly*, vol. V, no. 19 (1975).

Searle, J. R., ed., *Philosophy of Language*. (London: Oxford University Press, 1971),

Shaked, Gershon, *New Wave in Hebrew Fiction* (Tel Aviv: Sifriat Poalim, 1971).

Shalev, Mordechai, "Stealing the Gospel" in *Alpaiim*, vol. 1, June (1989).

Simmel, Georg, "On the Theory of Theatrical Performance", in *Sociology of Literature and Drama*, ed. Elizabeth and Tom Burns (Harmondsworth: Penguin, 1973).

Steiner, Rudolf, *Die Philosophie der Freiheit* (Dresden: Verlag Emil Weises Buchhandlung, 1936).

——, *Speech and Drama* (London: Anthroposophical Publishing Company, 1960).

Thomas, Dylan, *Under Milkwood* (New York: New Directions, 1953).

Tindall, William Yorkl, *Samuel Beckett* (New York: Columbia University Press, 1964).

Ubersfeld, Anne, "The space of Phedre", *Poetics Today*, vol. 2, no. 3 (Spring 1981).

Veltruski Jiri, "Basic Features of Dramatic Dialogue", in Ladislav Metajka and Erving R. Titunik, eds, *Semiotics of Art* (Cambridge, MA: MIT, 1976).

Wardle, Irving, ed., *New English Dramatists, Radioplays* (Harmondsworth: Penguin, 1968).

Webb, Eugene, *The Plays of Samuel Beckett* (Seattle: University of Washington Press, 1974).

Worth, Katharine, "Beckett and the Radio Medium", in J. Drakakis, ed., *British Radio Drama* (Cambridge: Cambridge University Press, 1981).

——, ed., *Beckett the Space Changer* (London: Routledge & Kegan Paul 1975).

——, "Beckett's Ghosts" in Steven E. Wilmer, ed., *Beckett in Dublin* (Dublin: The Lilliput Press, 1992).

Young, Jordan R., *The Beckett Actor* (Beverly Hills: Moonstone Press, 1987).

Zilliacus, Clas, "Act Without Words I As Cartoon and Codicil", in *Samuel Beckett Today/Aujourd'hui*, no. 2 (1993).

Zilliacus, Clas Zilliacus, *Beckett and Broadcasting* (Abo: Abo Akedemi, 1976).

Zuckerkandl, Victor, *Sound and Symbol* (New Jersey: Princeton University Press, 1969).

Index

Note: Main or detailed references are indicated in bold type. Works where no author is shown are by Beckett.